Henry Adams on the Road to Chartres

1.

Henry Adams on the Road to Chartres

Robert Mane

The Belknap Press of
Harvard University Press
Cambridge, Massachusetts
1971

To Pierre-Antoine and Michele

Preface

Writing "An Apology to Henry Adams" for the *Virginia Quarterly Review* (Spring 1962), Lewis Mumford rightly began by mocking "those who would cover their own shortcomings by revealing those disclosed by Henry Adams' scholarship, in his later work like *Mont-Saint-Michel and Chartres*."[1] A certain humility is required of one who approaches this imaginative reconstruction of the Middle Ages—the humility which must be felt in front of all great works of art. It is true, as will occasionally become apparent here, that Adams' scholarship did sometimes falter; but why should one attach more importance to "facts" than he himself did? *Mont-Saint-Michel and Chartres* is not a scholarly treatise, not a "text-book and guide-book." Indeed he would rather have burned it, he protested, "before I degrade it to such a fate. Our cult is esoteric."[2] Not that the book is arcane either. It is its common interpretation, exemplified by the subtitle appended to the French translation: *clefs du moyen-âge français,* which is misleading. If doors open, they give on to Adams' own imaginative world, to a world which like Wallace Stevens he could have called his *mundo,* and which he too made more real than reality, because what he wrote was in fact a poem. As early as 1936, Maurice Le Breton made this point quite clear: *Mont-Saint-Michel and Chartres* is undoubtedly Adams's greatest work; though not apparently related to his earlier writings, this inspired work of poetry is the crowning achievement of his severe and somber historical *oeuvre.*[3] In 1940, Oscar Cargill wrote to the same effect: "Absurdly futile, then, the scholar's effort to show that Adams used in the main secondary sources for his book. Equally futile also to suggest that Adams discovered a unity and order in France in the era of cathedral building which may not have been so apparent to contemporaries. And even a little ridiculous to charge Adams, as a modern historian, with neglect of economics in his study. The reference ought not to be from *Mont-Saint-Michel and Chartres* to thirteenth-century France, to test Adams's accuracy, but to contemporaneous works of literature, to fix the place and meaning of the book, for Adams's creation is a prose poem rather than anything else."[4]

How did Adams come to write this "poem"? To gain an adequate measure of its originality, it is necessary to begin by following the writer in his long and slow progress on the road to Chartres. In Ernest Samuels' admirably detailed biography such a theme naturally could not receive precedence above all others; more often than not it even gets lost. Here it will be isolated and developed, and so will the influences which molded the lover of the Gothic. To Ruskin he owed surprisingly little—at least directly; much more important was the enduring influence of his Harvard background, and of the New England milieu which he never really deserted. Above all, he was in debt to two men: the painter John La Farge and his own brother, Brooks Adams. Personal events also counted greatly. For without the tragic death of his wife, his reawakening to life in the South Seas, and his deep attachment to Mrs. Cameron, he would never have reached the portals of Chartres. And the result is the most personal book he ever wrote, even though a number of its pages were, as a matter of fact, more or less "cribbed" from various "authorities." Its power on the reader comes from its imaginative and emotional unity. Whether we can fully capture this unity is open to question, but we must at least try to get "a realizing sense" of what it all meant for Adams, exactly as he himself did with the emotion which was behind the Gothic. "To get a sense of what [he] had to say and a sympathy with [his] way of saying it" will be rewarding enough.[5]

Acknowledgments

My first thanks must go to Maurice Le Breton and Roger Asselineau, who showed me the fascination of Adams' Middle Ages and set me on the road to Chartres. Without them this book would not have been written. The same must be said of the American Council of Learned Societies, whose financial aid made possible such a venture, by allowing me a year of concentrated research in the United States. I am also deeply grateful to the staffs of the Massachusetts Historical Society, Houghton Library, and Wellesley College Library for their assistance. A very special debt is due to Richard Abcarian for his kindly criticism of my typescript. Ernest Samuels' work was an inspiration as well as an immense help. John P. McIntyre, S.J., guided me through the maze of Adams' theology. Indeed, whatever is good in my last two chapters comes directly from him; I know only too well that the errors are of my own making.

Contents

Part One
The Road to Chartres

1
The Makings of
Ignorance

BOSTON

Under the shadow of Boston State House, turning its back on the house of John Hancock, a little passage called Hancock Avenue, runs or ran from Beacon Street, skirting the State House grounds to Mount Vernon Street, on the summit of Beacon Hill; and there in the third house below Mount Vernon Place, February 16, 1838, a child was born and christened later by his uncle, the minister of the First Church after the tenets of Boston Unitarianism, as Henry Brooks Adams.

Nothing in these opening lines of *The Education* suggests that Henry Adams was to become a medievalist. On the contrary, he appears in his own words as "distinctly branded," condemned forever to remain a "child of the eighteenth century." The "prehistoric" nest of associations he describes represents but a few generations. Stretch it as much as he would, the ancestral heritage "crowding" on his "unconscious babyhood," or molding his character during his childhood, could never have taken him out of New England and further back than the seventeenth century.

The house in which he was born no longer remains. In January 1842, his family moved to "a larger one which his parents were to occupy for the rest of their lives in the neighboring Mount Vernon Street." Mounting from the river to the State House Archway, the street has a mellow charm with much of the London flavor. Its late Georgian-styled houses still breathe "the atmosphere of the well-ordered classicism that had spread over the continent and over England in the train of the new learning" in the eighteenth century and from there had come to America. For there could hardly have been anything redolent of the Middle Ages on Beacon Hill. The surroundings in which Adams lived until he sailed to Europe in 1858 were essentially classical. With its portico, its shining dome, Boston State House, built by Charles Bulfinch, the first American-born architect, remains a masterpiece of classicism. It is recorded that during his European trip in 1787, on entering St. Peter's, Bulfinch was "moved to tears." On his way to Italy, the only piece of French architecture which had impressed him was the Bordeaux Playhouse, newly built by Victor Louis. Judging from the letters Bulfinch wrote home, it seemed as though the Middle Ages had never existed, had left no monument, not even a stone; it was a past utterly foreign to the New Englander.[1]

The eighteenth century still ruled Adams' Boston "long after 1850." This was true not only of its society and of the architecture of its houses but of the frames of mind as well, at least of those in Henry Adams' family. In *The Education*, he pictures the very small boy that he was, standing on tiptoe in front of his grandmother's writing desk and peering through small glass doors at the "little eighteenth-century volumes in old binding"; in these books survived the spirit of his great-grandfather John Adams; they represented a family tradition. One might attempt to explain, as does Carl Becker, that the authors of these "little volumes," though living in the Age of Reason, actually dwelled in a medieval world, that they "demolished the Heavenly City of St. Augustine only to rebuild it with more up-to-date materials." However grounded in truth, such a paradox can hardly account for the fascination which the Middle Ages would one day hold for Henry Adams. Indeed Whitehead's formula, "a climate of opinion," which Becker applies to these philosophers' innermost beliefs, will just as well serve for the fundamental conviction an American citizen was bound to hold: "Do you see who have left all feudal processes and poems

behind them, and assumed the poems and processes of Democracy?" As it is here used by Whitman, "feudal" (or "medieval") is
not only the antithesis of democratic, it is the very opposite
of American. "Ruin'd cathedrals, crumble of palaces, tombs of
priests"—no such memories of a bygone and repellent age deface
America. Neither does she ring with the "chants of the feudal
world, the triumphs of kings, slavery castes." Couched in less
poetic phrase, this rejection of the past was already at the core of
the American Constitution.[2]

If the Founding Fathers felt any link with some distant past, it
was with that of Rome, of Greece, far beyond the Dark Ages.
Neither John Adams nor John Quincy Adams would later recollect
ever visiting a medieval cathedral when they were in Europe.
Politics and not the arts was for the first Adamses the ruling
passion. For Thomas Jefferson as well, politics was paramount.
Yet, "essentially, instinctively a builder," Jefferson also had a
"passionate love for architecture"; he seems to have been one of
the very few Americans aware of the fad for Gothic ornament in
England, near the middle of the eighteenth century, which culminated in Horace Walpole's Gothic extravaganza at Strawberry
Hill. As early as 1771 he jotted down notes for a "Burying Place"
at Monticello with these instructions: "in the center of it erect a
small Gothic temple of antique appearance." Toying with the idea
of a Gothic temple for his garden, he even made a small sketch of
the ground plan in 1807. Bricks were ordered for this Gothicism,
but it was never raised. These were merely passing whims. Jefferson's true love was the Maison Carrée, after which he patterned
the new Capitol of Virginia, at Richmond. "Here I am, Madame,"
he wrote from Nimes to the Comtesse de Tessé in 1787, "gazing
whole hours at the Maison Carrée like a lover at his mistress." Only
once before, he told her, had he been "so violently smitten"; it was
in Paris, with the Hôtel de Salm, a new structure of classical style:
he "used to go to the Tuileries almost daily and look at it." There
is not even a glancing mention in his writings of Notre-Dame or of
any other Gothic monument of the Old Continent.[3]

One of the first Americans of note who recorded his impressions
in front of a medieval structure is Emerson. "In seeing old castles
and cathedrals," he wrote in *English Traits* (1856), "I sometimes

say, as today in front of Dundee Church Tower, which is eight-hundred years old: 'this was built by another and a better race than any that now look at it'." In his essay on History, the same feeling is expressed in more general terms: "A Gothic cathedral affirms that it was done by us, and not done by us. Surely it was by man, but we find it not in our man." In other words, it yet remained an alien world. This feeling may be found even in his brilliant and frequently quoted definition of the cathedral: "The Gothic cathedral is a blossoming in stone subdued by the insatiable demand of harmony in man. The mountain of granite blooms into an eternal flower, with the lightness and delicate finish, as well as the aerial proportions and perspective, of aerial beauty."[4] How could Emerson have felt personally concerned with the poetry of these stones? George Herbert Mead has explained the "self-conscious setting of the past again" by the Romanticists as a reaction against the Napoleonic Age. "They returned to the Middle Ages with a sense of relief because the French revolution had meant disturbance, the most considerable war that had been waged in Europe for a long time, together with all that goes with continuous warfare." Medieval Europe had very little place for what we term "nationalism"; therefore by contrast it appeared as a safe harbor where the imagination could anchor. The Americans also had known war, but in an earlier decade, and its memories elated them with a sense of glory. Confident in the unlimited possibilities of the future, they had no reason to experience a passionate longing for "the security" of a past, with which their country had no connection.[5]

Yet the fashion for medieval designs which flourished in England about 1820, and then in France, also began blossoming a few years later in the United States. It found its best expression in the Gothic villas of the Hudson valley, making of it the American equivalent to the Rhineland.[6] One may still today see "Sunnyside," Washington Irving's picturesque Tudor country house in Tarrytown, designed in 1836 by the painter George Harvey; not far from it, at Irvington-on-Hudson, stands Paulding's mansion, designed in 1838 by Alexander Jackson Davies (1803–1882), the first American architect to have worked almost exclusively in the Gothic manner. It was by no mere coincidence that the most celebrated adepts of this new vogue belonged to literary circles. For the Middle Ages appeared distinctly linked with literature. One of the first houses built by A. J. Davies in the early thirties, just outside Baltimore, was Glen Allen; although ruined and deserted today, it remains an interesting landmark in the history of American taste, as a replica of Abbotsford, Walter Scott's baronial hall in Scotland. There is little likelihood that young Henry Adams ever saw Glen Allen or that he ever sailed up the Hudson River in order to gaze at the turreted landscape; but of his early and lasting love for the Waverley novels we have undisputed evidence. Unlike young Ruskin, he did not draw his sense of history from them; everywhere around him, history, modern history, was breathing. On the other hand, whatever notions he first gained of the Middle Ages probably came from Scott's novels, and, for that reason, they were very pleasant notions. Scott's influence on the future author of *Mont-Saint-Michel and Chartres* cannot be minimized.[7]

Indeed, we can find a sort of symbolic value in Adams' description of the happy hours, the "happiest," he says, of his boyhood, which were "passed in summer lying on a musty heap of Congressional Documents in the old farmhouse at Quincy, reading 'Quentin Durward,' 'Ivanhoe,' and 'The Talisman,' and raiding the garden at intervals for peaches and pears. On the whole he learned most then."[8] Already he had found a way of escape from nearer history—a discovery which would come of use in later days. Not that he then gained much factual information about the Middle Ages. In fact, as G. M. Young recently observed in a lecture on "Scott and History," "our positive knowledge, our popular knowledge of the Middle Ages" would not be less, had Scott never existed. Indeed, when we survey all his writings, we are quite surprised to notice how rarely he goes back beyond the Reformation, and, G. M. Young adds, "with how little profit . . . *Ivanhoe* is one of the best stories ever written, but for what it has to tell us of England in the reign of Richard I, it might be inscribed 'Scene—a forest. Time—as you like it.'" Thus, even when he was dealing with the medieval scene, "Scott himself never knew what treasures of record were lying just below the surface."[9] A Scottish lawyer with literary and antiquarian leanings, Scott was never a scholar aiming at a perfectly accurate reconstruction of the Middle Ages. Making a pilgrimage of sorts to Abbotsford, Ruskin was deeply shocked by the mongrel style of the place. The truth was that Scott had very vague notions of Gothic architecture. Like Strawberry Hill, his "castle" was a monument to fancy rather than to learning. The same may be said of his romances. Yet without Scott's picture of the Middle Ages one doubts whether in literature as in architecture such a fashion for medievalism could have sprung up during the nineteenth century. For the novelist greatly facilitated the Gothic revival by making the Middle Ages attractive.[10]

Medieval structures could never have become popular in the United States had there been no models in literature other than the murky castles sired by Edgar Allan Poe's fantasy. Emerson, for one, found little to praise in the "jingle man," but his letters abound with references to Walter Scott. "If you love romance you may read Scott's novels without sin or scandal," he advised a young woman in 1824. The novelist's Middle Ages were a "wholesome" holiday land into which a scion of Puritans could venture without the least fear of impropriety. It was such an ideal holiday land which, some eighty years later, in *Mont-Saint-Michel and Chartres* would also open out for young "nieces" under their benign uncle's guidance.[11]

The connection between the two writers is even more evident, when one considers Adams' attitude toward Scott in his later life. Writing to Henry Cabot Lodge in 1875, Adams noted that Leslie Stephen considered "Scott to be poor stuff." Feeling personally "a little awkward about literary judgment," he then offered no word of defense for the novelist, but it was obvious that he ranged him along with Pope, Gray, Cowper, and Goldsmith, for whom he still entertained "youthful prejudice or rather prejudice contracted in youth." In his old days, he no longer showed such diffidence in his open appreciation of Walter Scott. Four times he referred to him in *Mont-Saint-Michel and Chartres*. Writing in August 1913 to Charles Milnes Gaskell of his relish for twelfth-century songs, he wistfully added: "I wish Walter Scott were alive to share them with me, but he is my only companion in these fields, and I fear that even he never heard a note of music for Rebecca or Ivanhoe, or knew that it existed. He would have enjoyed the fun of Coeur de Lion and Blondel quite fresh from the Crusades, as good as the west front of Chartres."[12]

So the Middle Ages were *fun;* and they remained alive in Adams' imagination thanks to endearing heroes like Ivanhoe, whose story is significantly alluded to in *The Education* and in *Mont-Saint-Michel and Chartres* as well as in Adams' letters. "Human," "life-like," "understandable"—these are traits which typify all the characters whose acquaintance we shall make on our way from Mont-Saint-Michel to Chartres, whether they be Roland, the Virgin, or Abelard. Henry Adams was right in feeling closely related to Walter Scott. From him he "had learned most," for he retained the lesson brought out by Carlyle in his "Essay on Scott": "These historical novels have taught all men this truth, which looks like a truism and yet was as good as unknown to writers of history and others till so taught, that the bygone ages of the world were actually filled by living men, not by protocols, state papers, controversies and abstractions of men."[13] Truth and life, not a barren accuracy, were essential.

HARVARD

Little is known of Adams' earliest formal schooling. The chronicle of the years before he entered Harvard College remains, in Ernest Samuels' words, "incongruously barren." We may however, without great risk of error, assume that he never had the least instruction in medieval history; in spite of its literary appeal the subject had not as yet achieved academic prestige. The study of medieval history, the *London Times* declared in the 1840's, was "a foolish interference with the natural process of civilization and prosperity." How then could it fare better in New England, where, as may be judged from its status at Harvard, history at large had long been underprivileged?[14] From the year 1839 only dates the McLean Professorship of Ancient and Modern History, the first distinct endowment of that special branch in any American College. Jared Sparks, a minister then living at Cambridge and the author of a *Life of Washington* (published two years earlier and thoroughly modern in its outlook), was appointed to the chair. He insisted on being allowed to instruct by lectures, assigned reading, and essays rather than by set recitations, and "on having eight months out of every twelve free for his researches in European and American archives." To his regime belongs the introduction in 1846 of history among the requirements for admission to the freshman class. Thus, in the period 1852–1854, when young Henry Adams was drilled by Master Dixwell for the Harvard entrance examination, he had to study Worcester's *Elements of History;* "ancient history" was the part required.[15] By the time Henry Adams entered the college, however, history had again somewhat fallen upon evil days at Harvard. Appointed to the presidency in 1849, Jared Sparks had resigned in 1853, leaving the McLean Professorship without any incumbent. Until Henry Warren Torrey came in 1857, there was only James Jennison, "Tutor in History and Instructor in Elocution," to cover the entire field of history as best he could. With him, during the second term of 1854–1855, freshman Adams read Thomas Arnold's *History of the Later Roman Commonwealth from the End of the Second Punic War to the Death of Julius Caesar and of the Reign of Augustus; with a Life of Trajan.* This was all. No other courses in History were offered to his class until 1857–1858, when H. W. Torrey was appointed McLean Professor of History. This appointment gave new impetus to the study of history, reflected in a requirement that all seniors should spend three hours a week during the first term studying Guizot's *History of Civilisation in Europe,* the introduction to Robertson's *Charles the Fifth,* and Thomas Arnold's *Lectures on Modern History;* the second term was devoted to the study of the constitutional history of the United States. "Probably," says Ernest Samuels, "the most influential text of Professor Torrey's course," the *History of Civilisation in Europe* consisted of a series of fourteen lectures delivered by Guizot at the Sorbonne in 1828. Spanning the fall of the Roman Empire to the eighteenth century, these essays were brilliantly general; if they gave Adams an early interest in the twelfth century, a period more often alluded to than treated in several of the central lectures, it is not likely to have been a deep interest.[16]

Though time-hallowed (it had been first published in 1769), the *History of Emperor Charles V* came to have more immediate relevance to New Englanders, owing to a recent edition of the book brought out under the sponsorship of William H. Prescott. The bulk of the work itself, however, was not included in the syllabus; students had only to go through Robertson's introduction or "preliminary volume," entitled "A View of the Progress of Society in Europe from the Subversion of the Roman Empire to the Beginning of the Sixteenth Century." Some 200 pages of text supplemented by 160 more of "Proofs and Illustrations," this philosophic survey dealt in its first part with the "Progress of Society" until the fifteenth century. As such it could hardly infuse students with a nostalgia for the Middle Ages. Its author, William Robertson (1721–1793), was an avowed admirer of Hume and Voltaire, and his eighteenth-century bias naturally led him to dwell at some length on the "darkness" of the Middle Ages, a darkness which by the time of the crusades began slightly to dissipate. A good example of his bias is in what he exclaimed at that stage: "We have hitherto been contemplating the progress of that darkness which spread over Europe, from its first approach to the period of greatest obscuration: a more pleasant exercise begins; to observe the first dawning of returning light, to mark the various accessions by which it gradually increased and advanced toward the full splendor of day."[17] The "returning light" was a political one: governments began to assert themselves. But culture, as far as either Guizot's or Robertson's essays were concerned, did not flourish. Nor did any cathedral spring from the ground.

As a matter of fact, Adams was not to acknowledge the least indebtedness to the somewhat dreary textbooks from which he had received his first tincture of the Middle Ages. During his four Harvard years, he said, he learned "little and that little ill"—least, apparently, in history, which he did not even mention. Unlike Louis Agassiz's lectures on the Glacial Period and on paleontology, Professor Torrey's courses held no appeal for his imagination. Perhaps more than with the subject matter or the textbooks, the fault lay with the teacher. From *The Education* we learn only that he was a "charming" colleague in the seventies. Samuel Eliot Morison portrays him in his later period as "an excellent representative of the school of dear old gentlemen who taught history as an avocation" and merely "out of text-books." Although he was some years younger when Adams first came to know him (he had graduated with the class of 1833), Torrey had already behind him a career that included helping Frederick P. Leverett at the Boston Latin School with his *Latin Lexicon*, admission to the bar (which he never turned to account), and the founding of a school for girls. He certainly had no more of historical training than the future Professor Henry Adams and none of the latter's reforming enthusiasm. A member of the class of 1857, that is, someone who had left the college before Torrey came, recollected his four years with rankling bitterness: "I recollect no instruction which was not of the most perfunctory and indifferent sort. . . . The element of personal influence was entirely lacking . . . No word of advice or stimulus or encouragement was ever uttered . . . It was four years of monotonous routine going into the classroom, spending an hour and coming out."[18] Had this student stayed one more year and studied with Torrey there would probably have been no reason for him to alter his opinion.

Four years at Harvard College thus resulted for Adams in a "blank, a mind on which only a water mark had been stamped." Even if his resentment on the subject of his college education sounds exaggerated, it is nevertheless true that he was then little prepared for a career in medieval history. Seniors wishing to compete for the Bowdoin Prize in the academic year 1857–58 were offered a choice between two themes: "Saint Paul and Seneca" and "An examination of the evidence, historical and traditional, for the existence of Robin Hood." Though Robin Hood would one day be mentioned in *Mont-Saint-Michel and Chartres* with obvious sympathy, he failed to entice Adams, who opted instead for Saint Paul and Seneca. The only evidence we may find of an early interest in history is the purchase during this senior year of Michelet's *History of France;* the volumes bear a number of scorings and annotations, but these particular marks clearly belong to a later time, probably the winter of 1871–72, when Adams wrote a review of Freeman's *Historical Essays* and used his old college book to check on the genealogy of the last Carlovingians.[19]

Remembering his own years at Oxford, John Ruskin once asserted: "the whole time I was there my mind was simply in the state of a squash before it is a peascod." Yet Oxford did not lack in monuments apt to awaken a student's love for architecture. The Cambridge where Adams lived was a far less stimulating place. In an article he wrote on "Harvard College" in 1872, he could still remark: "Nature has not been prodigal to her; art has added but few attractions to the small number of those that nature conferred." This was a longstanding complaint. As early as 1836, in the *North American Review,* H. R. Cleveland deplored the stark ugliness of Harvard College buildings, "very perfect specimens of no known order of architecture; vast brick barns, destitute alike of symmetry, ornament and taste, and with all their plan and uncouth proportion there is a sort of horrible regularity and squareness about them which heightens their deformity."[20]

Anthony Trollope, who visited the college in 1861, found its dormitories and lecture halls "very ugly buildings standing here and there without order . . . It is almost astonishing that buildings so ugly should have been erected for such a purpose." One of the few redeeming features was the "handsome" library. Built in 1839–1842 and bearing the name of a former governor of Massachusetts who had bequeathed his fortune to the college "for the promotion of virtue, science and literature," Gore Hall might easily appeal to an English eye, since its model was no less than King's College Chapel in the English Cambridge. A "simplified travesty," it at least displayed none of the absurdities likely to mar many new structures going by the name of Gothic.[21] "It is not uncommon," H. R. Cleveland went on, in an 1836 article:

to see a church with pointed windows and a portico supported by Grecian columns like the orthodox church in Boston, Massachusetts, and many in the western towns of New York. Buttresses are almost unknown; and as for flying buttresses we do not believe there is an instance of them in the United States. The interior of these churches is generally still less Gothic than the outside. In very few is there any appearance of aisles; and if the gallery and pulpit are ornamented they are quite as often Grecian as Gothic. No distinction is made in the form of the building with regard to its being of the Grecian or Gothic order, and in general if the ornaments were not to be applied till the body of the edifice was finished in other respects, no one could tell, unless by the pointed windows, to what style of architecture it was intended to belong. As for the richer ornament of the florid Gothic, they are not to be found on any edifice in the country.

As A. D. Gilman in his turn complained, eight years later (also in the *North American Review*), Jefferson's saying that "the genius of architecture seemed to have shed a peculiar malediction over America" was still as true as in the early days of the Republic.[22]

Harvard itself offered little, as we have seen, which could improve the architectural taste of a student. Even Gore Hall, whose construction had been regarded as one of the college's greatest achievements, failed to be impressive. Stones kept falling from its jerry-built pinnacles, which had to be polled. Inside there were defects so serious that eventually it became necessary to pull down the whole building. One of Adams' classmates, who was to play an important part in his life, must easily have sensed these defects. Coming from New Orleans, Henry Hobson Richardson first intended to make civil engineering his profession, but he soon changed his mind and decided to become an architect. After graduating with Adams in 1858, he would go to study in Paris. Being very sociable and possessing great personal charm, he was a popular figure on the campus. As for Adams, he certainly had no acquaintance at Harvard he valued in after years so much as Richardson.[23]

Whether it may or may not be ascribed to Richardson's influence, Adams' first literary attempt was inspired by a piece of architecture. Before his first college year was over he had published in the *Harvard Magazine* of May 1855 a five-page article entitled "Holden Chapel." He was not moved by purely aesthetic considerations, as he made clear in the opening paragraphs: "Living as we students live among these College buildings, memorials of past generations, and coming every day into contact with them, connecting them with our remembrances of pleasant or disagreeable events, and keeping them in our minds merely as lodginghouses and recitation-rooms, it is not wonderful that we should lose, even if by any chance we had at first, any feelings of respect and veneration towards them. There are in reality few things in this country so well worthy of veneration as these walls, devoid though they be of any pretence to achitectural beauty, and though evidently intended much more for the wear-and-tear of every-day life than for the eyes of occasional visitors."[24]

There was one building which from the moment he saw it struck him with "its curious fashion and unpretending form." The casual visitor could easily miss Holden Chapel. Yet to Adams there was a "charm connected with it, . . . a charm which possibly the cherubs who seem in the act of leaping down from the walls to sport in reality on the grass may have their share in creating." Supporting a shield of vivid blue with an English coat of arms (probably those of a wealthy merchant through the generosity of whose widow the chapel was built in mid-eighteenth century), these cherubs remain the only sculptured figures adorning a wall on the campus. Rightly did Adams find them charming. After 1812, however, they were no longer the incongruous custodians of a holy place. When it became too small for the community, the chapel was turned to base uses and converted into a laboratory with a museum, providing students with the standard and rather tasteless joke: "My grandfather was a Harvard man. He is still here in a bottle in Holden." Far from indulging in such banter, the young freshman felt only reverence for the "most sacred and venerable spot in the possession of Harvard College." To him it was hallowed by the memory of the important events it had witnessed, for it was there that the first Massachusetts convention had met: "Let us go back in imagination ninety years—to the year 1764. It is the night of the 24th of January . . . Here we have a man who looks as though he were Governor of the province, so richly is he dressed . . . And now a third man approaches. He is short and stout, apparently yet young and quite good-looking. Mr. Hancock returns his salutation and says, 'Well, Mr. Adams, how comes on my law-suit?' "

A note is struck here which we will find again, amplified, in the first chapters of *Mont-Saint-Michel and Chartres;* that is, that the greatest charm of a monument for Adams does not lie in its art but in the personal associations it may conjure up. In none of the other essays he wrote during his college years do we find the same vein, for there was no other building which could thus take hold of his imagination. This first historical sketch is nevertheless important. Adams will have to traverse more than one ocean and nearly half a century before again communicating with his ancestors through the cathedral of Coutances; yet, between grandfather John Adams of 1855 and "our Norman grand-papas" of 1895, the link is obvious and quite strong.

ON THE GRAND TOUR

Toward the end of September 1858, Henry Adams, freshly graduated from Harvard College, set sail with "quite a delegation" of his class for a two-year stay in Europe. This journey was in the pattern of the time. Many young New Englanders before him, though not his elder brother, had also done their "grand tour"—an experience which in the words of the editor of Francis Parkman's journals was "the accepted part of every well-to-do young American's education in the mid-nineteenth century." Francis Parkman's adventures, which provide a good example of such a grand tour, will serve as a fitting introduction to Adams' own journey.

In 1843 Parkman went to Italy, a country then quite fashionable, especially with Bostonians eager to escape "from the frozen ocean of Boston life" and who found in Florence "the Boston of Italy," a "sort of continental Boston." Preferring Sicily, Parkman thoroughly covered the island and left no church or monastery unvisited; then he settled in Rome. As the home and center of Catholicism, the city proved quite outlandish to a young Boston Unitarian and yet strangely attractive to one whose ideal of life was already, he found, "a little mediaeval." He observed: "It is as startling to a "son of Harvard" to see the outstanding learning of these Jesuit fathers, and the appalling readiness and rapidity with [which] they pour forth their interminable streams of argument as it would be to a Yankee parson to witness his whole congregation, with church, pulpit and all shut up within one of the great columns to support the dome of St. Peter's—a thing which might assuredly be done."[25] Such was his fascination that he even spent a week in a monastery with the Passionist Fathers; but though these good men "horrified at the enormity of [his] disbelief" made him wear a holy medal round his neck, hoping that he might be favored with a miraculous visitation, to their sorrow, as he reported afterward, he "had no vision of the Virgin—at least of Santissima Maria."[26]

Sailing fifteen years later, Adams was bound for more serious shores; chance far more than tradition directed him. "As it happened by pure chance, the first door of escape that seemed to offer a hope led to Germany." One of the few professors who stimulated him at college was James Russell Lowell, Longfellow's successor in the chair of Belles Lettres. Upon his nomination Lowell had gone to Germany, as to the fount of all knowledge. According to Adams' testimony: "the literary world then agreed that truth survived in Germany alone, and Carlyle, Matthew Arnold, Renan, Emerson, with scores of popular followers, taught the German faith . . . All serious scholars were obliged to become German, for German thought was revolutionizing criticism. Lowell had followed the rest, not very enthusiastically, but with sufficient conviction, and invited his scholars to join him. Adams was glad to accept the invitation, rather for the sake of cultivating Lowell than Germany, but still in perfect good faith."

Thus the young man set out for Berlin by way of Liverpool, London, and Antwerp. Of all the cities on his route, Antwerp, with its thirteenth-century cathedral towering "above a sixteenth century mass of tiled roofs," impressed him most: "The taste of the town was thick, rich, ripe like a sweet wine; it was mediaeval, so that Rubens seemed modern; it was one of the strongest and sweetest flavors that ever touched the young man's palate; but he might as well have drunk out his excitement in old Malmsey, for all the education he got from it. Even in art one can hardly begin with Antwerp Cathedral and the descent from the Cross. He merely got drunk on his emotions, and had then to get sober as best as he could." A "poor, keen-witted, provincial town, simple, dirty, uncivilized and in most respects disgusting," Berlin must have had at any rate quite a sobering effect on the American youth.[27] Adams soon found that the gloom of Berlin's architecture was only equalled by the gloom of the Berlin winter. Senator Sumner, whom he then met and whose chief "hobby" happened to be architecture, could not direct him to any inspiring monument.[28]

Evidenced by the Gothic barracks and gasworks which graced Berlin, there then prevailed in Germany a distinct movement toward the Middle Ages. From an aesthetic point of view this *moyen-âge de pacotille* (brummagem Middle Ages), in Maurice Le Breton's words, was just as dreary as it was tasteless. Its interest lay in another direction. "As the nationalistic feeling grew in the German tastes," remarks Agnes Addison, "so spread the vogue for modern Gothic and the style was most extensively used in the period of national development from 1848 to 1871. To the historian the Gothic Revival in Germany is of particular interest, for it so closely parallels the growth of nationalism."[29] Since its foundation in 1810, the University of Berlin, which Adams proposed to attend, had been one of the most vital centers of German nationalism. The foremost historians who taught there—Niebuhr,

Droysen, Mommsen, Sybel Treischke—took an active part in politics, and the Prussian government rewarded these scholars with honors and positions. This alliance between history and politics continued until 1914. There was something particularly patriotic in the study of the Middle Ages, firing the Germans as it did with a pride for their past. German scholars made the publication of the early documents which gave a first-hand knowledge of the glorious achievements of their ancestors during the Middle Ages the outstanding labor of the century. The *Monumenta Germaniae Historica,* then in the process of publication under Georg Pertz's supervision, constituted in J. W. Thompson's words, "the greatest collection in the world," "the world's model for scientific history and scientific criticism." Henry Adams does not mention the collection in his letters; he does not even seem to have been tempted to drop in at one of the lectures of Professor Ranke, the most prominent historian Germany had ever produced. It was not, however, to his lectures that Ranke owed his "worldwide influence," but to what has been called "his genius" as a teacher in the historical seminar which he inaugurated at Berlin. As Thompson reckons: "Out of this seminar came directly or indirectly over one hundred eminent scholars . . . in the leading German universities, and they in turn created students in the Ranke tradition, supplying historians not only for Germany but also for America."[30] Adams, when in his turn he inaugurated an historical seminar at Harvard, would follow the same line; it is thus not unlikely that he had at least caught an echo of Ranke's method. His own seminars, it must also be noted, would be entirely devoted to the study of law and institutions. In this too, we may see a direct consequence of his sojourn in Germany. His purpose in coming to the University of Berlin was to study civil law. Though he eventually found himself, owing to his inadequate command of the "very repulsive language," unable to "join the university and make acquaintances there among the donkeys who walk around with absurd caps on their heads, rather more offensive than the soldiers," it is evident that he never forgot this early interest and his slight attempt at reading law.[31]

Did the Middle Ages exert a more powerful appeal upon Adams' imagination when he visited other parts of Europe? In April 1859, he deeply enjoyed a short tramp through Thüringen. Eisenach was a "delightful" place, and high above it there was, "covered with Romance and history until it's as rich as a wedding cake," the eleventh century Wartburg, where he would have liked to remain. Medieval Nürnberg, which he visited in July, also enchanted him. Probably more than any other German city, Nürnberg had preserved a medieval atmosphere, with its massive walls, castles with winding streets, halls, timbered houses, and oriel windows. Adams truly raved with delight, as he described the town to his brother: "Think me spooney if you will, but last evening as I wandered round in the dusk smoking a cigar in these delightful old peaked, tiled, crooked, narrow stinking lanes I thought that if ever again I enjoy as much happiness as here in Europe, and the months pass over bringing always new fascinations and no troubles, why then philosophers lie and earth's a paradise. Ben and I have passed the day in a couple of great churches, lying on the altar steps and looking at the glorious stained glass windows, five hundred years old, with their magnificent colors and quaint biblical stories. So fascinating these things are! . . . There's no use talking about it. Let it go. Nürnberg is Nürnberg. If I go on I shall be silly, even if I've not been already". (July 3, 1859) It is already apparent that he could rapturously lose himself in the atmosphere of the Middle Ages, provided it was not spurious. Circumstances also played a part in his delight. The weather was fine, the company pleasant. We will observe exactly the same conditions when many years later, in Normandy, he loses his heart forever to the Gothic. But for the time being he could only get drunk, as in Antwerp, on his emotions, and then sober up. We hear of no such raptures when, together with Mr. and Mrs. Charles Kuhn, during the summer of 1859, he "conscientiously did his cathedrals, his Rhine, and whatever his companions suggested." Back in Dresden, where he spent the following winter, he indulged in some Gothic humor, à la Horace Walpole, and to the dismay of his landlady, he determined to "hunt up a ghost, select a ruined castle" and "sleep there a night to see if the spectre will be hospitable. Of course it must be really romantic; otherwise it will only be a bore."[32]

As soon as spring returned, Adams gladly left Germany. From

Vienna, Venice, Bologna, and Florence in April, Rome in May, and Naples in June, he sent letters which appeared in the Boston *Daily Courier* under the title "Letters from a Tourist." Concerning himself with the "human" landscape, he wrote only about the people he met. What he then felt in front of the monuments of Rome, he kept to himself; "one's emotions in Rome were one's private affair," not to be displayed in a newspaper. But he would recollect them in *The Education*: "Italy was mostly an emotion and emotion naturally centered in Rome . . . The month of May, 1860, was divine . . . In 1860 the lights and shadows were still mediaeval and mediaeval Rome was alive; the shadows breathed and glowed, full of soft forms felt by lost senses. No sand-blast of science had yet skinned off the epidermis of history, thought and feeling. The pictures were uncleaned, the churches unrestored, the ruins unexcavated. Mediaeval Rome was sorcery." He was in love with the city, "Passionately, perversely, wickedly." There, about one century earlier, during an evening on the steps of the church of Santa Maria of Ara Coeli, Gibbon had conceived the idea of writing the *Decline and Fall of the Roman Empire*. The passage was quoted in Adams' guidebook. Often he would go and sit on the same steps of Ara Coeli; he "had no idea what he was doing. The thought of posing for a Gibbon never entered his mind." This was undoubtedly true. His emotions remained those of a young well-read Bostonian, intent on having an enjoyable time. How could he have then visualized himself becoming a professor of medieval history? In Antwerp, Nürnberg, Rome, he had been struck with the picturesqueness of the Middle Ages. His was a tourist's emotion, a passing excitement, not an "education."[33]

MUCH WENLOCK

"I rather fancy it was the biggest piece of luck I ever had," wrote Adams toward the end of his life. He referred to the seven years in England which we are now going to examine. After a not too successful try at journalism, he left the United States again in 1861 accompanying his father, Charles Francis Adams, who had been appointed minister to the Court of St. James, and whom he was to serve in the capacity of private secretary (without pay) during all the time this mission lasted, that is, until 1868. "It was a golden time for me and altered my whole life," he also reminisced. Indeed, more than during his actual studies at Cambridge, he now had, in Melville's phrase, his "Yale college and Harvard." The years in London are central to his life, just as they are to *The Education*.[34]

The psychological value of these years chiefly lies in the political education he received "with the most costly tutors in the world, provided for him at public expense." He found himself in the thick of action, though, to be sure, it was diplomatic action and not the fighting round Vicksburg or at Shiloh. He was only a minor participant, with limited responsibilities, but never again in his life would he feel so important. Actuality engrossed him. Machiavellian as British politicians were, however, or rather as they seemed to be, they could hardly, through the channel of imagination, throw him back into times as remote as the Middle Ages. We seldom find the word "medieval" in his writings dealing with his London experiences; coupled with "amusing," it is used to describe English dinner parties "sometimes coarse to a degree that might have startled a roustabout, and sometimes courteous and considerate to a degree that suggested King Arthur's Round Table." For though the Adams family had arrived like a "family of Christian martyrs about to be flung into an arena of lions, under the glad eyes of Tiberius Palmerston," soon enough Henry would be able to complain of "the rush and fuss of society" and describe himself "knocking about at dinners, balls, breakfasts from Rotten Row to Regent's Park."[35] Some parties had a distinct literary atmosphere, such as the one where he met Algernon Swinburne. "The name suggested nothing" to him, and on that occasion, while listening to the "wild Walpurgis night of Swinburne's talk," he felt quite conscious of the special quality of his "Boston mind which in its uttermost flights was never *moyenageux*," the latter adjective meaning "medieval with a grotesque turn."[36] Nothing could come out of such a chance encounter.

If Adams had any "poetic" inclinations, he drew on his Italian memories. "As for me," he wrote to Charles Francis Adams, Jr., in November 1863: "my old tendencies grow on me more and more. If we lived a thousand years ago instead of now, I should have become a monk and would have got hold as Abbot of one of those lovely little monasteries which I used to admire so much among the hills in Italy."[37] He apparently little thought there could have been any such monastery in England, or any medieval monument at all. There is not a single allusion to Westminster Abbey or the Tower of London in his Letters. When he traveled about the country he never saw, if we rely on his sole testimony, one of these Gothic cathedrals which Emerson had admired. The Middle Ages did not interest him in the least.

About a year after his wistful letter to Charles Francis, Jr., Henry could spend a weekend in a genuine monastic setting—an experience all the more pleasant since he was also in an English country house, verily "the perfection of human society." He was the guest of Charles Milnes Gaskell, an amiable young man whose acquaintance he had recently made. Of Yorkshire extraction, Gaskell's father sat in Parliament for the borough of Wenlock, in Shropshire, where he had bought the old Priory of Much Wenlock. The place was historic enough, with a longer past than any house where the young American had ever been invited to stay.[38]

There had been three monastic foundations on this very site. The earliest had been established about 680 A.D. by Merewald, king of Mercia, as a nunnery to be ruled over by his daughter, afterward known as St. Milburge. She died about 722 A.D., and the nunnery was destroyed by the Danes when they ravaged and conquered Mercia, probably in 784. Nearly two centuries later, about 1050 A.D., a minster church was established there by Leofric, Earl of Mercia, husband of the famous Lady Godiva, and a friend of Edward the Confessor. Well endowed, it was presumably a building of some architectural pretensions, but no part of it seems to have survived. Domesday Book, which was compiled in 1086, twenty years after the Norman Conquest, states that Roger de Montgomery, the Norman Earl of Shrewsbury, "has made the Church of St. Milburge into an abbey." Roger was a kinsman of William the Conqueror, who gave him practically the whole of Shropshire as part of his English estates, and was the founder of Shrewsbury Abbey as well as Wenlock Priory. The latter he gave to the French Abbey of Cluny, and that is why it is not strictly correct to refer to it, as Henry Adams does in *The Edu-*

cation, as Wenlock Abbey. However rich and powerful they became, all Cluniac houses ranked only as priories, dependent upon the parent abbey of Cluny. William of Malmesbury tells how when the new building was begun, the resting place of St. Milburge's remains was unknown, but a boy ran across the site, the ground gave way beneath his weight, and the grave of the saint was disclosed: "A fragrant odour of balsam breathed through the church, and her body raised high wrought so many miracles that floods of people poured in thither. Scarcely could the broad fields contain the crowds, while rich and poor together, fired by a common faith, hastened on their way. None came to return without the cure or mitigation of his malady."[39]

Nearly all the existing remains of the church date from a reconstruction of the thirteenth century, and enough survive to give some idea of the structure. Nave and choir were each 156 feet long, and the crossing which separated them and which supported the great central tower was 39 feet long. The whole church thus had a length of more than 350 feet; transepts and aisles gave it a proportionate breadth, and its height is indicated by the impressive portions of south aisles and transepts that still remain. It was one of the very few Shropshire churches to have a triforium as well as a clerestory. Henry Adams soon loved to "scratch" in its ruins. For after the monastery's dissolution in 1540, most of its buildings were pulled down. There only remained in its original state the Prior's Lodging, long left to decay as a farmhouse but now converted into one of the finest country houses England could boast. It was L-shaped. Jutting toward the Norman entrance and divided off by a thick wall and chimney-breast built in the fifteenth century when the main stone newel stair was built, the thirteenth-century Farmery had been turned into a study as pleasant as the one Henry Adams would one day visualize in the place of the charterhouse at Mont-Saint-Michel. Most of the rooms were in the fifteenth-century wing, a beautiful structure with a fenestrated gallery running its full length, ceiling timbers, and indented cornice.

Henry James, who, upon Adams' recommendation, was twice a guest of the Gaskells in 1877 and 1878 gave a delightful account of these visits in *Portraits of Places* (1877). Henry Adams never wrote so lengthily on his own experiences, but what he said in *The Education* had the ring of truth: "Like Catherine Olney in 'Northanger Abbey,' he yearned for nothing so keenly as to feel at home in a thirteenth century abbey, unless it were to haunt a fifteenth century Prior's House, and both these joys were his at Wenlock. With companions or without, he never tired of it." In point of fact, Henry Adams did not go to Much Wenlock as often as may be inferred from *The Education,* where time obeys Bergsonian rules; at Much Wenlock we are told "time sequences became interchangeable. One's instinct abhors time." Yet one must have dates. These are all consigned in a guest book, still in the hands of the Gaskell family.[40]

One of the first entries, dated "October 2, 1864," and written in the very clear, upright hand familiar to all those who know Adams' manuscripts, reads "Henry Adams, United States of America." He was the only guest on that occasion. His second visit was left undated, but since this particular entry in a slanting hand is situated between entries dated November 29, 1865, and January 18, 1866, it is reasonably certain that Adams had come for Christmas; together with him were three Oxford students. On July, 1866, a jocular "Henry Brooks Adams, Dux Massachusettensis" again appended his signature in his usual upright hand; the only other time he came during these London years was on May 31, 1868. These are naturally not the sole entries bearing his name. In after years, Adams still more than once repaired to the old priory. Thus we can find his name ("H. B. Adams, Washington, D.C.") three times in 1870 for June 16–21, August 9–24 and August 31–September 2, as though he were then taking a "refresher" in medieval atmosphere, to qualify for the professorship which was in store for him at Harvard. In 1872 (July 22-28) and 1873 (July 19-25) he brought Marian Adams to his friend's house. Eight years elapsed before his next visit on September 24, 1880, with Marian Adams, and then eleven more before he came back, a lonely widower, in 1891 (November 12), to return again in 1895 (July 30), 1898 (July 22-25), 1902 (September 23), 1907 (August 19, and also September 7-9), that year for the last time. The place had by then become sacred in his memory. "One's youth still has glamour, and mine owes most of it to you," he wrote to

Gaskell on June 29, 1909. "I do not know that I care to live over again any part of my life, but if I did, the part connected with Wenlock and you would be it,—the most pleasure and the least pain."[41]

Adams had a number of friends who played an essential part in his life. Had he not known John Hay, Clarence King, John La Farge, no doubt his *Education* would have been written along quite different lines. Less brilliant, less "intellectual," Gaskell probably influenced Adams far less than his other friends did; himself destined to a mildly distinguished career as a liberal M.P., he shared little of Adams' life after 1878, at least directly. Yet because of his innate kindness, his openhearted simplicity, he appears to have been the friend *par excellence*, to whom Adams sent his most spontaneous letters. He assumes an exceptional importance in this study. It was thanks to Gaskell that Adams really found a home in England, and it so happened that this home was redolent of the Middle Ages, a period which then became connected in his mind with happiness and fullness of heart. Only by a long—though not unwarranted—stretch of the imagination can Much Wenlock appear as, so to speak, the antechamber of Chartres. But it is obvious that by steeping the young American in a medieval atmosphere, it gave him the tincture, perhaps limited but altogether genuine, which was to justify his appointment as a professor of medieval history.

RUSKIN AND CLARENCE KING

"Art was a superb field for education," Adams observed while recounting his London years; according to his own testimony, he learned very little. Yet it was the period of his life when he was most exposed to English influences and more particularly Ruskinian art theories. How is it that he could not—or would not—ever acknowledge any kind of indebtedness to Ruskin? This is worth investigating, since, as Roger B. Stein remarks, in his study on Ruskin and aesthetic thought in America, *Mont-Saint-Michel and Chartres* was to be "the last great monument of the Gothic Revival in America," a movement intimately bound up with "Ruskinism."[42]

With the publication of the fifth volume of *Modern Painters* in 1860, not long before Adams' arrival in England, Ruskin had just completed his major work; his reputation stood at its highest point. "He has attained," stated a critic of the time, "the proud position of one of the greatest of all writers, living or dead, on the subject of art." Indeed, no man had done more to create the very taste by which he was admired. A vocal defender of Turner —his Earthly Master, as he said—he had also been most instrumental in the development of the Gothic revival. It had not originated with him, but by giving it the force derived from his resources of argument, imagination, eloquence, first in *The Seven Lamps of Architecture* (1848) and then in the three volumes of *The Stones of Venice* (completed by 1853), he had made it popular. "We do not remember anything in the history of art in England," wrote a reviewer in the *North British Review* of May 1854, "at all corresponding in suddenness and extent to the effect which the works of Mr. Ruskin have already exercised upon the popular taste directly and, through popular taste, on the taste and theories of artists themselves."[43]

The exceptional impact of these theories was in good part due to their being put on a squarely Protestant basis. A. W. Pugin, who, in his *Contrasts: A Parallel between the Noble Edifices of the Fourteenth and Fifteenth Centuries and Similar Buildings of the Present Day, Showing the Present Decay of Taste* (London, 1836), anticipated Ruskin's attack on the crassness of modern times when compared with the Middle Ages, exerted much less influence because his Gothicism seemed to be too closely linked with High Ritualism and the then three-year-old Oxford Movement. There is little doubt that his religious views cost him the leadership of the Gothic revival in England as well as in America, where his books were not reprinted. Ruskin, on the other hand, in addition to being a better writer than Pugin, could make the Gothic more generally acceptable by his specific appeal to the moral sense of his Protestant readers; he also stressed the civic side of medieval architecture.

Nowhere was the strength of Ruskin's words more felt than at Oxford, where Burne-Jones and Morris were undergraduates. Ruskin became for them, says J. W. Mackail, Morris' biographer, "a hero and a prophet," a position which was reinforced by the appearance of *The Stones of Venice* in 1853. "The famous chapter on 'The Nature of Gothic Architecture' long afterward lovingly reprinted by Morris as one of the earliest productions of the Kelmscott Press was a new Gospel and a fixed creed."[44] In the preface of the Kelmscott edition, in 1892, Morris was to tell the significance of this particular chapter which proved, he said, "one of the very few necessary and inevitable utterances of the century." "To some of us," he went on, "when first we read it, it seemed to point a new road on which the world should travel." This was not exactly the road to Chartres along which Adams would one day travel, but it did lead toward the Middle Ages. It may be here parenthetically noted that Adams never took notice of Morris as a fellow medievalist. He never mentioned his name. He never bought or (we may add with reasonable certainty) read his edition of "The Nature of Gothic Architecture," even though the chapter was issued again in 1899 with Morris' preface and had a large popular sale, at the very time he was himself engaged in the writing of *Mont-Saint-Michel and Chartres.*

To be sure, Adams read "something of Ruskin" while he was in England. But we know little besides the fact that he owned the original editions of *The Seven Lamps of Architecture, The Stones of Venice,* and *Modern Painters,* all probably acquired after his arrival in London. He did not record the dates of his purchases on the fly leaves, as was his wont with some of the books on which he set great store. Neither did he, at that time or in after years, score any line or scribble any entry in the margins, as he usually did, when his attention was arrested. Only once, in 1906, would he allude (quite apologetically) to this reading: "I pardon nobody for bad Gothic and Venetian taste. Yet once I read Ruskin and admired . . . Lord, but we date!" He may have then admired the "word-painter" for the luxuriance of his style. As to the fundamentals of his teaching, he does not seem to have paid much heed to them.[45]

One of the modern Gothic structures which Ruskin appreciated most was the Assize Courts at Manchester: "much beyond everything yet done in England on my principles," he wrote to his father in 1863. Adams traveled to Manchester, but he did not find any interest in the building which was being erected at that very time. In the seven years he spent in England, we may easily imagine that he visited Oxford at least once; his fellow guests at Much Wenlock during the Christmas holiday in 1865 were, as we saw, Oxford students. But, if he ever visited the town, he nowhere recorded his impressions, either of the old colleges or of the new museum whose carved foliage, Gothic forms, and generally rich decorative exterior all testified to Ruskin's direct influence on its architect.[46]

Indeed, until he began his visits to Much Wenlock, in late 1874, Adams does not appear to have been very interested in architecture. "As often as he could," we read in *The Education*, he ran over to Paris, "for sunshine" and convivial meetings with H. H. Richardson, now a student at the Beaux Arts; by his own admission, he caught very little of what lay in his friend's mind "because, to Adams, everything French was bad excepting for the restaurants." In England, on the other hand, while his father "would wander off on a Sunday to attend services successively in all the City churches built by Sir Christopher Wren," his own inclinations led him to Sotheby's, where he attended "sales of drawings, engravings and water-colors." For he claimed some connoisseurship in the pictorial arts because he saw, or "thought he saw," something in Turner. It is significant that even in this connection the name of Turner's most active champion does not come up. Neither shall we find the name of any other English contemporary painter. The Pre-Raphaelite Brotherhood, as far as Adams was concerned, never existed, a fact all the more noteworthy since, for the Americans, according to R. B. Stein, "the line between the Pre-Raphaelite Brotherhood and Ruskin was extremely blurred." Thus the "hit" of the first Pre-Raphaelite exhibition held in the United States in 1857 had been one of Ruskin's sketches. For all his sessions at Sotheby's (and we doubt there were many), Adams' connoisseurship exerted itself in what closely resembles an artistic vacuum.[47]

In addition to the young man's lack of genuine interest in aesthetics, we may find two other good reasons for his virtual ignorance of Ruskin. One was Ruskin's clearly expressed antipathy toward the Union's cause during the war. And besides, there was, since mid-1860, his shift to economics. Described by the *Saturday Review* as "eruptions of windy hysterics" and "absolute nonsense," his "Essays on the First Principles of Political Economy" (*Unto this Last*) had to be stopped after the third issue of the *Cornhill Magazine*, in 1860, because they were "seen to be too deeply tainted with socialistic heresy to conciliate subscribers." In 1863, another series of essays in the same vein which began to appear in *Fraser's Magazine* raised the same storm of protest and met with an identical fate. Always a missionary and a preacher, the man could now less than ever appeal to a self-styled "dilettante." Yet it so came to pass that at that very time, despite his anti-Union stand and his economic "vagaries," Ruskin was reaching the height of his American popularity. A group of young New York men who proclaimed him as their "leader" organized the Society for the Advancement of Truth in Art. Beginning in May 1863, they published an aggressive little journal called *The New Path*, which served as a vehicle for Ruskin's doctrines. Among them could be numbered the geologist Clarence King, later one of Henry Adams' closest friends.[48]

As King was away on his first geological expedition to the far West from April 1863 to January 1865, the part he played in the Society for the Advancement of Truth in Art and its journal (which ceased publication at the end of 1865) is not clear. But there is no reason to doubt his Ruskinism. We have an anecdote vouched for by John Hay and John La Farge, who were also to become close friends of Adams'. At a picture dealer's in London in 1882, King began discussing a canvas with an anonymous customer and "argued upon a number of subtle points which to him were evident." His opponent, whom he delighted with "the value and form of these sayings and criticisms," turned out to be John Ruskin. According to Hay, "Ruskin took him to heart, entertained him at Coniston and offered him his choice of his two greatest watercolors by Turner. 'One good Turner,' said King, 'deserves another,' and took both."[49]

What could make a scientist of a skeptical turn of mind (as is proved by his portrait, under the name of George Strong, in *Esther*) join a group of artists and give his lifelong adherence to their ideals? For "throughout his life," states Roger Stein, King was "never to be wholly free of the tension between his scientific bent and his Ruskinism." He cannot have been attracted by Ruskin's anti-Catholic stand (a major factor with the critic Charles Eliot Norton, who had been an ardent Know-Nothing), or by what Henry James would one day call his "moralism *à tout propos*" and "queer provincialities and pruderies." A reason may be found in Ruskin's amateur studies with Reverend William Buckland, which had led him to spread a veneer of geology over *Modern Painters* (Adams, who during his English years also dabbled in geology, would in his turn use such a veneer in *The Education*, but not, it must be stressed, in *Mont-Saint-Michel and Chartres*). Another reason was Ruskin's acute aesthetic sensitivity to landscapes, which was wholly shared by King and made the latter exclaim when he saw Mt. Shasta: "What would Ruskin have said, if he saw *this*!"[50]

Roger B. Stein has clearly pointed out the primary basis of Ruskin's appeal to the Americans at that time: "To the vast American public whose knowledge of art was very limited, to the young writers of the *New Path* who were unfamiliar with the wealth of European art of the past, upon which a philosophy of art might test its ideas, and to a nation which prided itself on its relation to nature and its freedom from tradition, Ruskin's dogmatic devotion to 'truth to nature' had a compelling force."

In other words, his appeal was essentially based on their American love of nature and not on their understanding of art, an understanding which, with most of them, remained tantamount to a kind of blissful ignorance. Adams' own ignorance at that stage, despite all his contacts with Europe, may serve as a case in point. Even so, however, it must be conceded that Adams showed little sign of that "Ruskinian Youth" whose ghosts, if we believe Roger B. Stein, he had to lay before he could write a book, "itself the last testament of a generation whose youth belonged to the nineteenth century," and Ruskin.[51]

The mule which, in one of the most heartfelt passages of *The Education*, leads her benighted rider to Estes Park and Clarence King perhaps leads him also to Ruskin. Whether we agree or not with Adams in his selection of the year 1871 as the dividing line in his life, when (he had been appointed at Harvard the summer before) he "stopped" his own education and began to apply it to practical purposes, the importance of the instant friendship he then struck up with Clarence King is obvious. It marks the real beginning of a second and (for our purpose) far more important "education": that of the artist in him. As he himself wrote, "King had everything to interest and delight Adams. He knew more than Adams did of art and poetry . . . The charm of King was that he saw what others did and a great deal more." Robert Spiller has stressed the part played by King in Adams' literary awakening: "It was largely under King's influence that Adams embarked upon his most profound exploration of human experience . . . It was King who stood behind his shoulder when he wrote *A Letter to American Teachers of History* and who first prompted the final pages of *The Education*."[52] This may be so. Yet, when the time came for these speculative adventures, King had already died, whereas he was still alive when his friend began *Mont-Saint-Michel and Chartres*. And even if he did not then physically stand behind Adams' shoulders, he was, and remains, unmistakably present. Indeed no "literary" influence could make itself felt more strongly; it was through such an influence that the book received whatever "Ruskinian" color it still has.

For we have to disagree with J. C. Levenson, who in *The Mind and Art of Henry Adams* traces the inception of *Mont-Saint-Michel and Chartres* to "the literary journalism of Jules Lemaître and Anatole France."[53] As will be my contention throughout this study, if Adams' Gothic pilgrimage was naturally bound to have a European setting, he nonetheless moved in an American intellectual landscape. One of the best examples American travel literature could offer was King's *Mountaineering in the Sierra Nevada*. Most of it appeared in 1871 in the form of articles in the *Atlantic Monthly;* it was to come out in book form the following year and again in a revised edition in 1874. King could not have been more saturated with his work than during that summer of 1871, when the two young men spent night upon night talking "till the frosts became sharp in the mountain," and when "history and science spread out," for Adams, under the stimulus of his new friend's talks, "in personal horizons towards goals no longer far away." One of these goals, though he did not yet see it, was Chartres.[54]

Mountaineering in the Sierra Nevada has been ranked by Van Wyck Brooks with *The Oregon Trail* and *Two Years Before the Mast:* "What made the book unique, as Parkman's and Dana's in their fields, one for the plains, one for the ocean,—was its special feeling for the mountains." Just as, let us add, *Mont-Saint-Michel and Chartres* would in its turn be made unique by its "special feeling" for the Gothic cathedrals. Here, in this account of an expedition undertaken in the flush of his Ruskinian enthusiasm in 1863, King exemplified what he meant when in 1869 he wrote of his "intense yearning" to complete his "analytical study of nature and drink in the sympathetic side." (Change nature for the Gothic, and this will perfectly hold for *Mont-Saint-Michel and Chartres* with its constant appeal to "sympathy." Unlike the Survey Reports of the U.S. Geological Expedition of the Fortieth Parallel, which he supervised, or his own *Systematic Geology* (1878), this work gave him a chance to project himself into his material. He did not content himself with quoting "facts" but, in his descriptions of western landscapes, showed all the emotional and imaginative capacities of the Ruskinian observer, faithfully adhering to his Master's Ideal of "Truth to Nature." By allowing what he called the "Juggernaut of the Intellect" to give way to an upsurge of feeling in front of Beauty, the scientist was setting up an example which a skeptical historian could one day follow.[55]

Did King also help Adams to a better understanding of the Gothic? He had as yet, in the early seventies, never been to Europe and had never seen a genuine Gothic monument, but he owed to Ruskin the conviction that the Alps furnished models for the early Gothic builders. In the Sierras, sharp roof ridges, flying buttresses, and jutting pinnacles naturally shaped themselves to his eyes. "To refuse to see the architectural suggestions upon the Snake canyon," he wrote, "is to administer a flat snub to one's fancy." His imagination (or "fancy," as it is called here) fed all the more freely on such associations that throughout his life he had an amateur interest in the Gothic. In 1885, together with the painter John La Farge, who himself had been an admirer of Ruskin's, he submitted plans for the tomb of President Grant. Although their project which called for the then revolutionary use of structural glass was rejected, his interest in the problem led him to air his views on architecture in an article called "Style and the Monument." What he then said about the Gothic, ten years, as we will see, before Adams had his true "Revelation" of the Gothic in Normandy, could serve as a motto to *Mont-Saint-Michel and Chartres:* "It seems to the writer that this is neither the age nor people to meddle with Gothic art. To do Gothic work requires a Gothic heart, a Gothic head and a Gothic hand. We are sophisticated, *blasé*, indifferent to nature, and conventional to the last degree. The men who awoke from the sleep of the Dark Ages and suddenly broke loose from monastic authority, prerogative, and precedent, and within fifty years created a style and carried it to the consummate flower of its whole life, were simple, direct, and religious. They made a passionate appeal direct to nature to help them in their new ideas of ornamentation, and she showered her favors upon them."[56] Whether King directly influenced Adams in these later years is immaterial. He had truly shown him the road to Chartres, which was the road of the heart.

2
Doctor Barbaricus

"TWO HUNDRED STUDENTS,
THE OLDEST IN THE COLLEGE."

According to *The Education,* Adams was a guest at Much Wen-lock when "he received a letter from President Eliot inviting him to take an Assistant Professorship to be created shortly at Harvard College." It came as a pleasant surprise; even a *Terebratula,* after "waiting ten or a dozen years for some one to show consciousness of his existence," would have been grateful for such a compliment. But, because he had no calling for such a position, Adams re-fused.[1]

In reality, when this offer arrived, Adams happened to be in Italy, at Bagni di Lucca, at the bedside of his sister Louisa, who was dying of tetanus; then, not just one letter from President Eliot, but two, reached him after having pursued him across Europe. It is, however, certain that he began by turning down the proposal. After his return home, "troublesome" pressure was put on him; concurring with the president and the dean of the college, "his father interposed, his mother entreated and his brother

Charles argued and urged" that he accept. "I hesitated a week, and then yielded," he wrote to Gaskell on September 29, 1870. "Now I am, I believe, assistant professor of History at Harvard College with a Salary of £400 a year, and two hundred students, the oldest in the College, to whom I am to teach Mediaeval History, of which, as you are aware, I am utterly and grossly ignorant . . . With the professorship, I take the *North American Review* and become its avowed editor."[2]

The circumstances leading to Adams' appointment have been analyzed by Ernest Samuels and Oscar Cargill; it appears that Ephraim Whitney Gurney, professor of ancient history and the university's first dean, was most instrumental in the matter. A tradition in the Hooper family has it, writes Ward Thoron, "that Gurney, after successfully tutoring Brooks Adams, Henry's younger brother, was recommended by Minister Adams to Dr. Hooper as an excellent person to teach his eldest daughter who wished to study Greek." Whether Helen Hooper learned much Greek is not known; in the autumn of 1870 she married her teacher, making him a rather wealthy man. No longer in need of the stipend attached to the editorship of the *North American Review* he had been saddled with during the last two years, Gurney was looking for a successor who would assist him in the newly reorganized department of history. Henry Adams seemed to him a fitting choice. Gurney had not only learned to appreciate the young man as a contributor to the *Review* but, by offering him a position, could repay a debt of gratitude to his family. And, in agreeing with Gurney, President Eliot (a classmate of John Quincy Adams, Henry's eldest brother) may also have been motivated by rather powerful personal considerations, since one of the most influential members of the board of Harvard Overseers was Charles Francis Adams, Sr. As a matter of fact, it was the latter's refusal of the presidency in 1869 (when President Hill resigned from his office) which left the post vacant for Eliot.[3]

So, in September 1870, "at twenty-four hours' notice," or practically so, Adams embarked upon a new career for which he had never prepared and signed a five-year contract which he did not intend to renew. A letter to his friend Gaskell, dated October 25, 1870, is indicative of his attitude and feelings at this stage: "Here

I am, fairly established and frightfully hard at work . . . I don't believe in the system of which I am made a part, and thoroughly dislike and despise the ruling theories of education in the university. So I . . . shall quietly substitute my own notions for those of the College and teach in my own way. There will be some lively history taught, I can tell you. I hardly know how I am getting on with the students, but I think we shall be on good terms. I have about a hundred, all more or less advanced, as to age at least, though as a rule they are supernaturally lazy and ignorant. I pound at them in vain nine hours a week. If it weren't that I am always learning I should soon grow fearfully tired of teaching." A major theme in this letter—as in nearly all the correspondence and the part of *The Education* dealing with these years—is the urgency of the task which suddenly confronted him. "The assistant professor had no time to waste on comforts and amusements. He exhausted all his strength in trying to keep one day ahead of his duties. Often the stint ran on, till night and sleep ran short." But, as he wrote to Gaskell in March 1871, he liked "being overworked. There is a pleasant excitement in having to lecture to-morrow on a period of history which I have not even heard of to-day."[4]

At any rate, studying was then practically his sole resource. As he complained in *The Education,* Cambridge life proved quite deadly. "Several of the best-educated, most agreeable and presumably the most sociable people in America united to make a social desert that would have starved a polar bear."[5] One of these men was Professor Gurney, "gracious, genial and scholarly . . . probably the best read man in the country."[6] In this gentle, dedicated teacher Adams found a very humane colleague whose house he could frequently visit; and by no means the least of his discoveries, he soon also found a brother-in-law. Within two years of his appointment, he had married Marian Hooper, Mrs. Gurney's sister. But this, Adams did not choose to recollect.

Another "most sociable" colleague was his former teacher, James Russell Lowell, who during the first two years shared with him the editorship of the *North American Review.* Though the disparity of age precluded an intimate friendship, there developed between the two associates a very easy relationship which made Adams rank Lowell among "the liveliest and most agreeable of men who tried to break out and be like other men in Cambridge . . ." Coming as he had to his professorship at the age of thirty-seven, after fifteen years of free literary life, Lowell, according to the portrait Ferris Greenslet draws in his biography, "was wholly devoid of academic mannerisms."[7] He always remained so, as he always remained capable of great, enduring enthusiasms, such as his love for the Gothic, and more particularly for Chartres. He had visited the cathedral on a glorious summer day in 1855, and the memory of the day, of the sublimity of the architecture, remained a haunting source of inspiration. Long after, in August 1869, it came to fruition with "something immense, as the slang is nowadays," running to more than 800 lines of blank verse. The poem had written itself; "all of a sudden it was *there*," Lowell told a friend; "it is a kind of religious poem and it is called 'A Day at Chartres'." James T. Fields, the publisher to whom it was dedicated and who brought it out for Christmas the very same year, in a "sumptuous" edition with "beautiful" engravings of a cathedral door and cathedral interior, preferred to rechristen it *The Cathedral*.[8] But as a contemporary critic remarked, "it would be difficult to devise any title sufficiently elastic to embrace very closely so capricious an outline of subject as the poem presented."[9]

Could the poem, such as it was, already have started Adams in imagination on the road to Chartres, just as Lowell's lectures, in his student days had sent him to Germany? "Filled with religious nostalgia and the anguish of the unwilling sceptic," comments Samuels, *The Cathedral* "could not help but speak directly to Henry's heart." It provided him with a "poetic chart," easy to follow.[10] Such is also the thesis of Oscar Cargill, who sees in this poem the very seed out of which *Mont-Saint-Michel and Chartres* was one day to germinate, a surmise which we would find difficult to support. There is no copy of the book in Adams' library, and his letters bring no evidence that he ever read it. No doubt he may have heard of Chartres from Lowell, thus gaining a faint and early interest in the subject, but it seems that the poet's influence then exerted itself in a different direction.

By a striking coincidence, it was in 1870, the year of Adams' return to Harvard, that Lowell began to teach French medieval literature, his latest passion. That year, not only did he start offering the seniors three hours of "elective studies in Bartsch's *Chrestomathie de l'Ancien Français,* but he also delivered a series of thirty-six "University Lectures," open to the public. Just as Adams was doing in his own field, Lowell was certainly breaking new ground. He later told of his experience: "When I first became interested in old French, I made a surprising discovery. If the books which I took from the College library had been bound with gilt or yellow edges these edges stuck together as, when ornamented, they are wont to do till the leaves have been turned. No one had ever opened these books before. 'I was the first that ever burst/ Into that silent sea.' "[11] Such a discovery must have taken place in 1869. Already in Lowell's *Cathedral,* Roland blows his "vain blast," as he would with Adams in the Abbey of Mont-Saint-Michel. We know that in the autumn the poet was busy preparing what he then visualized as a series of twenty lectures. The number expanded during the following months, as Lowell became more and more immersed in his reading. "All summer," he wrote on October 14, 1870, "I have been studying old French metrical romances, and have done an immense deal of reading." When these lectures were finally delivered, Longfellow occasionally sat among the audience. Thus we learn from his diary that on October 3, 1870, he heard "Lowell's introduction on Old French Poets." Another morning, on February 10, 1871, after reading Lowell's "new book," (that is, *The Cathedral*), he listened to his comment on Reynard the Fox, comments which must have been quite provocative, since in the afternoon we find Longfellow reading over "some passages in the poem and also Chaucer's Nonne's Priest's Tale, which is taken from Renard and idealized."[12] On neither of these occasions nor on any other does Adams seem to have been present. Whether the thought even occurred to him that he might attend one of these *causeries* is doubtful; he was far too busy keeping abreast of his own students, in preparing his own lectures. At any rate, when meeting Lowell in his capacity as co-editor, he still had an opportunity to hear the poet talk on his current interests, in addition to all matters concerning the Review.

Anyone calling on Lowell in these years, says William Dean Howells, was likely to find him engrossed in reading some old book. Indeed, if there was one thing Lowell loved anywhere near so well

Doctor Barbaricus

as reading books, it was, Greenslet remarks, "talking about them."[13] In 1872 he was still "plunged to his ears" in Old French, as may be judged from this letter: "Everything goes on here as usual. Three times a week I have my class . . . in Bartsch, *Chrestomathie de l'Ancien Français.* On Wednesday I have besides a University class with whom I read the *Chanson de Roland,* and I am now reading the *Roman de la Rose.* On my off-days, the first thing in the morning, I go over my work for the next day, and then renew my reading of old French."[14] In the early summer of the same year we may follow him to Europe, where he was to stay until 1874, sojourning chiefly in Paris. Although he had resigned his professorship before leaving, he kept working at Old French with unabated zeal and very often puzzled booksellers, he amusedly noted, with his mixture of *ancien français* and the modern lingo. Once back in Cambridge he regained his chair, and for three more years he again held his seminars on Dante and Old French poetry. These had become his specialties. He lectured on nothing else. And we may note that after his final departure in 1877, the same year as Adams' leaving, Old French ceased, at least for some time, to be studied at Harvard. Though the subject would eventually again enter the syllabus, no one in Cambridge could ever replace Lowell as a genial lover of Old French. "Never quite a scholar," says Greenslet, "in the German sense of the word, nor even in the modern academic sense," he was to an admirable degree a humanist with "the old-time scholar's deep imaginative perception of the unity and coherence of this various old world." Yet in 1889, two years before his death, he wondered about the usefulness of all these years of studying Old French; "I cannot see exactly what good it has done me or any one else."[15] The good he had done was to open a new world to a whole generation of Harvard students, and although Adams does not acknowledge this particular debt to Lowell, no doubt he, too, from his private conversations with the old master, had been able to gain some "imaginative perception of the unity and coherence" of medieval literature. Thus it would not be paradoxical to consider *Mont-Saint-Michel and Chartres* in its literary part as probably the best "paper" ever written by one of Lowell's pupils, even if at the time when Lowell delivered these courses Adams never sat in the audience.

"Between Gurney's classical courses and Torrey's modern ones, there lay a gap of a thousand years, which Adams was expected to fill." It was an enormous gap, even if slightly contracted to the dates 800–1649, between which, in fact, Adams was "absolutely free" to teach what he pleased.[16] Since the University records for 1870–1871 are not very clear, we shall draw upon the catalogues of the following years after the new assistant professor had fallen into his stride, to gain a notion of what was done in history. Five courses of instruction were offered for the academic year 1871–1872:

1—Roman and Mediaeval History (2 hours) *Prof.* Gurney.
2—The General History of Europe from the 10th to the 16th centuries (3 hours) *Asst. Prof.* Adams.
3—Mediaeval Institutions (advanced course) (3 hours) *Asst. Prof.* Adams.
4—History of England to the 17th century (3 hours) *Asst. Prof.* Adams.
5—Modern History—from the 17th century to the first half of the 18th (3 hours).

—from the second half of the 18th century (3 hours) *Prof.* Torrey. Though we will not go as far as Charles A. Wagner in stating that Adams "practically founded the History department with his presence at this time,"[17] it is quite obvious that he had to bear the brunt of the teaching. On the courses offered the previous year, the 1872–1873 catalogue gives some details for the guidance of the new students: "The studies pursued in 1871–72 by a candidate for the B.A. were partly *prescribed* and partly *optional*. The *prescribed studies* occupied the whole freshman year, about one half of the sophomore year, and about two-fifths of the junior year. In the senior year certain lectures and written exercises were required." All of Adams' courses were "elective." Now entitled "History of Germany, France and the Church (from the 8th to the 15th century), History 2 was the choice of thirty-three juniors who had to go through Hallam's *Middle Ages,* Menzel or Kohlrausch's *History of Germany*, Milman's *Latin Christianity,* and Student's *History of France* and hear "lectures" (unspecified). Seven juniors took History 3. The textbooks were Tacitus' *Germania,* Maine's *Ancient Law and Village Communities*, and Hallam's *Middle Ages.* "Lectures on Feudalism and Salic Law" are also mentioned. Finally, History 4 (attended by fifteen seniors) was based on Freeman's *Early English History*, Knight's, Lingard's or Pearson's *History of England,* and Stubbs' *Documents Illustrative of the Constitutional History of England.*

It is obvious that the emphasis in such courses lay heavily on Germanic or "Anglo-Saxon" history; the French Middle Ages were given short shrift. The only course dealing with the subject was History 2, which was also the only one Adams did not care to keep, no doubt because too many students took it. He taught it only one more year, in 1873–1874 (he had been "out of residence" the year before), to three seniors and sixty-five juniors, and then turned it over to Ernest Young, one of his doctoral candidates. Before doing so, he had prepared a six-page printed syllabus entitled "Political History of Europe from the 10th to the 15th century," which we may take to represent the final form this course had reached. Obviously inspired by the captions heading each of Hallam's chapters, 298 questions are listed, 105 bearing on Germany, the following 117 on the church. France comes last with a rather meager series of 76, none of which bore on its arts and letters. Students were expected to study maps of the north and south of France in order to be familiar with the location of many places such as La Hogue and the ford of Blanche Tache. Of Mont-Saint-Michel, of Chartres, however, there is no mention. In 1874 Adams ceased being concerned with the French Middle Ages and started a new course, History 5, on "Colonial History of America to 1789." The same year he also inaugurated a seminar in Anglo-Saxon law for Ph.D. candidates, the first history seminar ever held at Harvard.

Though this seminar was not exactly the first in the United States (Charles K. Adams had introduced the system at the University of Michigan five years earlier)[18] Henry Adams still deserves to be hailed as one of the most stimulating reformers in historical studies. Less than four weeks after his announcement to Gaskell, in October 1870 that he intended to quietly substitute his own notions for those of the college, he was able to boast to his friend of "smashing things here." "The devil is strong in me," he was also writing to another friend, "and my rage for reform is leading me into an open war with the whole system of teaching." Undoubtedly there was a great deal of pose in this attitude of a Saint George wishing to slay the dragon of scholasticism. Yet, fired with the enthusiasm well known to all beginners, he felt genuinely interested in his students (was he not still one himself?) and resolved on proving less boring to them than some of his own teachers had seemed to him. He soon had occasion to express these feelings in an article for the *North American Review*. While presenting long extracts from a diary written by President John Quincy Adams in his own Harvard days, the grandson was certainly thinking of the young men who sat in front of him in the lecture room: "One wishes to know what the student thought of himself, of his studies, and his instructors . . . with what spirit he met his work and with what amount of active aid and sympathy his instructors met him in dealing with his work and his amusements."[19] This *sympathy*, this *active aid* he felt duty bound to give, for he was "pleased with [his] lambs"; they were "lazy but not bad fellows" and quite "civil" besides; one of these young men, Lindsay Swift, later remembered him as an "affectionately-minded teacher," very genial, yet dignified in his attitude: "All was wholly unacademic; no formality, no rigidity, no professional pose, but you may be sure that there was never a suspicion of student roguishness or bad manners . . . He could make us laugh until we ached, but it was the laughter of a club, not a pothouse."[20]

In the classroom Adams was original, unexpected, and even explosive. His first aim upon assuming his functions had been to "get hold of the students' imaginations," and in this he often succeeded. The great political figures of the past were brought back to life. At that time, as in his book thirty years later, he was a "dramatist" of the Middle Ages. In a way, teaching was an amusement ("so long as I am amused," he wrote in November 1870, "I mean to go on with it"); it was a play in which he enjoyed acting a part. The students were his audience as well as his partners. Such is the feeling one gathers from his correspondence during his first months of teaching and from the memories of some of his best students. *The Education* sounds a different note: "he had no fancy for telling agreeable tales to amuse sluggish-minded boys." There is no real conflict, however, between these statements. Thinking over what he had tried to do at Harvard and the difficulties he had encountered, Adams also observed in *The Education*: "Any large body of students stifle the student. No man can instruct more than half a dozen students at once."[21] The attendance of 1873–1874 for History 2 was sadly in excess of this ideal number.

No doubt the teacher himself felt somewhat "stifled." He tried to protect himself by frightening away the "sluggish-minded." At the end of his first year he had intentionally given "papers so difficult that half the youths could do very little with them . . . It would be fun to send you some of my examination papers," he then told Gaskell. "My rules in making them up is to ask questions which I can't answer myself. It astounds me to see how some of my students answer questions which would play the deuce with me." In October 1873, he complained about being "put to my trumps to hold my own against my hundred students who think me too severe," a reputation, he added, he was "glad to foster." He was therefore glad to shift that burden to one of his protégés at the end of the year. When in 1876–1877 History 5 became in its turn too "popular" (it was elected by fifty-seven upperclass men), he had a potent reason to resign.[22]

Adams had a talent for stimulating and compelling the students to think for themselves. The theme runs through the recollections of all his pupils. Indeed, like Montaigne's, Adams' preference went to the *tête bien faite* rather than the *tête bien pleine*. In a letter he sent from London in 1873 to Henry Cabot Lodge, one of his first "disciples," and certainly his favorite, Adams made himself clear on the point: "For the present I was much less inclined to trouble myself about the amount you learned than about the method you were learning. I have no doubt more respect for knowledge, even where knowledge is useless and worthless, than for mere style, even where style is good; but unless one learns beforehand to be logically accurate and habitually thorough, mere knowledge is worth very little. At best it never can be more than relative ignorance, at least in the study of history." For such a reason, he had advised Lodge first "to master the scientific method, and to adopt the rigid principle of subordinating everything to perfect thoroughness of study." This, as he said in *The Education,* no doubt "smacked of German pedagogy," but in so doing he was "in the full tide of fashion."[23]

Blowing over the seas from Germany, the wind of reform in historical studies was beginning to ventilate American lecture rooms.[24] Adams was no lone pioneer, stumbling as if by mere chance upon some new and ingenious way of teaching. His originality lay in the fact that, to a greater extent than any of his fellow reformers, he was free from university tradition. Far from being absorbed in his speciality, he could stand somewhat aloof from his subject and assert that what one taught, after all, counted but little. As he was telling Henry Cabot Lodge in January 1873: "I propose no more to the fellows who are kind to think my teaching worth their listening to — those of them I mean who take the thing in the spirit I offer it in — than to teach them how to do their work. The College chose to make me Professor of History — I don't know why, for I knew no more history than my neighbors. And it pitchforked me into mediaeval history, of which I knew nothing. But it makes little difference what one teaches; the great thing is to train scholars for work, and for this there is no better field than mediaeval history to future historians. The mere wish to give a practical turn to my men has almost necessarily led me to give a strong legal bent to the study."[25] The last sentence is particularly interesting. Devoting, as we have noticed, scanty attention to the culture of the Middle Ages, Adams had plunged deeply into the study of its institutions which were not only the object of History 2, an "advanced course" for "candidates for honors," but also the sole theme of his "seminars" or "graduate courses," under the heading of "Anglo-Saxon Law" (1874–1875), "Early Mediaeval Institutions" (1876–1877). Organizing courses in this manner proved in keeping with a new trend at Harvard, whose law school was experiencing a revolution under its new dean, C. L. Langdell (also appointed by President Eliot in 1870). But Adams was also responding to an old family bent. The Adamses—no one more than John Adams, a great lawyer in his day—had always been a disputatious tribe; and now Brooks Adams, who would claim to derive his characteristics from ancestor John Adams, was also deep in law. Brooks had entered the Harvard Law School in February 1871; in April 1873, he was admitted to the bar; his studies naturally influenced his brother's interests at a time when they were living in close association. Henry turned to the law with relish; a most agreeable visit was one he paid during his European honeymoon in June 1873, to Sir Henry Maine, who then held the chair of comparative juris-prudence at Oxford.[26] He particularly liked recommending Maine's works to his students as fit objects of admiration as well as of criticism. "No writer . . . generalises more brilliantly. But every-one of his generalisations requires a lifetime of study."[27]

It was with genuine pleasure that Adams, about two years later, received the professor's last book, *Early History of Institu-tions*. In a letter of thanks he described how institutional history was taught at Harvard: "I have again this year taken a class through your *Ancient Law*, encouraging them to dispute, and overthrow if they could every individual proposition in it. Then we read the *Germania* and are now half way through the *Lex Salica*, translating and commenting on every sentence. They have had to read your *Village Communities*, McLennan's book, Nasse and everything else they could lay their hands on, including much Roman law and other stuff. They are deep in these on numerous abstruse points and argue in the lecture room by the hour." Of course, he very readily admitted, "except as an intellectual exer-cise," this work had little value and no practical result. One could only hope that, as a result, the students would "make better law-yers for the training." None of them as yet had been able to solve the riddles of archaic law. Neither, in point of fact, had their teacher, "in spite of having read more dreadful German lawbooks than a Christian community ought to tolerate."[28] Such exercises were nonetheless fraught with their own reward; the pleasure of the chase, of the investigation, and still more those of the battles of wit, when one pitted all the resources of his intelligence against another man's subtlety. The same zest for "arguing by the hour" still animates Adams' chapter on Abelard, in *Mont-Saint-Michel and Chartres*. What he said of his course on medieval institutions could very well apply to his later venture into the equally abstruse field of scholastic philosophy. He had no greater expectations for solving the riddle of archaic law than he had hopes for explicat-ing the mystery of the Trinity, but he immersed himself in the study and found it thoroughly "amusing."[29]

No one would dream of characterizing Adams as ebullient:

yet, to James Laurence Laughlin, who took his seminar in Anglo-Saxon law, he appeared "throughout this adventure in research . . . like a colt in tall clover." Books were really his clover. "The Nile is not a bad place for study, and I have run through a library of books there," he wrote during his honeymoon. At Harvard he maneuvred Sibley, the old, crossgrained librarian, into setting up a "Reserved Shelf" for all the books needed by students in his course, a system no one had ever thought of before.[30] During his first two years as a teacher he had been able to receive his smaller classes in his own quarters, two comfortable rooms on the ground floor of what is now called the Wadsworth House. After his marriage to Marian Hooper on June 27, 1872, and his subsequent year's leave of absence (a year which he forgot to deduct from the "seven" years of teaching referred to in *The Education*) he moved to Boston. There, in his own library, he used to hold his graduate seminars. Three students, Henry Cabot Lodge, James Laurence Laughlin, and Ernest Young, were preparing with him for the doctorate. "These were busy but halcyon days," Laughlin would remember: "We searched the early German code of the Visigoths, Burgundians and Salian Franks for the first glimmerings of the institutions which through the Normans and the Anglo-Saxons formed the basis of English and of course of American development . . . Besides the early codes and the writings of Weitz, Von Maurer, Sohm and other Germans we read and searched many times the whole collection of Anglo-Saxon laws and ploughed through twenty-five thousand pages of charters and capitularies in mediaeval Latin." Presumably it was grim work, but Adams took great pleasure in it. He was proud of "baking" a "batch of Doctors of Philosophy," Harvard's first Ph.D.'s. "I believe," he wrote in June 1876 to Cabot Lodge, "that my scholars will compare favorably with any others, English, German, French or Italian. I look with more hope on the future of the world as I see how good our material is."

The fruit of this common and arduous labor was a volume published at Adams' expense by Little, Brown & Co., *Essays in Anglo-Saxon Law*. Professor Herbert Baxter Adams of Johns Hopkins, who, more than any other teacher of his day, was familiar with academic activities in history, later called it "the first original work ever accomplished by American university students working in a systematic and thoroughly scientific way under proper direction." Indeed it was from this work that, according to President Gilman, H. B. Adams borrowed the idea of his own series of *Johns Hopkins Studies in History and Political Science.*[31]

An interesting episode must be noted here: so high was President Gilman's esteem for Henry Adams that, when the latter resigned from Harvard, Gilman invited him to come and take charge of the department of history at Johns Hopkins. Adams savored the offer a moment before turning it down in a letter he sent from Washington on January 21, 1878:

Had the invitation come from any other source, I should not have thought of it at all. I shall always be glad to do anything for you and the university and I am rather sorry to fail you now. At the same time I confess I would rather not talk about my own experiences as a teacher. They satisfied me so completely that teaching is and always must be experimental if not empirical in order to be successful that I was glad to find an excuse for abandoning any wild ideas I might have had of creating a satisfactory method of pedagogy. My only advice to my scholars who succeeded me in my branches of instruction was: "whatever else you do, never neglect trying a new experiment every year." It was a confession of failure, and all the more because it was intended to stimulate the instructor rather than the students.[32]

We can readily believe that Adams' experiments in pedagogy were devised just as much to stimulate the teacher as to keep the student alert. But, whatever reasons motivated him, his method of teaching appears to have been uncommonly successful.

PREACHING THE "NORSE DOCTRINE?"

Adams later disclaimed all title to his reputation as a great teacher; he felt rather as if he had been a fraud, and told John Franklin Jameson, in 1896: "I became overpoweringly conscious that any further pretence on my part of acting as instructor would be something worse than humbug, unless I could clear my mind in regard to what I wanted to teach. As history stands, it is a sort of Chinese play without end and without lesson."[33] If it was a play, his students had been well instructed in all the essentials of stage business, but had they not learned some cues as well?

The answer is given by what we know of the direction he steadily followed. In American historical studies, in the second half of the nineteenth century, not one but "two distinct and contradictory conceptions of scientific history" prevailed. The first was the belief that scientific history consisted in "a search for facts alone, with no laws or generalisations and with a renunciation of all philosophy"; the opposite belief was that historical laws and generalisations might be formulated.[34] Adams, as we know, had no respect for "facts alone," which "bored" him. This would become a leitmotiv in *Mont-Saint-Michel and Chartres*. But from his remarks on Maine's *Ancient Law*, it is obvious that he reveled in generalizations, even when he did not believe in their validity; he had a liking, said Laughlin, for "unusual and tentative explanations of puzzling problems." His theory was that: "History had to be treated as an evolution . . . We heard much of the Pteraspis of Siluria and the first beginning of things. There was in his mind an *a priori* assumption that the actions of men followed certain laws, and if Adams could not trace these laws or trace the expected evolution he was unhappy."[35] In this, as in his insistence on "method," Adams was in the tide of fashion. Nearly every issue of the *North American Review* during these years carried an article on some aspect of evolution; Adams himself had contributed one in 1868. But though "he felt like nine men out of ten an instinctive belief in evolution," his mind remained unresolved, since he professed, as we also read in *The Education*, "no more concern in natural than in unnatural selection." It was enough to believe in selection as such.[36]

For many historians of the day, selection was to take the guise of "Social Darwinism," in which they thought they could find the "lesson" of history. Analyzing the trends in nineteenth-century American historiography, Edward Saveth remarks on the then-prevalent worship of "Anglo-Saxonism"; by use of the comparative method a familial relationship among people of "Aryan ancestry" was supposedly demonstrated and "theories trading under the name of Darwin were called upon to justify the Anglo-Saxon ascendancy." Thus, when in 1890 Frederick Jackson Turner came for his degree at Johns Hopkins University, the historical department there proved to be "largely dominated by German methodology and by one of the weirdest delusions that ever afflicted American intellectual life, namely the Teutonic theory of history—the theory that the Teutonic race has been the prime mover of political liberty and popular government and that the roots of Anglo-Saxon democracy are to be traced back to tun-moots of barbarians in the forests of northern Germany."[37] It is interesting that Henry Adams had played a part in the development of these studies. "In the autumn of 1880," states Professor Herbert Baxter Adams, "had already begun a new departure in historical instruction at Johns Hopkins University in the introduction of American institutional history as a distinct branch of historical study . . . The continuity of the Germanic village community in England had been originally suggested to Sir Henry Maine by an article in *The Nation*, communicated by Professor W. F. Allen of the University of Wisconsin. It was determined as early as 1877, after consulting with Professor Henry Adams, to apply this principle of continuity to the town institutions of New England."[38]

It would therefore seem quite safe to assert, along with Ernest Samuels, that "the hypothesis of historical development which made the greatest impression upon Henry Adams was the Teutonic theory of history"; in employing this very hypothesis as "a touchstone in all his historical reviews," Adams aligned himself with "the so-called Germanist school of Kemble, Freeman, Stubbs and Green." In the "Medievalism of Henry Adams," on the other hand, Oscar Cargill very convincingly demonstrates that Adams' historical reviews were so many full-tilt assaults against the same "Germanist school." Indeed, as we are told in *The Education*, Adams "preached the Norse doctrine all his life against the stupid and beer-swilling Saxon boors whom Freeman loved, and who, to the despair of science, produced Shakespeare."[39] Between these various statements, the contradictions happen to be more apparent than real; they must nonetheless be elucidated, since they raise a question of paramount importance to the reader of *Mont-Saint-Michel and Chartres*: was one of the essential themes of his later work—the passionate pride in Norman ancestry—already deeply ingrained in his teaching and editing? How he had come to believe in the "Norse doctrine" seems easily explainable. Whether it had enough moment to give his historical studies a decisive bias may be somewhat more difficult to demonstrate.

Adams is not mentioned in Oscar J. Falnes' study "New England Interest in Scandinavian Culture and the Norsemen";[40] yet a link is certain between him and the various New England writers and men in public life who, from the 1830's to the 1890's, "took more than a passing interest" in the history and culture of the Nordic people. To use Whitehead's formula again, there existed a "climate of opinion" under whose influence Adams inescapably came. It all originated with the unearthing in April 1831 of the "Skeleton in Armor," thought to be that of a Norseman and on which Longfellow wrote one of his best poems; though the skeleton may well have belonged to an Indian (at any rate within ten years of its discovery it was destroyed by a fire together with the museum where it had been placed), its mysterious possessor had laid a sure hold on New England imaginations. Other pieces of evidence supporting the claims for an early settlement of the Norsemen in America were soon brought forward. From Copenhagen in 1837 there came a substantial volume bearing the title of *Antiquitates Americanae Sive Scriptures Septemtrionales Rerum Antecolumbianarum in America,* which aroused considerable attention. The notice in the *North American Review* (which also included prospectuses in one of its regular issues) ran to no less than forty-two pages. An introductory essay written in English by the editor of the book, Charles C. Raft, and reprinted in pamphlet form, was distributed by the thousands. The excitement over these discoveries was particularly intense at Cambridge; Longfellow contemplated (but the idea never materialized) writing a series of ballads or an epic poem on the subject. After the Civil War, public interest, which had never completely subsided, received new impetus with the publication in 1868 of the *Pre-Columbian Discovery of America,* by B. F. de Costa. Published in Paris six years later, Gabriel Gravier's *Découverte de l'Amérique par les Normands au Xème siècle* reinforced the thesis. A measure of the local support such theories received is shown by a petition which the inhabitants of Woods Hole, Massachusetts, addressed to the United States Post Office Department in 1875, requesting that the name of their locality be changed to the presumably nobler Wood's Holl. In connection with the approaching Centennial of American Independence, in December, 1876, a campaign was launched for the erection of a monument commemorating the first discovery of America. A "Leif Erikson Memorial Association" soon numbered such celebrities as Longfellow, Lowell, Holmes, Whittier, and President Eliot, whose joint efforts were to culminate eleven years later with the unveiling of a statue to Leif Erikson at the intersection of Commonwealth Avenue and Charlesgate East in Boston.

Though not a member of the Memorial Association, Professor Adams no doubt knew of its endeavors, and he must also have heard of the researches of Eben Norton Horsford, a Cambridge resident who for sixteen years had taught chemistry at Harvard College. Horsford had resigned his professorship in 1863 to spend the last thirty years of his life indulging his bent for archaeological and historical matters. "Living on the tidewater of the Charles," he found it convenient to interest himself in the story of the Viking settlement and launched into a crusade against what he called "the blind scepticism, amounting practically to inverted ambition, that would deprive Massachusetts of the glory of holding the Landfall of Leif Erikson and at the same time the seat of the earliest colony of Europeans in America." To him, it appeared beyond the shadow of a doubt that the Norsemen had settled in the very region of Cambridge, on the banks of the river Charles, a little west of Harvard Square. Many names in Massachusetts, he held, were of Norse origin, and even the word America could be traced to the Norse Eirikr.[41] One can only smile at such enthusiasm. Adams was far too critical to take the cult of the Norse discovery of America seriously. Not that he was totally skeptical. Reviewing under his editorship Gabriel Gravier's work, Henry Cabot Lodge admitted: "a glance at the map, and a comparison of the distance between Iceland and Norway with that between Iceland and our own coasts will furnish a probability that almost amounts to proof of the Norse visits to New England." But, Lodge went on, no doubt also voicing Adams' own feelings about the matter, very little purpose was served by depicting these hardy travelers as "American citizens and Members of the Young Men's Christian Association with the dress and manners of the tenth century."[42]

A "kindred race," sang Horsford, was now

> Dwelling in the very place
> Where the Norsemen moored their ships
> And left their names on savage lips.

With the first assumption Adams was to proclaim himself in full agreement. The Cotentin shore, we read in *Mont-Saint-Michel and Chartres*, "recalls the coast of New England. The relationship between the granite of one coast and that of the other may be fanciful, but the relation between the people who live on each is as hard and practical a fact as the granite itself." The kinship between Yankees and Normans (or Norse, or Norsemen—the words were loosely interchanged) was then deeply felt in New England. Who, asked Lowell in 1844, is "so meek a compeer of the Viking as the New England skipper?" Reviewing Frederika Bremer's novels, Lowell pointed out the similarities between New Englanders and Scandinavians: "The same niggardly soil, inhospitable climate, and energy of character which drove forth the old Norsemen to seek for happier seats; the same courage and constancy, which won them a rude welcome in every clime, and compelled fortune everywhere to open her arms to them, have not these, producing results modified only by the progress of events, made the Yankee accent a familiar sound over the whole globe? . . . To us the name of Yankee, nickname though it be, is associated with so much of energy, courage, independence and moral genius, as to make it not less poetical than that of Viking."[43]

No wonder such kinship existed. "If you have any English blood at all," Adams was to say (and who could feel more conscious of his English ancestry than a New Englander?), "you also have Norman." And it was this Norman blood, not the English, which counted. A few thousand adventurers, observed a *North American* reviewer in April 1858, sufficed to infuse a "sluggish original stock" with active, adventurous energy. Celebrating the eight-hundredth anniversary of the battle of Hastings ("the most important action that the modern world has known . . . Nearly all that is excellent in English and American history is the fruit of that action"), C. C. Hazewell, in the *Atlantic Monthly* (October 1866), could find only harsh words for the race that ruled in England, down to the day of Hastings, "a slow, a sluggish and a stupid race." There was little in the history of the Saxons that could lead one to "believe they were capable of accomplishing anything that was great." In contrast, the people who gave their names to what is called the Norman Conquest of England were "the most extraordinary race in the Middle Ages . . . They were superior in every respect to their contemporaries."[44]

The reviewers just quoted admitted they were drawing their inspiration from the *History of Normandy and England*, by Sir Francis Turner Palgrave (1788–1864). The son of a member of the Stock Exchange named Cohen, Sir Francis had the year of his marriage embraced the Christian faith and changed his name for the maiden name of his wife's mother, under which he was later knighted. After publishing a collection of Anglo-Norman *chansons* in 1818, he edited various volumes of Historical Documents and Records, still considered today quite valuable; curiously enough, Adams does not seem to have ever possessed any of them. Palgrave's popularity rose as a result of his four-volume *History* (1851–1864, the last two volumes posthumous) aimed to correct Augustin Thierry's *Histoire de la conquête de l'Angleterre par les Normands* (1825) "Now we cannot conceive," wrote E. A. Freeman in 1859,

two historians of equal power more likely to fail in appreciating and understanding one another than Thierry and Sir Palgrave. Each sees the causes of events, builds events, builds a theory . . . and remains blind to the other half. Sir Francis can see nothing but the agency of individuals and of institutions . . . With the history of the nation, he gives himself very little concern . . . Thierry . . . sees nothing but the broad facts of race, conquest and language. Sir Francis hardly believes that William the Conqueror was a foreign invader, because he called himself King of the English and did not formally abolish the old English laws; Thierry would have us believe that in the wars of the seventeenth century an Anglo-Saxon people was trying to throw off the yoke of a Norman King.[45]

The truth was that Palgrave had very little taste for racial theories; he even went so far as to assume that the Britons were of Germanic, not of Celtic stock and accordingly minimized the revolutions brought by each invasion.

At any rate, Palgrave, who spent all his energies on the earlier history of the Duchy of Normandy, never reached the period of the Norman conquest of England, leaving this part of history to be written by Edward Augustus Freeman (1823–1892). Modern critics see in Freeman "one of England's greatest scholars"; Adams beforehand readily concurred with this judgment, since in his review of Freeman's *Historical Essays*, in January 1872, he placed the author "in the very front rank of living English historians."[46] Yet no sooner had he paid homage to the man's merits than he started, as will be seen further on, belaboring him with undisguised animosity. There we have the crux of the problem, a matter of sympathies far more than of tenets. In "The Medievalism of Henry Adams," Oscar Cargill characterizes Adams as "a mere controversialist"; this was, maintains Cargill, how he had entered the medieval field, as "a partisan of Palgrave. His quarrel with Freeman began because the publication of the latter's study of the Norman conquest knocked Palgrave's earlier book off the stocks." However convincingly presented, such a thesis suffers badly in the light of facts. Adams could never actually have been acquainted with Palgrave, who died in 1861. Yet once he had struck up a close friendship with Charles Milnes Gaskell in 1863, he was often necessarily thrown together with Frank Palgrave, Sir Francis' eldest son and Charles' brother-in-law. No doubt curiosity led him to read *The History of Normandy and England* along with some other books which Frank recommended to him.[47] Frank, who was busy editing his father's third and fourth volumes, had thought it quite normal to ask Freeman's advice about the manuscripts, and the latter had "enthusiastically urged publication." Moreover, when the volumes came out, Freeman greeted them with an article in the *Edinburgh Review* (of January 1865) which would easily pass for a model of urbanity.[48] His own *History of the Norman Conquest of England, Its Causes and Its Results* began to appear in 1867, and by 1869 three bulky volumes had already been published (two more were soon to follow). In April 1870, the *North American Review,* under the pen of W. F. Allen gave a lengthy and on the whole exceedingly favorable analysis of these first volumes. Among the readers few were likely to be more interested than Henry Adams, now back in America. No doubt he had the opportunity to discuss the book with Gurney, the editor of the review, and to show some familiarity with the subject. That Gurney should have then thought him qualified to hold a professorship of medieval history appears in this light less surprising.

From what source, then, did Adams' animosity against Freeman originate? Freeman has been painted as a fanatic, a forerunner of Hitler's racial theories: "on his coat of arms were emblazoned the Anglo-Saxon militant, the Teuton rampant and the Aryan eternally triumphant."[49] In his view, the Teutonic heritage was best preserved not in Germany, which had suffered a Roman infusion, but in England, where, despite Roman and Norman invasions, the Anglo-Saxon institutions always prevailed. While the peoples of the continent were overwhelmed by all the calamities of the Carolingian age, England was at the height of her glory with a civilisation no other country could parallel. The Norman invasion, however, hardly disrupted the true course of history; Freeman made this point clear in the very first paragraph of the first volume of his *History:*

The Norman conquest is something which stands without a parallel in any other Teutonic land. If that conquest be only looked on in its true light, it is impossible to exaggerate its importance. And yet there is no event whose true nature has been more commonly and more utterly mistaken. No event is less fitted to be taken, as it too often has been taken, for the beginning of our national history. For its whole importance is not the importance which belongs to a beginning, but the importance which belongs to a turning point . . . So far from being the beginning of our national history, the Norman conquest was the temporary overthrow of our national being. But it was a temporary overthrow.

Within a few generations, Freeman went on (and in his review of the first volume, Charles Eliot Norton found the sentence "a little amusing in form"),[50] *we* led captive our conquerors; England was England once again, and the descendants of the Norman invaders were found to be among the truest of Englishmen." The sentence which Freeman most approved of in Palgrave's third volume was consonant with his favorite theme of the continuity of the English nation: "I must here needs pause," said Sir Francis (vol. III, p. 596), "and substitute henceforward the true and ancient word English for the unhistorical and conventional term Anglo-Saxon, an expression conveying a most false idea in our civil history. It disguises the continuity of affairs, and substitutes the appearance of a new formation in the place of a progressive evolution." Going much further, Freeman asserted "positively" that the distinction, in England, between Normans and Anglo-Saxons was but an invention of continental historians; actually there were only English and French, the latter being fated to loss and oblivion. The Normans themselves, who profoundly admired the beauty of the English race, had the luck to be fused into it.[51] The English had always been the superior race. And what's more, the blessings of their race transcended national boundaries, for the English had not one, but three homes: originally on the European mainland, then in England, and finally in America. "To me," wrote Freeman after a visit to the United States in the early eighties, "the English speaking commonwealth on the American mainland is simply one part of the English folk, as the English speaking kingdom in the European island is another part. My whole line of thought and study leads me to think, more perhaps than most men, of the ever-lasting ties of blood and speech, and less of the accidental separation wrought by political and geographical causes."[52]

During this trip to the United States Freeman was one night invited by the Bancrofts together with Henry and Marian Adams. The occasion must not have been altogether pleasurable for the Englishman, if one judges by Mrs. Adams' account:

At dinner, the great historian of the Norman conquest was on my right; Henry, *one* removed from my left. Ye gods, what a feast it was . . . The canvasbacks entered. *Three* of them—fresh and fair, done to a turn; and weltering in their gore. Says Mrs. Bancroft with a growing hauteur of manner as of a turning worm, "Do you appreciate our canvasbacks, Mr. Freeman?", "I cannot eat raw meat," he said angrily, while a convulsive shudder shook his frame. Then the *picador* which is latent in me when nature is outraged rose in me and I said to him, all unconscious of his theories and the scheme of his writing, "I wonder that you do not like rare meat. Your *ancestors* the Picts and the Scots ate their meat raw and tore it with their fingers." At which he roared out "O-o-o-o! *Whur* did yer git that?" Unheeding, careless of consequences, I said "Well your Anglo-Saxon ancestors if you prefer." He thereupon pawed the air and frothed at the mouth . . .

Never having read one line of Freeman, I did not know until the next day the exquisite point of my historical allusions. As I casually repeated them, Henry became purple in the face and rolled off his chair, and he, the husband of my bosom who is wont to yawn affectionately at my yarns, he at intervals of two hours says, "Tell me again what you said to Freeman about the Picts, the Scots and the Anglo-Saxons."[53]

If as early as 1872 Freeman seems to have become a sort of *bête noire*, it was not the Germanist per se whom Adams disliked;

it was the very Englishman who provoked him to the anger of "a Rolando Furioso." "A typical John Bull," as Professor Herbert B. Adams would affectionately describe him, with "a staunch biased English patriotism," the historian had little that might appeal "to such Americans as still entertain a prejudice against their English relations"; of those, Henry Adams remained certainly one, and he took no pains to disguise his animosity in his own articles for the *North American Review.* As an editor, observes Samuels, he was so violently unconventional that, "if he had dared, he would have flown a skull and crossbones on the mast of the quarterly"; when asking a paper from his friend Gaskell, he advised him to be fairly abusive: "Stand on your head and spit at someone." Freeman seems to have been for him an especially attractive target.[54]

A good example of the way Adams set on his fellow historian is provided by his January 1872 review of Freeman's *Historical Essays,* a collection of articles written during the Franco-Prussian war. "As usual with his controversial work," Adams revealingly remarked of the author, "he ends in producing a feeling of reaction against himself." Though no lover of the Napoleons, he himself was shocked by Freeman's "vicious" assault against the French Empire and his comments upon the emperor's use of the verbs "réunir" and "revendiquer," which were "one wilful, malicious and unjustifiable calumny of Louis Napoleon Buonaparte"; a calumny, Adams added with rather biting concern, which "must add a conerable sting to the sufferings of that unfortunate man . . . It certainly passes the limit of fair play, when Mr Freeman actually ventures to make the Emperor responsible for Mr Freeman's own French." The publication of a revised American edition of the *History of the Norman Conquest* gave occasion in January 1874 for even sharper banderillas at a writer whose judgment was seriously impaired by his inability to curb "his most inveterate prejudices," that is, "his patriotic enthusiasm for his Saxon ancestors, who were presumably the ancestors of New England." Any other writer, Adams remarked, would have been appalled "at the difficulties of inspiring enthusiasm for the English of the eleventh century, probably the only pure German race which was ever conquered twice in half a century and held permanently in subjection by races inferior to itself in wealth and power." With this race, he little cared to claim any common bond. Indeed, whether they ate their meat raw or not, it was obvious that Adams personally shrank from the Pict and Scot forbears of such a fanatic.[55]

Attacking Freeman, however, was not the main object of Adams' reviews. In nearly all of them, as well as in his classes, law remained his favorite theme, not to say his "hobby." It aggrieved him, he wrote in 1872, that the English should still "battle with desperate energy against the idea that the Germans as such, before they were either feudalised or romanised," had an actual system and propriety law of their own. Two years later, he noted sorrowfully: "The early history of this great system is still almost a blank . . . and it is to remain untouched until Germany has forced England into scholarship."[56]

For Adams' allegiance to Germany, it appears, was even greater than Freeman's, and it was an allegiance to the "great" Teutonic past as well as to the methods of the modern Germans. This allegiance he would proudly admit in the first lines of "The Anglo-Saxon Courts of Law," his own contribution to the *Essays in Anglo-Saxon Laws*. For a detailed analysis of this essay, one may turn to Ernest Samuels. It will here suffice to bring out the chief point, as it was already clearly defined by Adams in his review of Stubbs' *Constitutional History of England,* in the *North American Review* of July 1874:

The Angles and the Saxons who drove out the old English population brought to England a constitution of their own. In Germany they had adopted before the earliest historical period an organisation which bore the name of *hundred* . . .

If the clue offered by the hundred is once lost, or even if it loosely held, the entire history of the English judicial constitution becomes a confused jumble of words. The one permanent Germanic institution was the hundred. The one code of Germanic law was hundred-law, much of which is now the common law of England. The hundred and its law survived all the storms which wrecked dynasties.[57]

Grounding his argument on the "loose legal and geographical phraseology of the Anglo-Saxons" in their charters, he managed to trace through a series of verbal approximations and back to the seventh and eighth centuries the existence of several such "hundreds." The hundred and its court, he asserted in his essay, "were, of all Germanic institutions, the most long-lived, the most useful, from Iceland to the Adriatic." In great part, thanks to the survival of this liberal Teutonic element, England knew a golden age while the condition of Northern Europe, "with the deposition of the Emperor in 884," became chaotic. "It so happened that the precise period which was so fatal to the structure of European society was exceptionally favorable to the quiet development of England . . . Thus England passed in safety and content through the darkest period of modern history, when hope of happiness seemed extinguished in Northern France . . . There is no period in all early English history when the course of law seems to have been so regular as during this century of comparative repose." Unfortunately, about 100 years later, the situation of England deteriorated to the point of closely resembling a "situation of social and political anarchy" which had been characteristic of the continent. To no small degree the responsibility lay with Edward the Confessor, a king "half Norman by birth, and wholly Norman by education and sympathies": "His acts, not merely in reference to jurisdiction, but throughout his career show that he was not an Anglo-Saxon, but a Norman king. It was he who introduced the worst maxims of government into England; and whatever abuses may have existed before his time in the practice of judicial administration, it was he and his advisers who revolutionised the law."[58]

By elucidating the judicial value of the term "socnam" in medieval "sac and soc," Adams demonstrated that Edward recklessly granted the rights of jurisdiction to the church, a grant which may have seemed innocent at the time, yet which was "none the less fatal to the old Anglo-Saxon constitution":

The theory of the constitution was irretrievably lost. Justice no longer was a public trust, but a private property. The recognition of private tribunals for the church was a recognition of the legality of private tribunals in general . . . The entire judicial system of England was torn in pieces; and a new theory of society known as feudalism took its place. With the hopeless confusion of jurisdiction which followed the collapse caused by the Confessor in the Anglo-Saxon system, this is not the place to deal. From the moment that private courts of law became a recognized part of the English judicature the Anglo-Saxon constitution falls to pieces and feudalism takes its place. Yet whatever historical interest the manorial system possesses as a part of the English judicial constitution is due to the fact that its origin was not feudal, but Anglo-Saxon. The manor was . . . but a proprietary hundred, and as such has served, during many centuries to perpetuate the memory of the most archaic and least fertile elements of both the Saxon and the feudal systems.[59]

Before such evidence, how is one to agree with Cargill's definition of this essay as "a specific attack against the Freemanites?" It little matters that in a letter to Gaskell Adams did boast: "My own position will only bring your friend Freeman about my ears. I have contradicted every English author, high and low." This was essentially a pose and, while Freeman very rightly remained silent, other English historians expressed courteous appreciation. For as the author would admit in *The Education,* "he had obediently flung himself into the arms of the Anglo-Saxons." If we sense a contradiction between this admission and his other statement, also in *The Education,* which we have already quoted: that he "preached the Norse doctrine all his life" against Freeman's stupid Saxon boors, the contradiction appears to lie solely in his use of the word "Norse," which should be replaced by "Germanic," at least for the period under study. For it is clear that during all these Harvard years Adams felt little concerned with the Normans and held no particular admiration for them, even though the interest then prevailing in New England about the Norse may well have been sinking deep into his subconscious, ready to resurge at a propitious time, very long afterward; for the time being, far from equating Norsemen and Normans, he would see in the latter, just as the "Freemanites" did, *French* invaders whose influence had been totally disruptive. His quarrel with Freeman thus appears to have been in its essentials one between compeers, between fellow antiquarians, devotees of the same Germanic past; and the paradox sprang from his reluctance to admit that they were traveling the same road. It is true that once they reached the eleventh century, Adams swerved, or rather, he stopped short, as if the Middle Ages ceased to be of any interest to him or even to exist, when on their way to becoming "English." Playing the Dry-as-Dust was a game he practised well (his essay, E. Samuels comments, "would have done honor to any hair-splitting German seminarist"), but only in a limited field.[60] Adams had enough detachment to make fun of his own *tour de force* and write in monkish Latin an epitaph

one may take to mean that all intellectual curiosity—all "amusement"—had now died in him as far as the Middle Ages were concerned:

Hic Jacet
Homunculus Scriptor
Doctor Barbaricus
Henricus Adamus
Adae Filius et Evae
Primo Explicuit
Socnam.

Doctor Barbaricus might one day revive, but his journey would
then recommence on a very different road.[61]

3

The Best Traveling Companions

On August 23, 1890, with the painter John La Farge as a companion, Henry Adams boarded a ship in San Francisco, starting on a trip which was to take him to Polynesia and then around the world. Thirteen years had elapsed since his leaving Harvard, years which he professed to have enjoyed "amazingly" but which in truth had been blackened more than words—or even silence— could tell, by the suicide of Marian Hooper Adams in 1885. Almost mechanically he had gone on with his self-appointed task, completing his *magnum opus,* his *History of the United States of America during the Administrations of Jefferson and Madison,* and now, with the last volume committed to the printers, he felt tired and, "like a horse that wears out, he quitted the race-course, left the table, and sought pastures as far as possible from the old." Where he went was immaterial—or so he thought—since, as he would sum it up: "Education had ended in 1871; life was complete in 1890; the rest mattered so little!" And yet his true life—that of an artist—was just dawning. In the South Seas, Mabel La Farge perceptively comments: "A new world of perceptions opened out to him; and with his companion as a constant guide, the education of the senses began, that led him finally to his appreciation of the twelfth century glass, and the crossing of the chasm that divides the Anglo-Saxon mentality from the Latin."[1] Paradoxically, the road to Chartres for Henry Adams lay through Samoa and Tahiti, a quite unlikely but rewarding detour.

A "SCHOOL OF ART"

"Of all the men who had deeply affected their friends since 1850, John La Farge was certainly the foremost and for Henry Adams, who had sat at his feet since 1872, the question how much he owed to La Farge could be answered only by admitting that he had no standard to measure it by."[2] At any rate, to judge from this passage in *The Education*, Adams could tell when his "schooling" in art had got under way, long before the journey to the South Seas. It was after his marriage and through Marian's brother, Edward William Hooper, treasurer of Harvard, that he came into close contact not only with the painter but with two other men who in their own fields were to help him form his taste. "Every inch businesslike" in his severely unartistic capacity, Hooper was nonetheless an instinctive connoisseur, one of the first Americans to appreciate and collect Blake's works; he drew his new brother-in-law into a circle of his artist friends, giving him, H. D. Cater says, "a sort of life-membership in this 'school of art'."[3] Among these friends were Henry Hobson Richardson, Adams' old college-mate, now a successful architect, and John La Farge, recently appointed as a lecturer on art at the college, pleasant companions to be associated with. To be sure, Adams was still too much engrossed at that time in his own research on archaic law to gain in such company much more than an occasional and welcome relief from the stifling atmosphere of what he called the Cambridge "social desert." Yet, when one surveys Adams' career, this early "schooling" appears all-important.

Of the artists mentioned, precedence must be given not to La Farge but to H. H. Richardson. The architect was then living in New York, but he often commuted to Boston; what drew him there was Trinity Church, which he had been commissioned to build in July 1872. Though not quite finished, the church was to be consecrated on February 9, 1877. In the words of Richardson's first biographer, "When he began Trinity all his work had been merely tentative and it was itself but a great and bold experiment. When he finished it, he was already erecting other buildings which are mature and characteristic expressions of his power. When he began it, he was a very promising architect who had attracted a greater measure of popular attention than usually falls to the share of such a one in our day and land. When he finished it he was to his countrymen at large the best known and most interesting figure in the profession."[4] That he was "an interesting figure" is certain; Lewis Mumford characterizes him as "the Paul Bunyan of American architecture," and "a man who in his lifetime already assumed legendary proportions." Indeed, his popularity may have owed as much to his temperament as to his architectural talent, for Richardson was a full-blown romantic. His capacity for good fare, his love of laughter, his gusto for life were infectious; it was hard to resist him. "He is an ogre," Adams once said of him. "He devours men crude and shows the effects of inevitable indigestion!"[5] Since the erection of Trinity Church so neatly coincided with Adams' years at Harvard as a professor of medieval history, there is no doubt that during this period he was absorbed in his friend's neo-Romanesque adventure. Some years later, he would use the episode as the mainstay of a novel.

There is not, however, the least allusion in *Esther* to the architecture of the church in which most of the action takes place. It may be that Adams did not think highly of it. Richardson had as yet, La Farge would reminisce, "not taken hold seriously of the Romanesque problem. He designed a building which was intelligent but not what could be done and especially wanting in historical character."[6] And La Farge prided himself on having enabled the architect to improve the structure, at least its externals, by supplying him with photographs of Spanish Romanesque churches—Salamanca in particular, which gave Trinity its steeple. Hence originated that modified French and Spanish Romanesque going by the name of "Richardsonian." Even so, the church failed to be really impressive; and little wonder, since Richardson, whose most cherished ambition at the outset of his career was to design "a grain elevator and the interior of a great river boat," leaned much more toward secular than ecclesiastical architecture. "Apart from works of contemporary engineering, like Brooklyn Bridge," comments Lewis Mumford in a key strangely consonant with one of Adams' favorite themes, "it is in Richardson's architecture that one first receives a dramatic expression of the fact that man, thanks to his mastery of coal and steam and electricity, was now for the first time in control of colossal energies."[7] But here the architecture remained too cramped, too impersonal, to convey such a dramatic expression, and it was only when Richardson brought in La Farge, in the fall of 1876, to do the murals that Adams' interest appears to have been aroused—an interest, as is made clear in *Esther*, which focused exclusively on these frescoes.

Not that Richardson does not play a cryptic part in the novel. At the time of its writing, in the winter of 1882–1883, the architect happened to be a very frequent dinner guest of the Adamses in Washington. Late in 1881, while he was designing their friend Nicholas Anderson's house, their intimacy had been revived on a closer footing than during the preceding decade and now, fresh from a tour of France and Italy taken in the company of Phillips Brooks and two other ministers of the faith (they had spent the afternoon of July 15, 1882, at Chartres, "Mr. Richardson," it is reported, "being *very loud* in his admiration"), he freely expatiated on his projects for the improvement of Trinity. No doubt, as Ernest Samuels surmises, the debates between the painter Wharton and the minister Hazard in the novel echo the conferences which Richardson, La Farge, and Phillips Brooks (Adams' relative and the model for Hazard) held around the Adamses' table over the decoration of Trinity. But there is only one artist in *Esther*, Wharton, alias La Farge, vainly struggling with the trustees of the church "to get down to the thirteenth century." And Wharton deplores the fact that the place as such, that is, as a piece of architecture, "has no heart."[8]

According to Samuels, "Richardson, full of his theory of Romanesque architecture, opened Adams' eyes to the simple grandeur of the twelfth-century churches"—a statement which is supported by Adams' own admission when, long afterward, in a letter to Elizabeth Cameron, on September 18, 1899, he told of his "craving" for twelfth-century churches, and explained: "I caught the disease from dear old Richardson who was the only really big man I knew."[9] More than a disease, in fact, Richardson had given Adams a curiosity, planting seeds in his mind for the enthusiasms which were later, under very different conditions, to flourish. For like any well-to-do amateur, Adams could get a practical lesson by hiring the architect in his professional capacity. Not long after the completion of *Esther*, Richardson began work on a house for Adams in Washington. An old French house in the region of Troyes is supposed to have served as a model, but to one judging from photographs (the house has been long since pulled down to be replaced by a hotel), the result looks somewhat forbidding and justifies Montgomery Schuyler's quip that "Richardson's dwelling-houses were not defensible except in a military sense." It was "a relative failure," pronounced another architect.[10] Costly though it proved, this phase of Adams' artistic education remained limited; it made him aware of the massive quality of Romanesque architecture, even in its transmogrified American version; it enabled him to confront architecture as a living process, the more so since Richardson, not one to allow blueprints to bridle his inspiration, kept his "building in hand, as so much plastic materials"; he could also gain a feeling for material, which made him "ransack" the whole Smithsonian collection for a sample of the right kind of stone for his fireplace. That was all, and in the light of what still remained to be learned, not enough.[11]

The new house was not yet quite ready to be lived in when, on December 6, 1885, Marian committed suicide, dealing her husband a blow from which he would never fully recover. Then began what Adams called his "posthumous" existence, marked by a nearly endless series of journeys—an obstinate search for "some harbor of resolve where he could drop his anchor."[12] Such a harbor could not be found in Europe; the old continent was still too closely associated with happy memories, too "full of ghosts." In June 1886, in the company of John La Farge ("the rarest of animals is a companion," he would say, knowing how fortunate he had been), Adams set off on a five-month jaunt to Japan. The two friends were looking for a Shangri-la, a place where, La Farge hoped, they would find "a bath for the brain in some water absolutely alien." In Japan they settled in a "doll-house" with paper windows and matted floors near a waterfall; it all looked like a joke, and to Theodore F. Dwight, who was serving him as a secretary and who had been left in charge of the Washington house, Adams reported: "He [La Farge] avers that he is Huckleberry Finn, and I am Tom Sawyer. We certainly feel like those models. La Farge tries to sketch. I try to photograph. Our joint success leaves a margin for Tom Sawyer's imagination to fill in. Nikko is fascinating, but I am safe from one kind of bric-a-brac, at least; if not from the best. The one kind of which I have seen no specimen possible, is still the women."[13] For art, which had not yet become vital to him, he used one of his favorite terms, "bric-a-brac" or "curio" (he was shipping "tons" of them back home). But if he jocularly ranged women under the same denomination (unless he called them "very badly made monkeys"), the Tom Sawyer in him, with his pseudo-innocence, was at least casting off some of his prudery; he could break out "into carols of joy" at the sight of a whole village bathing starkly nude (here was a healthy survival of archaic mores), and the phallic symbol in one of the temples prompted him to the sagacious comment that "one cannot quite ignore the foundations of society."[14]

Under the veil of mock sententiousness, there showed the intellectuality which no bath in these alien waters could wash out. A letter which the painter wrote from Japan at the time is revealing: "My dreams of making an analysis and memoranda of these architectural treasures of Japan were started, as many resolutions of work are, by the talk of my companion, his analysis of the theme of their architecture, and my feeling of a sort of desire to rival him on a ground of fair competition. But I do not think that I could grasp a subject in such a clear and dispassionate and masterly way, with such natural reference to the past and its implied comparisons, for A[dams]'s historic sense amounts to poetry, and his deductions and remarks always set my mind sailing into new channels."[15] This is an admirable insight into character, a true perception of the paradox that Adams—the "Doctor Barbaricus" of not so long ago—was at heart a poet, as he would one day reveal himself to be, with his imaginative use of the Middle Ages. But what also appears is that at this stage Adams, still full of his late dabbling in architecture, is only capable of playing the don, as his own comment to Gaskell proves: "I took with me a well-known New York artist, John La Farge, an old acquaintance, and a very unusual man, who stands at the head of American art, but who interests me more as a companion than as a painter, for he kept me always amused and active."[16] In other words, La Farge's attention stimulated his mind to an enjoyable activity quite different from the creative rest, the pregnant passiveness it required. Five years must now elapse before Adams will really become the "pupil"—as he will style himself in his dedication of *Mont-Saint-Michel and Chartres* to La Farge. There will be a decided shift in their relationship, making their South Sea voyage of fateful importance in Adams' artistic development, whereas their first journey to the East had brought little more than a welcome change of scenery.

ADAMS' "REBIRTH" IN THE SOUTH SEAS

If, instead of keeping to his camera, Adams had as early as 1886 tried his hand at painting, he would not even then have been the first American writer to place himself under La Farge's tutelage. Henry James had preceded him in 1860, when along with his brother William, he studied in the studio of William Morris Hunt, at Newport; there, we read in James' *Notes*, La Farge was "quite the most interesting person we knew." Though James soon realized that he could never become a painter, he remained grateful to La Farge for showing him that "the arts were essentially one and that even with canvas and brushes whisked out of my grasp, I still needn't feel disinherited. That was the luxury of a friend and senior with a literary side—that if there are futilities that he didn't bring home to me, he nevertheless opened more windows than he closed."[17] The challenge of La Farge's personality was probably even more important than his lessons. "The La Farge to whom I would above all pay tribute," confirms Royal Cortissoz, his biographer, "is the La Farge who was in a sense greater than all his works, the La Farge who was to those who knew him well a lambent flame of inspiration. There was something Leonardesque about him, something of the universal genius."[18] To all appearances, as "geniuses" go, he and Richardson (who died prematurely of Bright's disease in early 1886) stood poles apart. Six feet tall, deep-chested, with long and slender hands, usually clothed in black, fastidious and ceremonious, even in his Bohemian ways, he seemed, as in the portrait Adams drew of him under the name of Wharton, in *Esther*, "to face life with an effort."[19] About the same age as Adams, he was a fit complement to him, and he could match Adams' chronic dyspepsia with his own array of illnesses; he often had to take to his bed out of sheer exhaustion; he also suffered from a slight lameness and was nearsighted. It was the man "inside," with his high intuitiveness, his mystical approach to life and art, that Adams admired and set above all others: "Of all his friends," he wrote in *The Education*, "La Farge alone owned a mind complex enough to contrast against the commonplaces of American uniformity, and in the process had vastly perplexed most Americans who came in contact with it."[20]

The son of a refugee from San Domingo, John La Farge (born in New York in 1835) had a lively sense of his French origins, which no doubt colored his temperament. His upbringing had been essentially French; he was steeped in the French language, in French ways and manners; his "jesuit" schooling (he had studied first at Mount Saint Mary's College in Maryland, then at Fordham, and his schoolboy letters reveal what a thorough grounding he had in Aristole and Saint Thomas) marked him profoundly.[21] Of paramount importance also were La Farge's years in Paris after his graduation; he had by then determined to become an artist and studied in Couture's studio. "At once," he would recall (and "pupil" Adams afterward made good use of this remark in *Mont-Saint-Michel and Chartres*), "one was asked what one held in regard to Delacroix and Ingres." Of course, he was for Delacroix.

For if his nearsightedness made of La Farge a halting technician, unable until the end of his life to draw the human figure properly, he was soon a master in the use of colors. The evanescence of light, the variability of weather and time of day fascinated him; he read extensively in scientific works on the subject of light. His interest in the phenomena of optics received a further and decisive impetus when he made the acquaintance of a fellow American artist, John Bancroft, who like him reveled in color analysis.[22] More scientific than poetic in their rendering of atmosphere, his earliest Newport landscapes thus anticipated the formula of Monet. At first, critics greeted his impressionistic paintings with hostility, but he gained full recognition in the seventies. His defective drawing was then excused on the ground that he was "less concerned with the external than with the hidden meaning it has for the soul." By the end of the century, it was commonly accepted that everything he touched had "the seal of genius."[23] His fame sprang not only from his pictures but from his colored glass. His years in France had taught him to love ancient glass, with its translucent colors, but it was owing to practical causes, because his pictures did not sell well enough (he was a married man and had nine children), that he took to window-making, finding a cheaper process thanks to the use of opaline glass. Among his first windows were those of Trinity Church. "There was," comments Royal Cortissoz, "something magisterial about his attitude toward glass . . . Self-assertion was, to be sure, abhorrent to La Farge's nature, but when he spoke on glass he spoke *ex cathedra*—and he knew it. He spoke and wrote with some copiousness on the subject." Two years after his trip to the South Seas, he published a booklet entitled *The American Art of Glass*. But his best work on the subject, he wrote vicariously; for it will not be a willful reading-in to find his heart and mind in Adams' own comments on glass in *Mont-Saint-Michel and Chartres*.[24]

Of his own part in the journey he made to the South Seas with La Farge, Adams once said that he wanted no record left: "for I can imagine few things more incongruous than my poor Bostonian, Harvard College, matter of fact ego jammed between the South Seas and John La Farge." Incongruous though the juxtaposition may have seemed, it proved highly beneficial, since it amounted for Adams to a new birth. "No future experience, short of being eaten," he wrote from Samoa, "will make us feel so new again." And from Tahiti, summing up the experience of the whole journey, he admitted "the secret truth," that "I am more like a sane idiot than I have known myself to be in these last six years past." He owed this renewal of the self to La Farge.[25]

No sooner had Adams, in August 1890, boarded the train for San Francisco on the way to Polynesia than he placed himself under his companion's tutelage. He had dragged him away, he said, "from half a dozen unfinished windows." No doubt he could hear much from La Farge about the subject of glass and glass-making, but what counted were the practical lessons in the rudiments of painting he started receiving. "I am trying to learn something about water colors," he wrote to his niece, Mabel Hooper, from onboard the train. "La Farge instructs me and I dabble already in blues and browns. All yesterday I labored to attain sage green for the sage bush. Of course I do not try yet to draw; all my ambition is limited to finding out what the colors are." Gradually his sense, which had been "cut down to a kind of dull consciousness," gained in power. Using La Farge as "a spectacled and animated prism," he discovered "the infinite variety of greens and the perfectly intemperate shifting blues of the ocean." From Honolulu, in September 1890, he could proudly report: "He [La Farge] has taught me to feel the subtleness and endless variety of charm in the color and light of every hour in the tropical island's day and night. I get gently intoxicated on the soft violets and strong blues, the masses of purple and the broad bands of orange and green in the sunsets, as I used to *griser* myself on absinthe on the summer evenings in the Palais Royal before dining at Véfour's, thirty years ago." While gaining the feel of art, Adams remained naturally aware of his own limitations; compared to La Farge's "wild daubs of brown and purple," his own water colors, he admitted, looked rather "like young ladies' embroidery of the last generation"; but, as he wrote from Tahiti on March 29, 1891: "I go on, trying every day to make pictures, and every day learning, as one does in a new language, a word or two more, just to show that the thing is laughable. Still, I have learned enough, from La Farge's instruction, to make me look at painting rather from the inside, and see a good many things about a picture that I only felt before."[26]

For once he ceased to be intellectual, he became intuitive, or at least "rather" so, gaining in the process, J. C. Levenson notes, "a sensuous responsiveness to both art and nature." No experience could be more crucial: "One does not receive the caress of beauty through the intellect," Sherwood Anderson would say, recalling one of the best moments of his own life, when he too felt free and glad in front of the Cathedral of Chartres.[27] Even before reaching the portals of Chartres, Adams knew this moment of priv-

ileged expansion. Though the South Sea interlude does not find
its place in *The Education,* there is at least a definite allusion to
its decisive influence in Adams' life. We find it in chapter xix,
"Chaos (1870)." With the death of his sister, Mrs. Kuhn, Adams
has received his first very great blow: "he did not yet know it, and
he was twenty years in finding it out; but he had need of all the
beauty" of the world. That was in the summer of 1870; twenty
years later Adams would be setting out for the South Seas, in La
Farge's company.[28]

If, in 1870, Adams already needed the beauty of the world (then
the Alps), it was "to restore the finite to its place." Recovering the
sense of sight in his 1890–91 voyage was part of the process toward recovering the sense of living. The disease he suffered from
was, as he well knew, *ennui,* "probably the result of prolonged
labor on one work and of nervous strain."; he wisely doctored himself with art lessons. "I am a painter," La Farge liked to remark
(and this remark would also find its way into *Mont-Saint-Michel
and Chartres*). "We painters are in a certain way like children; we
delight in anything seen." They delight in sheer life. Adams had
not left Hawai when he could already own: "I enjoy myself and
the sense of living, more than I have done in five years." It was like
sailing to another planet; Japan in his earlier journey had already
helped him to shed some of his inhibitions; now Samoa, in Ernest
Samuels' phrase, would soon "sweep him off his Puritan feet."[29]

Much amusement can be gained from the letters in which he
describes himself with La Farge, "up to our necks in old gold and
hand-in-hand," and, as he states further on, "all mixed up with
naked arms, breasts and legs, yet apparently as innocently as little
children." The sight of the *Siva* dance made him gasp with "the
effect of color, form and motion," while La Farge's spectacles
"quivered with emotion"; it was all, he again and again insisted,
"innocent and childish," even though, as he told John Hay, "any
European suddenly taken to such a show would assume that the
girl was licentious and, if he were a Frenchman, he would probably ask for her."[30] If Adams never lost what he called his "Bos-
tonitis," he nonetheless relaxed considerably, as his letters prove.
Many charming passages have been unfortunately excised from
the letters by their first editor; out of these suppressed passages

some lines at least are worth quoting: "Only unlucky men, with a skeptical turn of mind who have unwillingly betaken themselves to the study of history for want of having had an education to fit them for better employment are likely to treasure the facts of an ideal archaic Arcadia and to feel their meanings."[31] These "facts" were the proportions of two native beauties, Aloa and Alele, whom he had carefully measured around all parts of their bodies (bare —except for the hips—and "a little allowance must be made for the thickness of the *siapa*"). To be sure, here was pleasant research, though somewhat incongruous when compared with the severe documentation which had gone into the making of the *History;* what also appears is that Adams, even half in jest, can already use themes which will be found again at the core of his great works, not only the complaint about the failure of education but the nostalgia for an ideal Arcadia where woman was enthroned.

In Tahiti Adams was soon adopted by an old chiefess, "the greatest woman in the whole of Polynesia," and for weeks he listened to her, while she recounted her family history. His mind reveled in a society where "women shared equal sovereignty with men; where they not only caused wars, but directed them." And if, from Washington, his old friend John Hay wrote: "I have just read Daudet's *Port Tarascon*—It is a definite Waterloo—everything is *manqué.* Now is your chance! Do a South Sea book, *comme il n'y en a pas,*"[32] this "South Sea book," which was to take more than two years in the making, could not be a mere novel *à la* Daudet. Printed "ultissimo privately" in Washington at the end of 1893, *The Memoirs of Marau Taaroa, Last Queen of Tahiti* represents an astonishing tour de force of scholarship in which Adams successfully threaded his way through the tangled genealogies and incessant tribal struggles of the remote Pacific island. For he could not content himself with simply transcribing the old queen's memories, as they were told him. On his way home from the South Seas, Adams went the round of Paris and London bookshops in search of material on Tahiti; he brought into his new undertaking the same meticulous scholarship which had been the forte of the Harvard professor of medieval studies. The severe genealogical charts he drew of the island "chiefly" families closely resemble those he had used for his Harvard lectures on the French kings, just as they prefigure the dynastic outlines we shall find interspersed in the pages of *Mont-Saint-Michel and Chartres.*

For it was not the dry medieval world of *sac* and *soc* in which Adams steeped himself but one far more attractive, instinct with life, where family lines were all-important. His *Tahiti,* as he liked to call it, actually provided the necessary link in the "evolution" of the Harvard professor into a lover of the Virgin, an evolution which had been obscured by all the years devoted to Madison and Jefferson: "For the literary historian Tahiti supplied the contrasts, the absence of which had so troubled Adams in the writing of his nine-volume *History.* In the United States the individual did not count; the family did not count. The patrician elite was rootless. In Tahiti the individual and the family were everything."[33] No wonder that in January 1894, just after publishing his "South Sea memoirs," Adams told Gaskell that they had *amused* him much more than "my dreary American history which is to me what Emma Bovary was to Gustave Flaubert." It was a standard joke with him: "American history is so dull; there's not a woman in it." Tahitian history proved refreshingly different. But the truth went much deeper. In his *History,* Adams had tried (not that he always succeeded!) not only to exclude personal feelings but to keep clear, so to speak, of his own family. No such barriers existed here. Yet telling the story of the glorious days and decline of a great family in this remote island must have had infinite resonances in his mind; it was so easy for him to bring into parallel what he and his brothers considered as the "decline" of the Adamses—the grievous loss of their prominence. No doubt Tahiti became all the more sacred because it could offer ground to a secret and personal parable. And so in their turn would the Middle Ages, now that the historian's imagination had received its first liberating impetus.[34]

THE SOURCES OF CONSERVATIVE
CHRISTIAN ANARCHY

Even though at this stage the spires of Chartres stand distinctly in the offing, there remains a long distance to cover, with another quite unlikely detour, before Adams is ready for them. At the origin of *Mont-Saint-Michel and Chartres,* there must still be traced the play of the determining emotions; one was the violent distaste which welled up in Adams upon his return to the "civilized" world. "Yet I remember," he wrote in the spring of 1901 to his friend Cecil Spring-Rice (at that time he was not only deep in his book on Chartres but busy with a revised edition of *Tahiti*), "how I came back from the wilderness ten years ago and what consternation and horror I felt at seeing so-called civilisation." There, he said, "was the source of the C.C.A.," the Conservative Christian Anarchy—as he pleasantly designated his own personal philosophy—which he henceforth was to parade;[35] but if his feeling of revulsion was all-important (during the following years before he discovered Chartres, he would keep fleeing to "primitive" countries, going to Cuba twice in 1893 and 1894, then making a tour of Mexico and the Carribean Islands from mid-December 1894 to mid-April 1895), other emotions played an equally essential role in determining the movement of his mind.

There was his frustrating relationship with Elizabeth Cameron, the young wife of the Senator for Pennsylvania, on whom he had been increasingly dependent ever since Marian's death. Things had come to such a pass between Adams and Mrs. Cameron that, in part, it was the impossibility of finding a solution to their hopeless entanglement that sent him away on his South Sea voyage; fourteen months later the solution was not any nearer, and an all too brief encounter in Paris, in October 1891, turned out to be an excruciating experience. Reality had to be faced. "I am not old enough to be a tame cat," he would soon write to her; "you are too old to accept me in any other character. You were right last year in sending me away." He had by then taken refuge at the Gaskells' in Shropshire. His "long tearing wild jaunt," he told her, "had finished at Wenlock Abbey in a sense of ended worlds and burnt-out coal-and-iron universes." In the old priory, musing among the peaceful ruins, he could dream of a time when the world was harmonious, and to Elizabeth Cameron (he would never again write so frankly), he bared his heart:

Progress has much to answer for in depriving weary and broken men and women of their natural end and happiness; but even now I can fancy myself contented in the cloister, and happy in the daily round of duties, if only I still knew a God to pray to, or better yet a Goddess; for as I grow older I see that all the human interest and power that religion ever had was in the mother and child and I would have nothing to do with a church that did not offer both. There you are again! You see how the thought always turns back to you.[36]

For his thoughts dwelt on Mrs. Cameron not just as a radiant young woman but as a mother who had achieved a fulfillment which his own barren marriage had not. In Scotland, where he went after his stay at Much Wenlock, a kindly host suggested that he should get himself a "*Frou-Frou,* a companion,"[37] but this was not the solution his mind craved and which would eventually be achieved by elevating Elizabeth Cameron to the height of a symbol and worshipping her as a Madonna with child. At any rate, once back in Washington in early 1892, he seems to have fairly reconciled himself to his role as "tame cat"; it was in this position that he joined the Camerons at Chamonix the following year, planning to pass the month of August with the women of the party after the Senator had gone back to Washington; but bad news from the United States compelled him to follow hard upon Cameron. In the story of Adams' progress on the road to Chartres, this journey home, and the summer he spent at the "Old House" in Massachusetts with his brother Brooks, will appear just as fateful as his journey to Polynesia had been.

"A kind of exaggerated *me,*" was how Henry Adams once characterized his brother Brooks, ten years his junior.[38] Nervous, moody, opinionated, "a little unhinged" in the mind, as his friend Theodore Roosevelt was later to complain, Brooks, even in his childhood, had always been wearing, and from Germany, in 1859, at their mother's entreaty, Henry appealed to his other brothers: "I think myself we ought to tolerate the child who is really a first-rate little fellow apart from his questions, and we ought not to snub him." Tutored, as we know, by Gurney, Brooks in his turn entered Harvard College, which he did not find much more inspiring than Henry had. Yet, at least one subject, history, captured his imagination; this he evinced in a letter he wrote to his father, in 1868:

Between my studies and amusements I am historical enough and medieval at that. I don't know how it is but I find and always have found, that medieval history was more to my taste than Greek or Roman just as I can't help confessing to myself that a Gothic cathedral, or ruined castle, pleases me more than a Roman ruin.

I always find myself looking at Greek and Roman remains with a feeling that I have no personal interest in them, that they are of another civilisation and are separated from me by a barrier that I can't get over. On the contrary, in a dirty, quaint, crooked-streeted and dear old Rhine town, I feel as if I had a personal lively connection, with not only the town itself, but the people who lived there.

I don't mean by this that Roman and Greek things don't interest me. They do intensely, but somehow with an entirely different and not half so warm a feeling.

This is I know a very degrading confession, but I can't help it, the dawning of our civilisation has, and does now, interest me more than all the splendour of the ancient.[39]

Though his brother's subsequent appointment to a professorship of medieval history could not but enhance this interest in the Middle Ages, Brooks chose a different avocation: he read law and then twice set up legal partnerships which soon dissolved, while he sought political office with even less success; added to these disappointments, his failing health drove him into a gloomy retirement, where he undertook what was to remain his life's chief pursuit: the formulation of a philosophy of history that would solve—or so he hoped—the major problems of the human race. Thus, he said, he "became the author of 'The Emancipation of Massachusetts' which greatly scandalized all the reputable historians of Massachusetts and elsewhere."[40]

For this Social-Darwinist study of the Puritan era, which he published in 1887, not only proved to be quite unorthodox but was doctored with all the deeply ingrained prejudices of a brilliant but erratic Adams who, even more conscious than his brothers of the "decline" of their family, wanted to read the lesson of a similar decline in all his interpretations of history. Henry Adams, who, since Marian's death, relied more and more on flight to avoid tension, could not bear the company of his argumentative brother; when the latter proposed to join him at Quincy, where he happened to be, in October 1887, he rushed away to prevent the wrangling discussions through which Brooks would certainly stalk him. No doubt Brooks was bitterly disappointed. "My dear fellow," he said a few months later, in June 1888, to Spring-Rice, who had shown him some kindness, "I'm a crank; very few human beings can endure to have me near them, but I like to be with those who are sympathetic, the more so since they are so few."[41] And now, in 1893, it happened that the two brothers were thrown together for weeks on end. As Brooks afterward recalled, "Henry and I sat in the hot August evenings and talked endlessly of the panic and of our hopes and fears, and of my historical and economic theories, and so the season wore away amidst an excitement verging on revolution." That was a memorable summer, which, in Brooks' own words, truly "changed all [their] lives."[42]

It was the financial panic of 1893 which had compelled Henry Adams to return home. Throughout the country that year, there were over 15,000 commercial failures; 572 banking establishments collapsed, including those in Kansas City, where his brother Charles Francis had deposited large sums of money. It seemed as if the Adams Trust itself, set up at the death of their father in 1886 for his surviving children, was doomed to bankruptcy, and they were to go beggars. If, in *The Education,* Henry Adams was blandly to assert that he would have easily lived "on the income of bricklayers," nothing could have been more unsavory to him.[43] Facing sudden poverty at the age of fifty-five was a grueling experience, and though, a month after his arrival, he was able to report to Gaskell the cessation of the scare, the strains of these weeks and the sensation he had then of being caught in a ruthless trap would never be effaced. The villains in the affair, he and Brooks soon convinced themselves, were the Eastern bankers (the "Gold bugs," as he took to calling them, since they were against the use of silver as a legal tender), who by cornering the gold market had engineered the crisis. Once already in 1870, with "The New York Gold Conspiracy," he had attacked the monetary powers; now his ancestral quarrel with State Street, of which he was to make so much in *The Education,* became acutely personal, while assuming international proportions. For the chief conspirators, he saw it all clearly, were the financial lords of Lombard Street; his old anti-British feelings (had not his London years, as he reminded his brother Charles, turned him "into a life-long enemy of everything British?") revived with a rare intensity, making him wish to hang Rothschild from a lamppost in the company of the Lord of the

Exchequer. Such a vengeful mood would still be strong enough about a decade later to color *Mont-Saint-Michel and Chartres;* for under the influence of Brooks it acquired a solid philosophical basis.[44]

During these tense days at "the Old House" Adams tried to remain calm by playing solitaire in the "President's library." There, one evening at the beginning of his stay, his brother came in with history, and I am inclined to think it sound." This cautiously quite mad." He read it. "Your work," he reassured Brooks, "is not the dream of a maniac. It is an attempt at the philosophy of history, and I am inclined to think it sound." This cautiously phrased approval (such it was reported by Brooks) ill expresses the passionate interest the work immediately aroused in Henry.[45] He endlessly discussed the ideas in the manuscript with his brother, constantly approving the concepts but despairing at the quality of the style, and this went on until, unable to stand further arguing, he ran away to the World's Fair in Chicago. Not that his departure could bring an end to this meeting of their minds. If the brothers were too full of restless energy not to become enraged with each other during any session of talk, they could confront their ideas, expound their beliefs, and even disagree bluntly by mail; thus until death cut it short, they would carry on their debate, castigating the world and its ways, while predicting events with rather uncanny foresight. At first their letters revolved about the manuscript which Brooks assayed, chapter after chapter, upon his brother. "But for you," he would write him a few years later, "I never should have printed it. Most of what has attracted attention has been the result of your criticism. The form is, I think, wholly yours." Though Henry Adams disclaimed all parentage to the ideas of the book, it is true that much of his time, during the intervals of compulsive traveling in 1894 and 1895, was taken up with the manuscript, which he carefully revised. "All I can say," he added upon giving his final approval, "is that if I wanted to write any book, it would be the one you have written."[46]

We have no idea of the form of the manuscript in 1893, but we may safely guess that its author's philosophy of history, based on the analysis of the vicissitudes of men in the grip of an ever-tightening gold currency, was already clearly delineated. As Brooks

Adams then told Henry Cabot Lodge, he was treating of "the origin, rise and despotism of the gold bug."[47] Around that one motif, the influence of money on the fortunes of the world, he now wove not only a tract, *The Gold Standard* (probably culled from the original manuscript), which he published in Boston the following year, but his full-length treatise: *The Law of Civilization and Decay,* in the writing of which Henry Adams played an important part. Brooks, Henry Adams summarized in *The Education,* "had discovered or developed a law of history that civilization followed the exchange, and having worked it out for the Mediterranean was working it out for the Atlantic." In Brooks' own words, his book demonstrated that:

The economic center of the world determined the social equilibrium, and . . . this international center of exchanges was an ambulatory spot on the earth's surface which seldom remained fixed for any considerable period of time, but which vibrated back and forth according as discoveries in applied science and geography changed avenues of communication and caused trade routes to reconverge. Thus Babylon had given way to Rome, Rome to Constantinople, Constantinople to Venice, Venice to Antwerp and finally about 1810 London became the undisputed capital of the world. Each migration represented a change in equilibrium, and, therefore, caused a social revolution.[48]

And so the banker was now supreme master, as he had been in ancient Rome, and was heading society toward the same catastrophe. Brooks' wife suggested calling the book: "The Path to Hell: A Story Book," but such a title, Brooks said, would have been fallaciously optimistic, since he could not even promise anything "so good as a path to 'Hell.' " There was nothing but chaos in sight. For, to quote again from *The Education:* "Among the other general rules, [Brooks] laid down the paradox that in the social disequilibrium between capital and labor, the logical outcome was not collectivism, but anarchism; and Henry made note of it for study."[49] Another point Henry duly "made note of" was the view which his brother expressed of the thirteenth century, as the most brilliant epoch in European history: "It was then the French communes had their rise, and Gothic architecture culminated. It was then the cathedrals of Paris and Bourges, of Chartres and Rheims, were built, and it was then that the glass of the windows of the Sainte Chapelle was a commercial article. It was the golden age of the

University of Paris when Albert the Great, Saint Thomas Aquinas, and Roger Bacon were teaching, and when in Italy Saint Francis of Assisi preached. It was then that the kingdom of France was organized under Saint Louis, and English constitutional government began with Magna Charta."[50]

In *The Law of Civilization and Decay,* as already in *The Emancipation of Massachusetts,* Brooks, while venting his hatred of religion, professed admiration for some of its work. In the earlier volume he praised the clergy for developing an educational system; now it was for the growth of architecture. He rhapsodized over the time when "the monks took no thought of money," and their art "was no chattel to be bought but an inspired language in which they communed with God or taught the people, and they expressed a poetry in the stones they carved which far transcended words." For these reasons, Gothic architecture in its prime was spontaneous, elevated, dignified, and pure. But he also pictured these same clerics turning into merchants of the temple, solely concerned with the money value of the "miracle"; even the most beautiful products of human imagination had become debased. Greed had revealed itself as the impelling force driving a mercenary world to its doom.

The Law of Civilization and Decay was a gloomy book indeed. Houghton Mifflin turned it down in Boston, and Henry Adams had to arrange its publication with a London firm. As he foresaw, it was savagely attacked; but this did not change his high opinion of the book. "I think it is astonishing," he wrote to Mrs. Cameron on October 4, 1895: "Indeed it is the first time that serious history has ever been written. He has done for it what only the greatest men do; he has created a startling generalization which reduces all history to a scientific formula, and which is yet so simple and obvious that one cannot believe it to be new. My admiration for it is much too great to be told. I have sought all my life those truths which this mighty infant, this seer unblest, has struck with the agony and bloody sweat of genius. I stand in awe of him."[51] He had found what he henceforth liked to call his "Bible of Anarchy." All his own later works were to be influenced by it.

4

Ignorance Triumphant

THE "NORMAN PARADISE"

It was in the summer of 1895, at the time when *The Law of Civilization and Decay* was finally coming off the presses, that Henry Adams really "discovered" the French Middle Ages. He had come to France after staying over a month in England. "I am going over," he had written from Washington to Gaskell, in late June, "with Mrs. Brooks Adams's sister, Mrs. Cabot Lodge. The Lord only knows what has induced the Senator of Massachusetts to go over with wife and sons, to Europe, where he has not been these five-and-twenty years, and which he detests almost as much as I do; but go he will . . . I shall drift about also, and I suppose my brother Brooks will come over later, as he wants to print his book. We shall be a little family party." Brooks did not leave the United States that summer. As for Adams, he was right in warning another English friend that "dyspepsia has seized me." London, where he arrived on July 10, disagreed with him at once; it "sits with my stomach like a Welsh rabbit at midnight," he complained the following day. "London was decidedly too much for me; it tired me, not so much physically as mentally," he averred a fortnight later, also protesting that "the Englishman is too much for me. The Englishwoman is much too more."[1] He had by then sought refuge at Much Wenlock for a week; after another calm week in Scotland he rejoined the Lodge family in London, and the party soon left for France, where by way of Amiens, Rouen, Caen, Saint-Lô, they reached Coustances "in time to see the sunset from the top of the cathedral."

The day was Friday, August 23, 1895, probably the most important day in Adams' life as a medievalist. There and then, he experienced a Pascalian "surprise," which, he wrote to his niece Mabel Hooper, "humbled my proud spirit a good bit." He said, "I thought I knew Gothic. Caen, Bayeux and Coutances were a chapter I never opened before, and which pleased my jaded appetite. They are austere . . . I never before felt quite so utterly stood on, as I did in the cathedral at Coutances. Amiens has mercy . . . Coutances is above mercy itself. The squirming devils under the feet of the stone Apostles looked uncommonly like me and my generation."[2] The squirming devils are a piece of fantasy, and so are the Apostles, Coutances being, as Adams said, too "austere" to allow such figures on its fronts and columns. Yet they have their place in the imaginative construct which he was already beginning to build. Nowhere as much as in the letter he sent to John Hay two weeks after this experience are we made conscious of the intensity with which his imagination started working in Normandy:

Our trip there was very successful. Not for several days or more have I enjoyed happier moments than among my respectable Norman ancestors, looking over the fields which they ploughed and the stones they carved and piled up. Caen, Bayeux, St. Lo, Coutances and Mont St. Michel are clearly works that I helped to build, when I lived in a world I liked. With the Renaissance, the Valois and the Tudor display, I can have had nothing to do. It leaves me admiring, but cold. With true Norman work, the sensation is that of personal creation. No doubt Amiens and Chartres are greatly superior architecture, but I was not there. I was a vassal of the Church; I held farms—for I was many—in the Cotentin and around Caen, but the thing I did by a great majority of ancestors was to help in building the Cathedral of Coutances, and my soul is still built into it. I can almost remember the faith that gave me energy, and the sacred boldness that made my towers seem to me so daring, with the bits of gracefulness that I hasarded with some doubts whether the divine grace could properly be shown outside. Within I had no doubts. There the contrite sinner was welcomed with such tenderness as makes me still wish I were one. There is not a stone in the whole interior which I did not treat as though it were my own child . . . Nearly eight hundred years have passed since I made the fatal mistake of going to England, and since then I have never done anything in the world that can begin to compare in the perfection of its spirit and art with my cathedral of Coutances. I am sure of it as I am of death.[3]

The rest of the trip, though highly satisfactory, did not achieve the same emotional value. On Saturday, August 24, the party arrived at Mont-Saint-Michel; they found the Mount milling with tourists of, Adams said, "many kinds of repulsiveness": "Odious French women, gross, shapeless, bare-armed, eating and drinking with demonstrative satisfaction; and dreary English women, with the usual tusks; and American art students, harmless and feeble, sketching from every hole in the walls. The mob was awful, and the meals hog-pens. Romance and Religion are a long way from Madame Poulard's kitchen in these summer weeks." Still, he was ready to concede, "the castle was worth many hogs," and they stayed on until Monday, "enjoying it from all sorts of points."[4] Then, as he summed up to Mrs. Cameron, they went across country to Vitré, "called on Mme de Sévigné, who was quite entertaining," slept at Le Mans, and proceeded to Chartres, where they spent two hours, "and after thirty-five years of postponed intentions, I worshipped at last before the splendor of the great glass Gods. Chartres is a beautiful gate by which to leave the Norman paradise, as Amiens is a beautiful gate to enter." They were in Paris on August 28; less than a week later, they had left again for Touraine, "a violently over-admired country," he found; "Francis I and Henry VIII are brothers, and should have been cooks. They look it. Their architecture looks it." It was all "mercantile, bourgeois and gold-bug," and made him homesick for Normandy. His only keen pleasure was the glass windows in the cathedral at Tours: "I am not quite sure that there is much religion in glass; but for once I will not require too much. The ultimate cathedral of the 13th century was deliberately intended to unite all the arts and sciences in the direct service of God. It was a Chicago Exposition for God's profit . . . It was the greatest single creation of man . . . The more I study it, the more I admire and wonder. I am not dis-

posed to find fault . . . Even its weaknesses are great, and its failures, like Beauvais and Le Mans, are because man rose beyond
himself."[5] Thus, by the end of the summer, in 1895, some of the
great themes of *Mont-Saint-Michel and Chartres* had already taken
possession of Adams' mind.

It is necessary at this stage to pause and analyze the conditions
which led to such a discovery. "And so it chanced," Adams states
in *The Education,* "that in August one found one's self for the first
time at Caen, Coutances, and Mont-Saint-Michel in Normandy."
What was there in this "atmosphere" which could give him, in his
own words, "the touch of a real emotion," the emotion out of which
his book really originated? And how could he suddenly receive the
revelation, not only of a whole new world of architecture but also
—and above all—of a spiritual country where like an O'Neill
character stumbling at last upon his long-sought-for identity he
would henceforth *belong*? Of course he was already quite familiar
with Gothic architecture; as he told Mabel, "I had not thought myself so ignorant or so stupid as to have remained blind to such
things, being more or less within sight of them now for nearly
forty years." He did not owe his acquaintance merely to books.
Amiens, where he "passed Monday in the cathedral" before going
on to Normandy, he was thus visiting for the third time—"but it
is always newer and more wonderful every time—and it never
seemed so fresh as now or so marvellously perfect." Rouen was
also "old grounds, but interesting, and we might well have stayed
longer." Yet no more than on former occasions, for all the pleasure
he took in these new visits, was he carried away as he would be at
Coutances. And even at Chartres, which he then discovered and
found "fascinating," his judgment remained quite sober. "The
other sights," his letter to Hay continued, after the rapturous paragraph on Coutances, "were a pleasure but not the same. I enjoy
them—but in an intellectual kind of way."[6] How was it that in
Normandy, and especially at Coutances, he experienced such an
emotional upsurge?

There may well have been physiological reasons. Thus the
weather, which he reported "cool," "charming" (in blessed contrast with the oppressive heat in London the week before), contributed not a little to the "success" of the trip.[7] Arriving as they

did at Coutances just after sunset, he could enjoy the balmiest part of the day—and this enjoyment proved all the sweeter if, as is likely, they then had the cathedral all to themselves, or practically so. Less of a tourist haunt than Bayeux or Mont-Saint-Michel, Coutances, particularly at that time of day, must have been free of those herds of "cattle on two legs" so obnoxious to Adams. The tourists (but what was he, if not one himself?) set Adams' nerves on edge, marring a good deal of his pleasure at Mont-Saint-Michel, or even, though he does not say so, at Chartres. All his letters that summer ring with his hatred of the species, hatred which further contact in the Loire valley intensified. "To be a tourist," he burst out on his return from Touraine, "is to lose self-respect and to invite insult."[8] But in tranquil Coutances he was not provoked to such fury, and, feeling benignly at ease, he could even more easily fall under the charm of the place.

"I have rarely felt New England at its highest ideal power as it appeared to me, beatified and glorified in the cathedral of Coutances," Adams afterward wrote to Brooks,[9] for he really found himself at home. The austerity of Coutances proved congenial to his puritanical disposition, whereas the "exterior magnificences" of Amiens, Rouen (and he also included Chartres) left him not only cold, but somewhat antagonistic. His letter to Brooks explains this dissatisfaction: "The Gothic church, both in doctrine and expression, is not my idea of a thoroughly happy illusion. It is always restless, grasping and speculative; it exploits the world, and makes profit; it is the legitimate parent of Lombard Street; the legitimate child of the Jews." Coutances was different; it was Norman; it was English; it was un-Jewish. For one must realize, even if it comes as a shock, that the mainsprings of Adams' rather complex emotions at Coutances were racist, not artistic.

To one who reads *The Education,* the author's antisemitism (though more covert than in *Mont-Saint-Michel and Chartres*) soon becomes apparent. Yet one of the most explicit passages, in which we see the young man, "an American of Americans," coming back to his native land in 1868 and faring less well there than any "Polish Jew fresh from Warsaw or Cracow," any "furtive Yacoob or Ysaac still reeking of the Ghetto" happens to be misleading. To heighten the drama of his own return Adams has telescoped into the picture a situation that then did not yet exist and feelings he had certainly not yet come to entertain. After all, we must remember that in England his best friend Gaskell was connected with the Palgraves, alias Cohens, whom he admired greatly. And in Tahiti, Arii Taimi, the old Chiefess, happened to be the widow of a London Jew. This did not prevent Adams from being on the best of terms with her son, Tati Samon.[10] As a matter of fact, his antisemitism appears to have welled up together with his intense feeling against the "gold-bugs" in 1893, the Jews providing him with an obsessional symbol destined to haunt his imagination with the vividness which the *Pteraspis,* and then the dynamo and the Virgin, would achieve. In the Jew he started crystallizing all his hatred of the world.

"I am myself more than ever at odds with my time," he tells Gaskell on January 23, 1894. "I detest it, and everything that belongs to it, and live only in the wish to see the end of it with all its infernal Jewry. I want to put every money-lender to death, and to sink Lombard Street and Wall Street under the Ocean." Springing as it did from economic causes, his animus was now taking a markedly racist coloring under the influence of such writers as Karl Pearson and Max Nordau. "The other day," he writes again to Gaskell in June 1895, just before leaving for England, "I thought I saw myself, but run mad and howling. I took up a book without noticing its title particularly and read a few pages. The vertigo seized me, for I thought I must be inventing a book in a dream. It was Nordau's *Degeneracy.*" In 1896 he would complain: "The Jew has got into the soul. I see him—or her—now everywhere, and wherever he—or she—goes, there must remain a taint in the blood forever."

During the Dreyfus affair, he passionately committed himself to the *anti-Dreyfusard* side. Hay, who was then traveling with him, remarked that he "now believes the earthquake at Krakatoa was the work of Zola and when he saw Vesuvius reddening the midnight air he searched the horizon to find a Jew stoking the fire."[11] Considering the intensity with which Adams' splenetic imagination had been aroused at Coutances in 1895, it is easy to find a substratum of truth in his friend's pleasantry.

"His revulsion from Lombard Street to the Middle Ages was violent, emetic," Ernest Samuels comments, and with these terms we shall agree.[12] Adams took to the Middle Ages in what clearly appears as a neurotic reaction. Had he gone straight to Normandy, his reaction might have been less acute. London, as he said, "over-irritated" him, not only by making him "groan inwardly with the reminiscences that make life seem a nightmare," but by exacerbating what, since the summer of 1893 and his conversations with Brooks, had become his maniac grievance against the gold bugs. "I am interested only in the city," he reported on August 13, 1895. "There I go to inquire the progress of my brother Brooks's book, which is now almost ready, and which is my Gospel of anarchy. There too I go to consult an Ebrew Jew about silver and gold—a Jew such as I respect and admire for his splendid contempt of mankind." Thus, as he was about to cross the Channel, his conviction that the world was on the brink of "cataclysm" brought about by the manipulations of the moneylenders was reinforced: "We may have the collapse precipitated next week by a panic or we may have it postponed six months, but it is made the worse by pretending to ignore it." Europe, he added, "may burst with gold without helping us"; and by Europe, he meant England as well as "International Jewry," the two notions now going together in his mind. This detestation colored everything he saw; "between British taste and Jewish taste, nothing survives untouched," he said of the London scene.[13] Combining with his antisemitism, his disgust with England and the "oceanic vulgarity" prevailing there prepared his mind for the emotional turmoil he was soon to experience. "He had gone," Ernest Samuels explains, "almost directly that summer from his interviews with the London bankers to view the Cathedral at Chartres. Escape from the present had been imperative."[14] Accurate in its essentials, such a synopsis nonetheless appears too abrupt, since the most important point on Adams' road was Coutances, not Chartres; and it does not take into account the part played at that stage by Senator Henry Cabot Lodge—a part which has never been sufficiently stressed.

HENRY CABOT LODGE

"Cabot beamed with satisfaction in history," Adams told Mrs. Cameron at the end of his journey through Normandy, and he added that rather wistful comment: "He ought to have been Professor at Harvard College as I meant him to be when I educated him. He showed it at Mont St. Michel where the church is not so religious as military."[15] Indeed, the roles seemed to have been reversed, with old "Doctor Barbaricus" now sitting under his former pupil's mentorship, making good note of what he heard in order to use it later in the first chapters of *Mont-Saint-Michel and Chartres;* but the exposés he most profited by were not on architecture.

"Lodge's plumage was varied," we learn from his portrait in *The Education,* "and like his flight, harked back to race. He betrayed the consciousness that he and his people had a past, if they dared but avow it, and might have a future if they could but divine it." Instead of choosing the academic profession, he had entered politics, a field in which he was eventually to distinguish himself as the man whose decided stance against the Versailles Treaty prevented its ratification by the Senate. Throughout his political career, as a matter of fact, he consistently defended ultranationalistic positions, encouraged in that stand by Brooks Adams, his brother-in-law and close associate. At this particular stage of his career, he was the most active spokesman in the Senate advocating the restriction of immigration. If, prior to the eighties, immigration from Russia and Poland had been "but a minuscule fraction of the total," while the Irish practically submerged the electorate Lodge had now to court, Jews from all over Slavic Europe were now flocking into the States by the hundreds of thousands, arousing mounting fears in this electorate. In 1894 an "Immigration Restriction League" was formed in Boston whose mission was to save the United States from mongrelization; naturally, Lodge was one of its members.[16]

Unlike many old New Englanders, however, the Senator did not pride himself on his English parentage. His "inborn Yankee disinclination toward Great Britain" had been strengthened by the ambiguous policy of the British during the American Civil War—in the same way that Henry Adams had then acquired his profound distrust of "that besotted race."[17] Luckier than Adams, Lodge could clearly trace back his ancestry to non-English sources. Giles Lodge, his great grandfather, who was on one side of Huguenot extraction, belonged on the other to the Ellertons, a family which had settled in England after the Norman Conquest. As to Anna

Sophia Lodge, his mother, she was decended from George Cabot, a member of the Massachusetts Convention which adopted the American Constitution and one of the first representatives of his state in the U.S. Senate. Henry Cabot Lodge felt particularly proud of this ancestor; writing his biography was the first task to which he had settled himself after graduating. In the very first lines of *Life and Letters of George Cabot* (Boston, 1878) he traced his Norman filiation: "Among the names on the 'auncient role' . . . of 'the chiefe Noblemen & Gentlemen, which came into England with William the Conquerer' is that of Cabot." The Cabots, he proclaimed twenty years later, "were of that Norman race which did so much for the making of England, and sprang from the Channel Islands which have been a part of the kingdom of Great Britain ever since William the Conqueror seized the English crown." No wonder that, as their traveling companion reports, the Lodges "breathed native air in the Normandy of 1200," though the year was 1895. "And through the Lodge eyes, the old problems," Adams adds, "became new and personal."[18]

What was it that they could reveal to him and which was so important? The answer is in the speech delivered in the Senate on March 6, 1896; with Carlyle as an authority, Lodge asserted that the Normans who had civilized England were not Frenchmen. On the contrary, they were "Saxons who spoke French . . . the most remarkable of all the people who poured out of the Germanic forests . . . To them we owe the marvels of Gothic architecture, for it was they who were the great builders and architects of Mediaeval Europe. They were great military engineers as well and revived the art of fortified defence . . . They were great statesmen and great generals, and they had only been in Normandy about a hundred years when they crossed the English Channel, conquered the country, and gave to England for many generations to come her kings and nobles."[19] Does not this read like an outline of the Norman chapters of *Mont-Saint-Michel and Chartres*? Thus it may well have been that Adams received his first literary "cue" from Lodge during their 1895 tour. But the elation which then seized him ("going back now to the old associations," he writes to Gaskell, on September 1 of that summer, "seems to me as easy as drinking champagne") was not of an inspirational nature. It was, as he said, "personal." He had found his *true* ancestry, a perfectly satisfactory one. "I am sure that in the eleventh century the majority of me was Norman," he explained to his English friend in the same letter, adding in what seems to us rather merciless banter, "so we conquered England, which was a pretty dull, beer-swilling and indifferent sort of people."[20] Needless to say, in his judgment, the English had little changed, except for their becoming completely dominated by the Jews.

Playing with the idea of "an evolution which did not evolve," as he had when dabbling in geology, Adams saw the Norman part of himself (a part which unlike the Lodges, though, he could only assume on the strength of feelings, not of historical facts) remaining through the ages perfectly safe from the English taint. And it was a part which had never been French, never been but pure Norman or Germanic, the emphasis being on the word *pure*. Distinctly marked with racial prejudices, the "Norman paradise" turns out to be, so to speak, an Aryan as well as an atrabilious Valhalla. It did not trouble Adams very much that, through an historical accident, the paradise was now French. After all, as he wrote from London to Brooks Adams, on October 3, 1895: "On the whole France impressed me favorably. The signs of decay are less conspicuous than in any other country I have visited. Capitalistic processes are less evident. The small man has a better chance. The people understand the age better, and still make a fight." He added, and this was a most important point: "Of course, the Jew is great, but he is not yet absolute as he is here." The following year, "blushing to confess" the keen pleasure he took in reading "the extravagance of Drumont's *France juive, libre parole,* and all," he advised Gaskell: "Suppose you try *Dernières batailles* or *La Fin d'un monde,* at least it will take you out of an English atmosphere."[21] But to such an end, as far as he himself was concerned, nothing could have ever surpassed in effect this first trip to Normandy.

"BROTHER BROOKS" AGAIN

Except for a rather confusing passage in *The Education,* Henry Adams never acknowledged his indebtedness to Lodge; the Senator's influence on him was incidental. Seen in the broad continuum of the medieval pilgrimage which was to end with *Mont-Saint-Michel and Chartres*, only one influence really counted; to his brother Brooks Adams alone could Adams write as he did, on June 5, 1905: "You started me ten years ago into this amusement, you mapped out the lines and indicated the emotions. In fact I should find it difficult to pick out of the volume what was yours from what was mine." And it is indeed fascinating to watch how Brooks after the summer of 1895 actually set out "indicating" the emotions for the benefit of his senior; apparently, it was with very little result, Henry then remaining just as he described himself to Gaskell on September 1, 1895, "by no means an imaginative or emotional animal but rather a cold and calculating one," looking out in true Norman fashion "for the actual with a perfectly cool head."[22] Thus while one brother, keeping a dispassionately clinical attitude, seemed interested chiefly in pointing out all the signs of decay in modern Europe, the other would ecstatically keep reverting to his moments of communication with the past.

Never one with steady nerves, Brooks was then on the verge of a breakdown; the tense feelings which had accompanied the publication of *The Law of Civilization and Decay*, coupled with his excitement at his brother's loud acceptance of him as a genius, had shaken him tremendously.[23] With pathetic eagerness, he seized upon Henry's "discovery" of the Gothic as one more common bond between them. Some seven years before, he had gone through a somewhat similar experience; medieval architecture now became more than ever vital to him, and in letter after letter (most of them still unpublished) he described his aesthetic and spiritual thrills. Although Henry could not, then or later, ever exactly realize his brother's sensations in a Gothic church or at any rate ever duplicate them, no doubt, as Arthur Beringause maintains, he used Brooks' raptures "for an ever deepening poetic sense of his own" out of which *Mont-Saint-Michel and Chartres* would come one day.[24] "In modest imitation of you," he had written Brooks on September 8, 1895, "we have taken vast draughts of Norman architecture." Dated September 21, came an excited reply:

I am delighted to hear that you have been making a Gothic pilgrimage. On the whole, the parts of my life which I look back to with the greatest delight are those I have spent among the churches and castles of the Middle Ages. If I have a particularly weak spot it is for Le Mans, I suppose because it was there I first came to understand what the great poem meant. I remember the day well. I came to Le Mans largely by accident, and on strolling up to the cathedral I found some great function was at hand. I asked what was on foot, and they told me they were to sing the mass of the Fête-Dieu. I had never heard a great mass in a Gothic church, and I sat down in the nave to listen. The bishop and chapter came in and the service began. The light was blazing through those thirteenth-century windows of the choir, and lighting up that marvellous glass of the twelfth century of the nave, the arches were misty with incense, and the mass was sung by a choir of boys, under the lead of one of the canons with a simplicity that is impossible outside of France. As it went on and on, and they sang their hymns, I confess that I disgraced myself. I felt for half an hour as I know the men must have felt who stained those windows, and built those arches. I really and truly did believe the miracle, and as I sat and blubbered in the nave, and knelt at the elevation I did receive the body of God . . . To me the Gothic is the greatest emotional stimulant in the world. I am of it, I understand it, I know how those men felt, and I am in feeling absolutely at one with Saint Anselm or Godfrey de Bouillon.[25]

Only once during the following months did Henry revert to the past summer's experience, and then merely by way of a brief allusion, in a letter dated October 3: "We did, I believe, all the great Gothic cathedrals. I quite agree with you as to the effect they produce. It is overwhelming."[26] It was as though he otherwise deliberately shirked the subject. But there was no way of containing his brother's excitement. On October 13, Brooks, who was then still staying at "the Old House," poured out his disgust with contemporary New England:

It is hard to live in such an atmosphere and after a time I grow to yearn with a longing that is almost like hunger to go off to some place like Palestine where I shall live again in that land of dreams which has become more real to me than reality. It is now just eight years since I crossed the threshhold of that land. I found it by accident one September in Paris; year by year I have gone back to it and fed on it and I have been more and more shut out from active life at home. I have lived more and more in the Middle Ages. Till you went to France this year, except my wife, there has not been one living soul who has seen what I have seen, or felt what I have felt.

The "land of dreams" had now become a family demesne which no one else—and especially not La Farge, whom he now felt he was supplanting in his close relationship with Henry—could enter: "Even the artists, men like La Farge, don't see the heart of the great imaginative past. They see a building, a color, a combination of technical effects. They don't see the passion that this means or meant, and they don't feel that awful tragedy, which is the sum of life,—the agony of consciousness."[27]

In India, where he had gone to spend the winter in search of further symptoms of the decay spreading across the modern world, fever combining with nervous exhaustion brought Brooks so much down that his wife Evelyn feared his immediate death. As soon as he had recovered sufficiently they started back for Europe. "It seems to me that I have crossed a great bridge in the last few months," he wrote from on board the ship, on March 25, 1896; that was a bridge which led directly to the medieval "land of dreams" which he would soon haunt. An opportunity to renew these raptures with an increased intensity provided itself as the travelers, on their voyage home, stopped over for several weeks in France. It was "hard work," though, at the beginning; Brooks complained to his brother on April 22, 1896: "For me the Gothic is a dream of my own, I do not think it is a reality and my dream will only be dreamed when I have time and can sit by myself long in quiet. If I have time and quiet and sit near or in a church, after a while, the vision will begin more or less strongly, but it won't appear if I am not at ease, so that my attention is distracted. We stopped at Dijon and Autun but the weather was so cold we could not sit or stand still and we gave it up. I got absolutely nothing." But taking up the very same letter after a visit to Notre-Dame de Paris, he could joyfully go on: "As I saw once more the towers of Notre-Dame I had a shock of delight, as though it were new. There is nothing like it—no, nothing. The Gothic in its prime is I believe the greatest effort of man. The magnificence and the dignity of the nave, the glory of the rose, the fire, the fancy of the whole west church leaves everything done by Greek or Roman, by Egyptian or by Arab dead and cold. At least, I feel it so." For days he was to remain in this exalted state of feelings, experiencing, every time "he trod the nave of the great church," his biographer notes, "a knife-edge thrill of blissful exaltation and communication which cut so deep into his vitals that his nerves tingled for hours in ecstasy." Such was indeed his agitation that Evelyn Adams felt more anxious than ever to pursue the journey home.[28]

Politics soon engrossed him after his return to the States. Whether, with the change of interests, his exaltation had naturally calmed down or whether his brother's disinclination to commune had discouraged him, he ceased to expatiate upon the Gothic. Only in a letter from Dresden, dated October 29, 1899, did he revert to the subject which Henry had this time brought up: "Reading what you say of the Twelfth century made me horribly homesick. It is now just twelve years since I discovered the French Middle Ages and I shall never forget my excitement and my delight. For three years I wandered over France and Syria absorbed in the remains and I look back on those days as the most charming of my life. I suppose I have been twenty times to Chartres. I made repeated tours from Paris to Normandy, Champagne, Nevers and Picardy, and I have always hoped to go back."[29] By then Henry Adams was, as he said, "living in French Gothic." Instead of making "repeated tours" that is, flinging himself into the Middle Ages by passionate "fits and starts," he had come gradually into the "land of dreams," but to dwell there permanently. "The form is never arbitrary," he would say in *The Education;* "but it is a kind of growth like crystal-lization."[30] In such a Stendhalian way, by a process of slow accretion, was *Mont-Saint-Michel and Chartres* to take shape; it would be hard to believe that Brooks' rapturous descriptions in his 1895–96 letters, though apparently unheeded, did not, at least a little, contribute to this growth.

IN SEARCH OF A "HOBBY"

"Whence comes a law, drawn from Brother Brooks: All true imaginative art belongs to the imaginative period which must be religious and military," Henry Adams remarked for the sake of Mrs. Cameron, on September 12, 1895. In another letter which he sent to her, the following summer, from Italy, where he was then traveling, he again played with the theory:

As you may remember, or forget, my brother Brooks and I, in our historical discussions on the theory of his book, have been greatly exercised by the fact that the Roman Empire, one day, about the year

400, dropped to pieces without any apparent causes . . . Yet it showed very curious energy for a corpse. It adopted a new and very strong, centralized religion just at that time. At Byzantium, which happened to survive, Justinian, a hundred years later, . . . built the church of Saint Sophia in an entirely new form of architecture which is still our admiration. The empire did many other things not usual for corpses to do, and among the rest, built Ravenna, which was the reason I wanted to see it. So we went there, and I found what I wanted. Ravenna is a startling discovery to a poor American searcher for conundrums. Except the great Gothic churches like Chartres and Amiens, with their glass and sculpture, I know nothing to compare with the religious splendor of the Ravenna churches with their mosaics. They are a revelation of what can be done by an old civilisation when the gold-bug breaks down, and empires expire.[31]

Thus, for all his apparent apathy when Brooks urged him to share his emotional attitude toward the Gothic, he was more than willing to let his brother "map out the lines" of his thoughts. *The Law of Civilization and Decay* still greatly engaged his interest. In 1895 he had kept with him copies of the book which he went on annotating in view of the New York and Paris editions. Of all his suggestions, only one, according to Ernest Samuels, resulted in a "major change": "Henry felt that the ultimate and costliest disaster which befell the Western world was aesthetic, the decline of the arts through the impoverishment of the imagination. 'An entire chapter,' said Henry, 'should be given to arts.' Brooks adopted the suggestion."[32] In the first American edition brought out by Macmillan in 1896, he considerably enlarged the conclusion and now wound up the essay with a lament over the death of true art.

No poetry can bloom in the modern arid soil, the drama has died, and the patrons of art are no longer even conscious of shame at profaning the most sacred of ideals. The ecstatic dream, which some twelfth-century monk cut into the stones of the sanctuary hallowed by the presence of his God, is reproduced to bedizen a warehouse; or the plan of an abbey, which Saint Hugh may have consecrated, is adapted to a railway station. Decade by decade, for some four hundred years, these phenomena have grown more sharply marked in Europe, and, as consolidation apparently nears its climax, art seems to presage approaching disintegration. The architecture, the sculpture, and the coinage of London at the close of the nineteenth century, when compared with those of the Paris of Saint Louis, recall the Rome of Caracalla as contrasted with the Athens of Pericles, save that we lack the stream of barbarian blood which made the Middle Age.[33]

Henry professed himself highly pleased with the "mostly new" chapter which "relieve[d his] mind" (he used the expression at least twice on October 6 and 9, 1896), and saved him "the bother of saying the same thing, and repenting it." Of course in these additional paragraphs, his brother particularly dwelled on the Gothic. Henry himself, that very summer, some weeks before the New York edition of *The Law* came out (he was just fresh from his journey through Italy), had again visited Chartres, spending a Sunday afternoon there, "with the glass and the afternoon service," as he reports in his letter of August 3, 1896, to Mrs. Cameron: "In my sublimated fancy, the combination of the glass and the Gothic is the highest ideal ever reached by men; higher than the Mosaics and Byzantine of Ravenna, which was itself higher, as a religious conception, than the temples of the Greeks or Egyptians. Our age is too thoroughly brutalised to approach or understand any of these creations of an imagination which is dead. I am myself somewhat like a monkey looking through a telescope at the stars; but I can see at least that it must have been great."[34] He still shrank from any closer exploration. Byzantium only (perhaps because he found it more accessible) then seemed to attract him, and more than once he reverted to the subject in his letters to Brooks. "But as for me," he wrote to Mabel Hooper, on December 30, 1896 (spending his winter as usual in Washington), "I read Byzantine history and the early Christians." And if just a few days later he complained to Gaskell: "I have exhausted my Byzantine books, and have nothing to read,"[35] he still did not think that he could turn to a regular study of the French Middle Ages.

It was by midsummer or in the very early autumn of the year 1897 that Henry Adams contracted the interest in French medieval literature which he was to retain until the end of his life. He was then staying in France. "Reeking" though it was in summertime with Yankees, whose "weird spectacle" made him dream of some "new St. Bartholomew," Paris had become for him "after all . . . the best watering-place in the world."[36] He had arrived there at the end of May 1897, looking for a "spot" where he could "camp" his nieces (Edward Hooper's daughters), soon due to join him for several months. He rented a villa on the heights of Saint-

Germain-en-Laye. For their first Sunday in France, he took the girls to Chartres; but that was, it seemed, a very perfunctory visit, just to escape the crowds swarming for the Grand Prix. In the whole summer's correspondence there is not the least mention of another cathedral. Life was very tranquil and studious at Saint-Germain-en-Laye. Writing to Brooks on July 29, 1896, Henry painted himself as "buried in forgetfulness of time and worry"; his intellectual efforts did not go "beyond French subjunctives and Valois kings"; he was seeing nobody, hearing nothing. "I can vegetate, but not feel," he told Mrs. Rebecca Gilman Rae a few days later. Engrossed in his avuncular duties, he recorded: "We study French and French history, and have birthdays and eat a great deal." On August 26, he could likewise report to his brother: "We have all had school and worked solidly on everything French."[37]

Was his interest in Old French a natural outgrowth of his drilling sessions in grammar with his nieces? Or did he turn to medieval literature out of sheer *ennui*? ("Even Rochefort and Drumont and Paul de Cassagnac are dull. Even I am dull," he had complained in June.) At any rate, in late October of the same year (the Saint-Germain villa had been vacated, and he was established in Paris, Rue Christophe Colomb, still "keeping house with two nieces . . . a mild sort of Euthanesia"), he could burst forth with a "*Damnedieu!* as my chanson says." Once the nieces had departed, he settled for a winter in Paris, keeping up with "long hours of study over *Chansons de Geste* and French prepositions." It was an utterly private divertissement; it simply did not occur to him that he could hire a tutor or might attend public courses at the Sorbonne or Collège de France. Even when quite deep in his medieval studies, he would never get in touch with a French specialist. As far as he was concerned, Paris was then "very solitary" but "all right"; "I study a great deal and write," he told his niece Mabel, on December 3, by which he meant he divided his time between Old French literature and letter writing.[38]

"Vaguely a new work, the *Mont-Saint-Michel and Chartres*, was beginning to take shape in his mind," states Ernest Samuels; if so, it could be but very vaguely indeed. The only literary pursuits he was for the time concerned with were those of his brother, who came over in mid-December to bring out a French edition of

The Law. Bent on using Henry's suggestion, Brooks had resolved to expand the section on Byzantium. No doubt, during these winter weeks in Paris, their discussions ranged far and wide, inescapably bringing them back to the Middle Ages, for Henry Adams kept to his medieval reading. "As for me, I read only *Chansons de Geste,*" he wrote to Mabel, on January 1, 1898, just before "settling down to a nice, long, quiet evening of French"; and to John Hay, on January 11, he pictured himself sitting up by his little wood fire and reading "about Lancelot or Parthenopeus of Blois." Not all evenings were so tranquil, since he naturally had numerous sessions with Brooks. As usual his junior's argumentative temper soon proved a little too much for him, and in February he was glad to join the Hays for a trip up the Nile.[39]

Before leaving Paris, Adams placed an order for bookbinding with his bookseller which showed how deeply he had already delved into the Middle Ages. The list of books included such items as "*Adam de Halle, Roman von Lancelot, Wace, Roman de Rose, Guillaume d'Orange* and Bartsch's *Chrestomachie.*"[40] It does not appear, however, that at this stage he contemplated making literary use of his new scholarship. From Athens, which he reached by way of Turkey, pursuing his journey alone after a month of Egypt with the Hays, he advised Brooks on April 2, 1898: "As for the book, I don't know what better you have to do than to work over it. I wish to the Lord I had such hobby to ride. So far from finding it a *corvée*, I think you are extremely happy to have such an occupation, and that you had better prolong it all you can."[41]

"A TWELFTH-CENTURY MONK IN A NINETEENTH-CENTURY ATTIC"

As a matter of fact, we may observe an intermission in Henry Adams' playing with his medieval "hobby." The chief reason for this apparent loss of interest is that he did not stay in France after his Mediterranean tour but went to England for the summer. From there, in November he sailed for the United States. He could hardly have continued with his "schooling" in Old French during all these months, taken as they were by the resumption of his old social routines. Even when back in France the following year, he did not at once recommence his scholarly habits. "I find Paris much where I left Washington,—flat and tired," he wrote to Brooks, on April 6, 1899, a week after returning there. Within a few days he started on a trip to Italy with the Lodges. "Sister Anne" (the Senator's wife) was not of the party, but with Cabot Lodge and his two sons, Bay and John, there came along another young man, Winty (Winthrop) Chanler. And so, as in 1895, and in not such different company, he could once more fall under the spell of the Normans.[42]

The highlight of the journey was Sicily, a Norman dukedom in the twelfth century, where, as we shall be reminded in *Mont-Saint-Michel and Chartres*, the cathedral of Monreale is as truly an exemplar of Norman art as the Abbey church on Mont-Saint-Michel. Writing from Rome on May 12, Adams told Mabel Hooper of his new experience: "We made our trip to Sicily, and did our Greeks and Normans satisfactorily. One or two of the things there—such as Monreale or Taormina—are an education in themselves, and impressed properly the emotions of our youths. Also the fleas impressed them considerably." The tone is somewhat detached. There is nothing here of the passionate intensity which filled Adams' letters after his discovery of Norman architecture at Coutances. His Sicilian trip had only served to impress upon him further a truth of which he had by now long been convinced: "Nobody but the French ever knew anything about religion. There is nothing worth knowing in Europe but the Greek and the Norman—and Michael Angelo who was the first great anarchist."[43] And since, as he had observed a little earlier, "one Greek temple is just like another when it is ruined"; since, in addition, the world of modern art that began with Michelangelo did not please him ("there is no peace, or protection, or repose about it," he wrote on September 5, 1899. "They won't even let me be damned in quiet"), only the Norman, that is, twelfth-century Gothic, remained open to him.[44]

With renewed zeal Adams immersed himself in the French Middle Ages, now focusing his interest on architecture, though not entirely losing sight of literature. Announcing, on June 12, his intention to "pass the summer quietly alone" in Paris, he naturally resorted to the image he had used several years earlier:

"On the whole, if one must be alone, Paris is the best water-place. One can invent hobbies, and run them here even better than in London." Indeed, to someone stationed in Paris, riding the medieval hobby was easy. As he explained to Gaskell, about four months later: "I am making a collection of twelfth-century spires. They are singularly amusing, and, for afternoon walks or drives in summer, are quite delightful. There are dozens within easy reach of Paris, all culminating in the Chartres spire. I find that I always get back to the twelfth century when left to myself."[45] In this way he amused himself during all the summer months, and the fun would keep, he hoped, "at least a year or two more." His correspondence of this period constantly refers to this "amusement." He *craved*, he said, his "eleventh-century Norman arch"; it was "a disease"; it "had become a habit like *absinthe*." Not that he could, even when most excited, show the least signs of artistic inebriety. "I must and will not be agitated," he insisted in July and again in September in his letters to Mabel Hooper, no doubt thinking of his brother's reaction to the Gothic. He himself wanted nothing but "peace," "repose"; his life was "cloister-like," spent in (relatively) "utter solitude."[46] But he often left his "cell" (Mrs. Cameron's apartment on the Avenue du Bois de Boulogne) to "drag" friends on a tour of "Norman *clochers* and *flèches*" or to "attend services at Chartres most of the Sundays." There also he went on one particular October Tuesday, when "he passed a long day" in the cathedral, "studying it out so as to square it with the books."[47]

For, of the "various ways of wasting time by study," reading was still assuredly the best. Adams devoted four to six hours a day to the study of Old French, heartily cursing, on August 21, the preposition *à*, "the basest and most servile relic of the Roman decadence" for all the trouble it gave him. A few days later he told Gaskell of his being deep in "Wace for facts." But, supplementing his architectural tours, technical treatises came more and more to supersede the *Chansons de Geste* in his reading. Thus, on September 18, he could warn his *propriétaire* about the "gay library of twelfth-century architecture" cluttering her rooms. And to her too, on October 23, he wrote: "My photographs too are an occupation, and by the way a fairly expensive one. The mere *clochers* and *flèches* number hundreds in the Monuments Historiques series alone. Your rooms are becoming a school of romanesque architecture. Volumes lie about the floor. Last evening Joe Stickney and St. Gaudens dined here, and floundered in architecture on all the chairs."[48]

When did he actually begin to write *Mont-Saint-Michel and Chartres*? He first alludes to it in jest, that summer in 1899. "I am seriously thinking of writing at last my *Travels in France with Nothing to Say*," he confides on August 28, "I have it all in my mind. It would cost a year's work and about a thousand dollars." At that time we find him following "William the Norman and Harold the Dreyfusard" with delight while reading Wace. Is he also putting his hand to the chapters on the Mount? What he is contemplating, he says on October 2— and we are getting further along on what will turn out to be the main thread of his story— "a drama of the Second Crusade with Queen Eleanor of Guienne for heroine and myself to act Saint Bernard and reprove her morals." On November 22, he again states: "What I do want is to write a five-act drama of the twelfth century, to beat Macbeth."[49] How far he had by now advanced in the writing of *Mont-Saint-Michel and Chartres* is immaterial. It is clear that he was definitely at work on it.

The year 1899 thus marks the end of a long turning in Adams' life, a turning in which he had engaged as early as 1893, when during the summer days at Quincy the first draft of *The Law* came into his hands. Indeed, this particular work appears to have influenced his own literary career to such an extent that one may wonder whether the publication of its French translation, in March 1899, did not actually trigger the writing of *Mont-Saint-Michel and Chartres*. The claim has been made by Brooks Adams himself in "The Heritage of Henry Adams." According to his brother's account, Henry felt dissatisfied: " 'Don't you see, Brooks,' he would say to me again and again . . . 'that you, with your lawyer's method, only state sequences of fact, and explain no causes?' " Summoned to write a "scientific summary," Brooks felt unequal to the task: "Therefore I declined Henry's suggestion to join him in Paris and work at the scheme which he proposed, and went back to my old life in America. From that time Henry lost interest in my further publications. On the other hand he took up "scientific history" himself, and soon became immersed in it. The result may be read in "Mont-Saint-Michel and Chartres."[50]

In fact, when *La Loi de la civilisation et de la décadence* came out, Brooks was not in Paris; as for Henry, who arrived there two weeks later, and "immediately" went to the publisher's, he expressed great satisfaction with the book. "I see no reason," he wrote to Brooks, on April 6, "to find fault with anything."[51] This very same year Brooks, crippled with gout, decided to take the waters at Bad Kissingen, in Germany. We can assume (there is no evidence of it) that on his way he stopped over in Paris, were it only to see his brother and repeat the words of gratitude he had poured into a letter from Quincy, on July 5, 1899:

> I do not know that anything I have ever done, or ever shall do, will be of much moment—probably of none at all—but certainly all there is is due to you.
>
> Six years ago you read my manuscript. But for you I never should have printed it. Most of what has attracted attention has been the result of your criticism. The form is, I think, almost wholly yours. The translation is yours. On looking back over my life I cannot imagine to myself what my life would have been without you. From the old days in England when I was a boy, you have been my good genius.

There is not, in the extant correspondence, the least indication that Henry then tried to prod Brooks into writing another essay. Neither do we find, as a matter of fact, many allusions to the Middle Ages. On September 10 and then again on October 12, Henry wrote of his "amusement" with twelfth-century churches, prompting his brother's reply dated October 29, 1899, part of which has already been quoted. Brooks not only spoke of his "horrible homesickness" for the Middle Ages, he also offered a piece of advice which was to prove his last great contribution to the making of *Mont-Saint-Michel and Chartres:* "One part of the period which never seems to have attracted you, but which fascinated me was the Monastic philosophy. My old friend Haureau's book, I have always loved, as one of the best books I ever read."[52]

"LES MIRACLES DE LA VIERGE"

"All day long I read metaphysics and study St. Thomas Aquinas, it is as amusing as Punch," Adams informed Gaskell on July 27 1900. "A sideplay" to his interest "in twelfth-century spires and

Chartres cathedral," this *passe-temps* considerably absorbed him all summer. An order of books placed at the beginning of that same month of July evidences that he was becoming the possessor of another "gay library." Rich with such works as "Adgar's *Marienlegenden,* Remusat's *Abélard* and Jourdain's *Philosophie de St. Thomas d'Aquin,*" it also contained many other items, one of them being Houreau's *Philosophie scholastique.*[53] On his return to Paris, in early May 1900, after four months in Washington, Adams immersed himself again in the Middle Ages, turning to the study of scholastic philosophy and using Thomas Aquinas, he wrote on July 25, "like liquid air for cooling the hot blood of my youth." Such reading must have served more literary purposes, since in the same letter he playfully asked Mrs. Cameron to tell her daughter (then aged fourteen) that "my metaphysical chapter is nearly done and I want to send it for her to read and tell me what she doesn't understand, so I can correct it." To the same young lady, in October, he reported that "St. Thomas and the Virgin have got married,"[54] by which he meant he had completed the first draft of the volume, though he still worked on it for some time that year, polishing his translation of Thibaut de Champagne's ballads to Queen Blanche and the Queen of Heaven. In the main, the summer of 1900 appears to have been highly metaphysical; Brooks' suggestions were turned to good account.

But Adams' incursion into scholastic philosophy and Marianlore proved more than a summer's amusement. The "angelic doctor" grew on him so much that, two years later, when the Lodges had a son, he insisted on calling the boy Saint Thomas.[55] As so often with him, facetiousness was rooted in deep earnestness. It was the time when, in a letter to Brooks, he pleasantly styled himself as "a dilution of a mixture of Lord Kelvin and St. Thomas Aquinas." The expression was fanciful, not the conjunction of the medieval philosopher and of the modern scientist whose theories were soon to find their way into the last chapters of *The Education.* Both men, with the systems of thought they stood for, had become equally vital to Adams, prompting him to admit a "weakness for science mixed with metaphysics."

As a matter of fact, throughout the years, we can discern a contrapuntal movement in his interests which will be reflected in his work. A salient juxtaposition of the Middle Ages and of modern times—a device which we shall find constantly and effectively employed in *Mont-Saint-Michel and Chartres*—occurs in a letter sent from Washington to Mrs. Cameron, in February, 1900: "Every day opens a new horizon, and the rate we are going gets faster and faster till my twelfth-century head spins, and I hang on to the straps and shut my poor old eyes. As for having views or ideas as to what one should do, or what is going to happen, I no longer pretend to do it. The machine is beyond all control." Still more dizzying horizons opened in Paris when, with his friend Langley as a guide, toward the end of the summer, Adams visited the Great Hall of the Dynamos at the *Exposition universelle*. Of this World's Fair, which was closing its doors in November 1900, he remarked to Hay that it had been "an education." As may be sensed from his use of the term, he had then gone through another experience nearly as important from a literary point of view as his "discovery" of Coutances in 1895. His letter to Hay is worth quoting: "You are free to deride my sentimentality if you like, but I assure you that I,—a monk of St. Dominic, absorbed in the Beatitudes of the Virgin Mother—go down to the Champ de Mars and sit by the hour over the great dynamos, watching them run as noiselessly and as smoothly as the planets, and asking them—with infinite courtesy—where in Hell they are going. They are marvelous. The Gods are not in it."[57] Now in full possession of the imagery for which he had been fumbling all these years, he soon began to draw on it: "by way of relief from boredom," he told Mrs. Cameron in February 1901, "I have returned to verse and have written a long prayer to the Virgin of Chartres." Combining his symbols of both the Virgin and the Dynamo, composing a prayer within a prayer, it unified the two major themes which had preoccupied him since the summer of 1893. For all the intensity of feeling that went into the making of the poem, it was an aesthetic achievement, not "an act of faith"; and under such a light, in the second part of this study, we shall have to see *Mont-Saint-Michel and Chartres*, which it condensed while already announcing *The Education*.[58]

When Adams composed his "Prayer to the Virgin of Chartres," early in 1901, he was in Washington, quite "relieved" by his de-

cision "not to return to Paris," and feeling "not the smallest wish
or desire to go there any more." But how could he long adhere to
such a decision? On June 1, he once more found himself in Paris,
there to stay, except for the summer months, which he spent
traveling about Europe, until December; and there again, each
following spring, until the outbreak of the first World War brought
an end to this practice, he would arrive and not depart before the
heart of winter. Yet we have no reason to doubt his sincerity when
he announced his intention not to return to France. After such an
intense absorption in the French Middle Ages and also such a long
period of creative outburst (the first, with the exception of the
Tahiti interlude, in many years), he may well have felt some emotional weariness. He reverted to the study of science, swamping
himself in "tubs of geology, working up to date after twenty years
of neglect." After a tour of Russia, he traveled as far as the North
Cape. But before going he had shown what he then called his
"Miracles de la Vierge" to La Farge and rested secure with his
friend's admiration. He would soon come back to them. Thus, in
January 1902, he was passing his time "entirely in the 12th-cen-
tury, as far away as mind can get," and in April he could proclaim
himself "perfectly square with the Virgin Mary, having finished
and rewritten the whole volume."[59]

But this was not exactly so. For Adams truly resembled a medieval architect in that his work "like a Gothic cathedral compelled further embellishment even when seemingly finished. The
metaphysical chapters were as restless as the Gothic arch and
lured him to further study."[60] In order to respect his own norm of
establishing the causal sequence for an historical phenomenon
(here, the building of Chartres by the worshippers of the Virgin),
he had conceived of representing the energies prior to and following that of the love of Mary. Scientific history and literary contrast demanded this. And if, for the first part, the chapters on
Mont-Saint-Michel which he had polished off as early as 1899
suited his purpose, the concluding "metaphysical" chapters required considerably more labor. Only in December 1902, he
acknowledged: "I've finished Thomas Aquinas and the Thirteenth
Century. I'm dying to know how it would look in type . . . One
copy for me alone." But the manuscript, "swelled and swelled to

the size of an ox," does not seem to have been quite ready until the end of the winter of 1903, when on March 15 Adams told Mrs. Cameron: "My great work on the Virgin is complete even to the paging, and I've no occupation." Even then, a few months were to elapse before he could decide (in January 1904) to have it set in print.[61]

As with so many of Adams' previous volumes, this was to be a private printing. It began with a severe mishap. On February 7, the premises of the Baltimore firm, J. H. Hurst, which had been commissioned to do the work, burned down with, Adams grieved, "my Chartres manuscript and the money to print it." Actually, "only a few chapters had been lost," and he started hoping that what he called the "Chartres snare" would soon straighten out, only to despair at the end of the month: "Chartres is still in the fire, or at least not out of it. Printers are my devil."[62] Finally printed in Washington, the first edition of *Mont-Saint-Michel and Chartres* (100 wide-margined quarto copies) did not come out before late December 1904. Copies went immediately to "nieces in fact and in wish" for whom the book was meant. Mabel received hers dated January 1, 1905. Perhaps Henry Adams was a little tardier with his male friends and even with his brother Brooks, but Brooks did not sound the less enthusiastic when on May 12, 1905, he voiced his feelings:

I have this moment finished your book. I have read the concluding pages to Evelyn in my study here at Quincy with an admiration, delight and emotion which I can never hope to feel over any work of literature again. Mixed with my delight in the intellectual effort and the great art, is gratified pride and ambition. I have long felt shame that our generation had achieved nothing of the first merit. Now I am content. No book in our language written within a century surpasses it. It is a gem of thought, of taste, of creation. I perhaps alone of living men can appreciate fully all that you have done, for I have lived with the crusaders and the schoolmen—but this book of yours will stand, believe me, even in this dying age—for Henry, we are dying.[63]

Brooks had only one request—that a proper edition of the book be issued. But this was for the moment out of the question. "If you asked me to find out five hundred persons in the world to whom you would like to give the volume," Henry answered, "I could say only that, as far as you and I know, five hundred do not exist—nor half that number—nor a quarter of it. . . . There are already some fifty copies afloat, and I'll bet ten to one that half of them have not been once read."[64] The true course of events was to prove somewhat different.

The purpose of this first part was to show how Adams came to write *Mont-Saint-Michel and Chartres,* the chief influences which played on him, the men who helped him most on the road to Chartres. What became of him and his book afterward does not really fall within the purview of this study. It has been told by Ernest Samuels in the last chapters of *Henry Adams: The Major Phase* and by Moreene Crumley in "The Reputation of Henry Adams."[65] Only a few more details are therefore needed.

In 1904, while the book was going its troubled course through the printers' shops, Adams returned as usual to France for the summer. Landing at Cherbourg on Saturday, June 4, he hastened to Coutances, "to wander peacefully there" and attend mass on the following day in *his* cathedral; he then proceeded to Paris, feeling apparently no wish to make a detour via Mont-Saint-Michel, and there is no evidence either that later in July, when he motored through Normandy to Brittany, "hunt[ing] windows like hares," he stopped at the Mount.[66] Yet, he did return there, again on a Saturday, May 29, 1908, well before the summer crowds, and in the pleasant company of "nieces." "By immense luck," he reported, "the evening was warm and fine and so was the next day,—Sunday—which we devoted to doing our Abbaye thoroughly, all by ourselves with a sympathetic guide and plans, till they learned all about it and got it by heart in time to start off at four o'clock." In spite of the charms of this quiet weekend, Adams felt dissatisfied; the Mount, he complained to Mrs. Cameron, was "no joke,—an awfully fatiguing pigsty—Mme. Poulard has sold out to a joint-stock company, and the company is not improved or likely to improve it."[67] The 1908 trip to Normandy —the last he was to make—had its own rewards, however. For Adams could at last discover Cerisy-la-Forêt, "a remote abbey that," as he also wrote to Mrs. Cameron, "I have been trying to visit for years, like St. Pierre-sur-Dives where I was stopped on the road five years ago by running over a laborer and having a long debate with him afterwards. I was repaid for all my sufferings of travel by seeing these two things which complete my twelfth-century pilgrimages."[68]

This did not bring an end to Adams' medieval "pilgrimages"; he kept making short tours to Gothic churches within easy reach of Paris, "automobiling *d'outre-tombe* like Chateaubriand," in July 1913. And if ill health prevented him from going, he could still make his visits vicariously, as we learn from a letter he was writing to Gaskell on November 1, the same year: "I have sent all my young women today down to Chartres to bid goodbye to Our Lady, whose chansons we now sing by the score. One of them I translated years ago in my Chartres, before I ever knew that the music still existed. *On est bête à faire peur.*"[69] What is also seen here is that Adams had found another "hobby" which was to keep him "amused"—and even fairly happy—till the end of his life.

For he continued to crave hobbies. "I am only in despair," he wrote in 1907, "that they run off their legs so quickly." A good, steady "plaything" was French medieval literature; after translating Richard Coeur de Lion's Prison Song (this would eventually find its way into a new edition of *Mont-Saint-Michel and Chartres*), he passed on, in the summer of 1911, to the Chanson de Willame. "It is so fascinating an amusement," he told Professor F. B. Luquiens of Yale University, with whom he had started a correspondence, "that I hope to make it last the rest of my life." Unfortunately his heart attack, in April 1912, "put an end for all time to any serious study either of the French literature, or any other."[70]

Aileen Tone became his secretary-companion, playing the role of "niece in residence" while supervising all domestic details. In her luggage she brought a book of medieval songs she had just been given. They delighted Adams so much that the following year, when after his recovery he again went to France, he hired two specialists to search the Bibliothèque Nationale and the Arsenal for other items. Miss Tone sang them for him in the Gregorian manner. He found them "fascinating" and, he added, "like the glass-windows, their contemporaries, all our own, for no one else will ever want to hear them." They were the "fun" he wished, in a letter quoted in the first chapter of this study, he could have shared with Walter Scott; he never tired of hearing them, even on the eve of his death in 1918. "Dear child, keep me alive," were his last words to Miss Tone.[71]

He still lives through *Mont-Saint-Michel and Chartres*. "I, vastly to my surprise," he observed in December 1912, "find myself a leader of a popular movement, with my *Chartres* for Evangel . . . They will beatify me after all."[72] His first 1904 edition had long been distributed, and, in the intervening years, he had received so many requests for copies that during the winter before his stroke he revised and reprinted the book. This second edition of 500 copies was again private. Apart from changes in punctuation and typography, as well as the addition of titles for the chapters, the text remained very much the same as in the first edition; his main revisions, as we shall see, were confined to the chapters dealing with the cathedral of Chartres. He made no more changes when, in 1913, under the urging of the architect Ralph Adams Cram, he finally agreed to let the American Institute of Architects officially sponsor the publication of *Mont-Saint-Michel and Chartres* by Houghton Mifflin. He even donated the royalties of the book to the Institute of Architects. Among the projects which have since been financed with the returns, one seems particularly appropriate. It was the commissioning, some years after World War II, of a stained glass window for one of the side aisles of Chartres, depicting the life of Saint Fulbert, who first built a Romanesque church on the site. At the bottom of the window, American skyscrapers can be seen juxtaposed to the Romanesque church. Thanks to the iconography, the centuries are bridged; America is in Chartres. It is doubly so, since this had already been achieved by Henry Adams and his book.[73]

Part Two
Chartres

5

A World of Architecture

"Voyages autour de ma chambre"

Beneath the title of the first edition of *Mont-Saint-Michel and Chartres* Adams wrote the simple legend: "Travels/ France." There was no name, only the anonymous uncle of the "Preface," who, after landing at Cherbourg or Le Havre, goes with one or several nieces "across Normandy to Pontorson, where with the evening light, the tourists drive along the *chaussée* over the sands or through the tide, till they stop at Madame Poulard's famous hotel within the gate of the Mount."[1]

Any Frenchman slightly familiar with Mont-Saint-Michel, and who will join the party the following morning, that is, at the outset of the real journey, is likely to be surprised. It all begins with a flourish: "The Archangel loved heights," the past tense being designed, J. C. Levenson explains, to "warn us that the speaker is recovering a meaning that has been lost."[2] What we notice is that the description, in this opening paragraph, of the Archangel standing, as he has "for centuries," at the top of the Mount, hap-

pens to be a factual description of a statue set up in 1897, two
years after Adams' first journey to Normandy. No statue had ever
stood there before.[3] But let this pass as a poetic simile. More confusing is the second paragraph, where our attention is directed
to the church door: "one needs to be centuries old to know what
this mass of encrusted architecture meant to its builders." With
the exception of St. Michael's statue, no part of the edifice is more
recent than this commonplace facade erected by the Maurist
monks in 1780; its only beauty lies in the scars left by the fire
which in 1834 nearly destroyed the church, after it had been
turned into a prison workshop. Of course, as Adams wrote to
Henry Osborn Taylor on January 17, 1905, commenting upon his
book: "To me, accuracy is relative. I care very little whether my
details are exact, if only my *ensemble* is in scale."[4] His purpose
was to steep the reader in the Gothic; hence the necessity to begin
with an imaginative leap, without caring for any extraneous details. The facts about the facade will be set right twice (page 7:
"In 1618, the whole facade began to give way"; page 10: "We
have not even a facade") before the end of the chapter. Yet the
question remains whether the imaginative leap is successful.

A good point of comparison is provided by Adams' description
in *The Education* of his first contact with the Gothic at Antwerp.
The passage reminds us not a little of Flaubert's *Education senti-
mentale*, when Frédéric Moreau's moods subtly change as he sails
up the Seine. Young Henry Adams experiences a similar psychological progression as he steams up the Scheldt on the "Baron
Ory." The sight of the peasants dancing on the bank of the river
makes him think of Dutch or Flemish paintings. History and art
take life. ("Ostade and Teniers were as much alive as they ever
were, and even the Duke of Alva was still at home.") Suddenly
a sentence discloses that Adams has come face to face with a revelation that may one day alter his whole life: "The thirteenth-century cathedral towered above a sixteenth-century mass of tiled
roofs, ending abruptly in walls and the landscape that had not
changed."[5] What is important here is that the Gothic is being apprehended not only in the midst of life but as part of its natural
setting. Adams is then too inexperienced to get much beyond the
shock of recognition conventionalized by Washington Irving; he

nonetheless makes an essential discovery which is, as Henri Focillon will put it, speaking of Chartres: "The settings and landscapes in which Gothic thought evolved are an integral part of it."[6] Why does not the "uncle" today, as he proposes to lead us into the heart of the Gothic, begin by pointing out such basic truths as those which he had himself sensed spontaneously when a young man?

For we wonder how Adams' party has reached the platform in front of the church without first ascending the picturesque "Grande Rue." Indeed, how have they managed to reach the Mount itself driving "along the *chaussée*" without even noticing the landscape? Few travelers would have been willing to miss the beauty of the approach to Victor Hugo's "pyramid of the seas," the "vertiginous" abbey which Michelet saw as a "gigantic shrine against a screen of fire."[7] No doubt one of the finest sights in France, its faraway silhouette rising in the middle of the immense estuary between the coasts of Normandy and Brittany is as tantalizing as that of Chartres cathedral for the tourist journeying by road and seeing its spires appear and disappear according to the undulations of the wheat fields. "One cannot assume, even in a niece, too emotional a nature," we have been told, "but one may assume a kodak."[8] Yet at no time, either the evening of the arrival or when we all leave the Mount in (we may presume) broad daylight, does our pretty companion appear to be tempted or is she invited to use her camera.

The unreality of these "travels" will become even more apparent in the later part of our journey, when we drive (how else could we visit all these "little churches" on our way?) to Chartres. Suddenly we find ourselves posted in front of the cathedral, with our eyes riveted on to the towers; we never saw them from afar; we did not even cross the square to come to their foot. The beginning of our visit is static, like the one at Mont-Saint-Michel, and when our tour is ended, we will not "loiter" through the town and on the banks of the Eure, as James Russell Lowell does in *The Cathedral*. Just as, outside Mme. Poulard's Restaurant, there seems to be no house on the Mount, the town of Chartres is conjured away. The reason why both the abbey and the cathedral are thus isolated from even their immediate vicinity has been given by Adams in his letter to Mrs. Cameron, dated October 23, 1899: "I went to Chartres last Tuesday and passed a long day studying it out *so as to square it with the books*."⁹ For it is a fact that Adams' Gothic monuments now stand out, not against their own natural landscape, as at Antwerp, but against a landscape of books—the "books and guides" revealingly mentioned in that same second paragraph of the opening chapter.

In order to realize how much indeed of what we find in *Mont-Saint-Michel and Chartres* is simply based on secondhand information, it suffices to bring into parallel Adams' and Ruskin's ways of "studying" a monument. No methods could be more antithetic. When preparing *The Stones of Venice*, Ruskin did regular "fieldwork." According to E. T. Cook: "He carried with him little square note-books of a size easily pocketable, in which he entered measurements, contours of mouldings and the like, occasionally with slight notes of colour . . . In the evening Ruskin entered up his memoranda and impressions in larger note-books."¹⁰ At the Massachusetts Historical Society, there is an identical pocket book, called the "Chartres book," in which Adams entered his own notes when he visited the cathedral. These are startlingly meager: no measurements, no drawings, not the least perceptive comment. Adams contents himself with counting the figures round the Virgin Enthroned on the South Porch or in the Rose de Dreux.¹¹ And he soon shifts to quotations from Poincaré or Haeckel which have nothing to do with the Gothic and were certainly not transcribed during the visit. If he had had to depend on this sole pocket book, he could hardly have written anything on Chartres. On Mont-Saint-Michel, we do not even find a note—and no wonder, since Adams visited the abbey only once before writing *Mont-Saint-Michel and Chartres*. That was in 1895, several years before he actually sat down to serious work on it. The account he gave in a letter of his second visit, in 1908, after the book had been completed and published, is nonetheless of direct interest: "We devoted Sunday to doing our Abbaye . . . till *they* [his companions] learned all about it."¹² As far as he was concerned, he apparently did not then in the least expect or try to learn anything new about the abbey, though in the last thirteen years important discoveries had been made there by the architect in charge of its restoration.

The knowledge on which Adams rested so secure all came from the "gay library" of architecture which cluttered Mrs. Cameron's apartment when he was writing *Mont-Saint-Michel and Chartres.* It included not only volumes but photographs, which had become for him, he then said, "an occupation." This is why in chapter iv, on our way to Chartres through Normandy and Île de France, we will not be surprised when we are advised to "begin a photographic collection." One of its first items should be the church at Cerisy-la-Forêt, a church, as we happen to know, which Adams had not yet been able to visit at the time. Yet we have to make a detour to see it, because "it matches that on the Mount, according to M. Corroyer." And for Adams, having Corroyer's judgment upon it is just as good as having personally been there.[13]

We may still look into his finely bound copy of Edouard Corroyer's *Description de l'Abbaye du Mont-Saint-Michel* (Paris, 1877). The total absence of scorings and annotations must not lead us to infer that Adams made little use of the book. Indeed, to resort to one of these architectural similes which he liked, it was, with "the sacred sources of Viollet-le-Duc" (i.e., the *Dictionnaire raisonné de l'architecture française*) and with the Abbé Bulteau's *Monographie de la Cathédrale de Chartres,* one of the three main pillars on which he built his own edifice. In this bulky volume of 434 pages is to be found not only "the chief source of all one's acquaintance with the Mount," but, as will soon appear, a pattern for our imaginary visit.[14] A disciple of Viollet-le-Duc, Edouard Corroyer was the first architect appointed by the French government, in 1874, to start the restoration of the building, a task to which he applied himself with a rather heavy hand and some shocking lapses in taste. For a quarter of a century, however, he remained the best authority on the abbey, till his works were superseded by those of Paul Gout, a new architect appointed in 1898. As a matter of fact, Paul Gout's *Histoire de l'architecture française au Mont Saint-Michel* (Paris, 1899) is also in Adams' library. There is no way of knowing whether it was acquired during the 1908 trip (as is likely), or at some earlier date, but we may safely assume that Adams had by then completed his own description of Mont-Saint-Michel. He never mentions the book; neither does he seem to have ever turned to it to check upon any detail. Such as they stood, the opening chapters of *Mont-Saint-Michel and Chartres* satisfied him so well that when he later revised his work, he left the whole part dealing with the Mount untouched.

Adams could understandably be content with his description of Mont-Saint-Michel. It is typical of his *manière*, of his way of—to use terms which will endlessly recur throughout *Mont-Saint-Michel and Chartres*—getting "poetry" out of "facts." Indeed, these opening chapters set the imaginative pattern for all his visits of "monuments," whether they are architectural, literary, or theological. This is why it is necessary to follow this first visit somewhat in detail, Edouard Corroyer's book in hand.

From "facts" to "poetry"

If, at the beginning, we found ourselves standing on the Terrasse du Plomb au Four (Adams does not burden us with its name), it was because Corroyer had chosen to start from this very point, a way of proceeding which he held "le plus rationnel et le plus sérieusement utile," though it meant running counter to the topography of the Mount. After casting, just as the architect does, a glance over the sea, we enter the church. All borrowed from the *Description*, the information we are now given, concerning "this mutilated trunk of an eleventh century church,"[15] sounds so learned that it takes a little time to realize how much is left unsaid. And the missing details are naturally those which will interest us most, on account of what they reveal about Adams himself.

A first striking characteristic is the practically total unconcern about the architecture overhead. At Chartres, because the towers and then the stained glass windows are going to captivate our attention, we shall be less aware of this characteristic. Yet even then, when describing the windows, Adams will never pause to make us admire the tracery of the triforium gallery just beneath their level. Here, in the abbey, the only upper part he cares to mention is the timber ceiling, and it is as a thing which is no longer there. Nothing is said of the triforium, nothing of the two side aisles, both rib-vaulted, the one to the north with broken arches, for it was rebuilt in 1103, with, it may be perceived, less daring and more care for solidity. Comparing the skill of their two architects might have proved an interesting topic, which Adams shuns decidedly: "The subject of vaulting is far too ambitious for summer travel . . . we must not touch it," he declares at another stage of the visit, and laying still more emphasis, a few minutes later: "The vaulting is a study for wiser men than we can ever be."[16] The truth is that Corroyer himself, who merely makes a fleeting reference to these aisles without in the least observing on their vaults, seems to have had little relish for the subject.

Another omission in our itinerary here as at Chartres is the roof. Ascending the "lace stairway" built on the raking part of a flying buttress, on to the upper balustrade, would have been an exciting experience for the niece, but she is not even allowed to admire the flamboyant Gothic Chevet from afar. "We have not time to run off into the sixteenth century," our guide will say, by way of an excuse when, going down instead, he hurriedly crosses "the splendid crypt . . . called the Gros Piliers, beneath the choir."[17] But why then do we not visit the other chambers beneath the abbey, which all date back to the eleventh century or earlier?[18] We would easily understand Adams' contempt for what so many tourists consider as prime attractions, the dungeons and the ancient ossuary now housing the huge windlass used by the prisoners to hoist in all the supplies for the abbey, when, from the Revolution till 1863, it was a penitentiary. Yet there are fine crypts under the transepts, little defiled by this past; and those he also refuses to enter. Indeed, it seems as though he felt even more reluctant to venture into the lower parts than to ascend to the upper stories.

In the chapters on Chartres we will vainly look for a description of the crypt, though Adams can mention it twice now, while still far away in Normandy: it "rivals the church above," and together with that of Saint Denis "would serve to teach any over curious tourist all that he should want to know about such matters." Not over curious himself, he dismisses the matter.[19] A probable reason for his dislike of crypts is their lack of light, which he must have found oppressive. The one exception he is going to make seems to prove the rule, since the Aquilon, which belongs to the beginning of the twelfth century and where we are now invited to tarry on our way to the Merveille, though erroneously called a crypt by Corroyer, is a gallery lighted by windows.

It was the first Almonry; poor pilgrims used to sleep on its floor. Setting apparently little store by this piece of architecture and its companion, the monks' *promenoir*, situated just above, Corroyer treats them in a most cursory fashion. Adams, who here has fed his imagination on "such photographs as those of the Monuments Historiques," is much more appreciative, even pausing to admire "the astonishing leap in time and art" between one and the other vault. Had he been aware that the Romanesque ceiling of the upper room, damaged by fire, was entirely rebuilt about 1150, no doubt such a discrepancy in styles would have seemed to him less amazing. As it is, a good deal of his interest springs from this very misinterpretation which provides him with a brilliant parallel: "another *pons seclorum*, an antechamber to the west portal of Chartres which bears the same date (1110–25). It is the famous period of the transition, the glory of the twelfth century, the object of our pilgrimage." Time and again he will stress such historical links between the various chapters of his "study in unity," so as to make this unity all the more manifest. But there is also perhaps another less scholarly reason for this interest. A patron of the opera when in Paris, he may well have been tempted, as he was engaged in the writing of *Mont-Saint-Michel and Chartres*, to attend a performance of Meyerbeer's *Robert le diable*. It had just been restaged, and its Norman hero was bound to appeal forcefully to his imagination. One of the most impressive pieces of scenery happened to be a replica of the Aquilon. Thus Abbot Roger II's construction proved after all a perfect transition, for it led not only into the realm of light but into the realm of romance as well.[20]

Both light and romance are going to inform the second part of our tour, when at last we reach the Merveille. Built at the beginning of the thirteenth century, this impressive pile, rising on the north face of the Mount, is the part of the Abbey which Adams obviously prefers. Of it he speaks most feelingly and on the whole accurately, once allowance has been made for his confusing, after Corroyer, the Guests' Hall where the Abbot entertained distinguished visitors with the monks' refectory, actually situated just above, on a level with the cloister and the church. Not yet fully restored at the time of his visit, the latter room, which had served as a dormitory for the prisoners, held little charm for him; therefore only the "so-called refectory" or Salle des Hôtes and its neighbor, the Salle des Chevaliers, will "concern us." As Adams describes them, he more and more evinces the passion for light which, throughout *Mont-Saint-Michel and Chartres* appears to be the chief motive of his quest. The Salle des Chevaliers is "beautifully lighted"; the lighting of the adjoining hall is "superb"; and both halls are a "preamble to the romance of the Chartres windows"; for, when we reach the cathedral, "the great book of architecture will open on the word 'Fenestration.' Fenêtre—a word as ugly as the thing is beautiful; and then with pain and sorrow, you will have to toil till you see how the architects of 1200 subordinated every other problem to that of lighting their spaces. Without feeling their lights, you can never feel their shadows." There were little shadows, and Adams felt neither pain nor sorrow, only peace, we sense, while resting, as he probably did for a blissful moment during his grueling 1895 visit, on one of the stone benches in the window embrasures where we now "sit at ease . . . looking over the thirteenth-century ocean and watching the architect" at work. All the details are so "simple and apparently easy" that we soon feel at one with the man who devised them.[21]

There is no better way, Adams held, to enter into the spirit of the Middle Ages than thus to bring "into relation with ourselves the picture they still present."[22] Reliving his visit in the secrecy of his study, Edouard Corroyer's book in hand, he could let his imagination run away with him and, for an instant, picture himself as one of the monks who once lived there, but as Van Wyck Brooks notes, "if he dreamed of being a monk, then he was the abbot."[23] So he became the lord of this palace. Nearly all the kings in Christendom would be his guests. But most of the time he would be quite content to sit in such a setting, dreaming and writing as he was then doing. On page 169 of the *Description*, there is a drawing in vertical section of the west end of the Salle des Chevaliers, with one of "the huge and heavy *cheminées* or fireplaces" already duly noticed in the course of our visit; to the left of this drawing is another, representing the *chartrier,* a little room hardly more than a cubbyhole, on a slightly higher level than the Salle des Chevaliers, where the monks used to store their manuscripts.

Confused by the rather misleading caption, Adams, who obviously had never set foot there, took the whole figure to represent "Le Chartrier"; he saw the "large stone fireplace" (indeed it is ten feet broad) and the beautiful windows in this chimneyless and rather dark closet, thus turning it into a "gem," where in imagination he set up his study: "To contemplate the goodness of God was simply a joy when one had such a room to work in; such a spot as the great hall to walk in, when the storm blew, or the cloisters in which to meditate, when the sun shone; such a dining-room as the refectory; and such a view from one's windows over the infinite ocean."[24] We doubt whether he realized his error at the time of his second visit, "thorough" as it was; but supposing he did, his feelings may have been like those of Voltaire, who, being reproached with some such glaring invention, simply answered: "Oui, sans doute, mais avouez que c'est bien mieux comme cela." And so every summer American tourists at Mont-Saint-Michel will harass puzzled and sometimes irate guides, asking to be shown into this "gem" currently used as a lumber room by the masons at work in the abbey. Denied admittance, they will go away, still believing in a wonderful island of peace, mysterious as "the little room" in Madeleine Yale Wynne's story. Adams would probably enjoy the humor of this, even though he did not in the least intend it as a joke.

A private literary demesne and a stage

How are we to construe this imaginary visit? As we paused at an early stage of our tour, the author seems to have revealed the end which he himself pursues: "Here is your first eleventh-century church: How does it affect you? Serious and simple to excess! is it not? Young people rarely enjoy it . . . but men who have lived long and are tired—who want rest . . . feel this repose and self-restraint as they feel nothing else . . . They come back to it to rest, after a long circle of pilgrimage—the cradle of rest from which their ancestors started."[25] But, even in such a setting, repose proves "none too deep." Perhaps we ought to look further than the architectural reasons to account for this disquieting element in the church and trace it to Adams' memories of his 1895 trip through Normandy. Indeed, if he then did find a cradle of rest, it was at Coutances, and not in this tourist-ridden abbey. This is why, today, at Mont-Saint-Michel, chosen for its sheer prestige to be the starting point of our architectural journey, we can easily feel how contrived, how fabricated the whole journey is; and we find it fitting that our guide should seem most at ease when focusing his attention on the *chartrier*, practically a figment of his imagination.

Yet, has not the place a reality of its own? Is it not Montaigne's *librairie*, or the "peaceful hermitage" found by Milton "in some high lonely tower," near the "studious cloister's pale" where *Il Penseroso* also likes to "walk"? Of a certainty, it is the lonely study where, "a twelfth-century monk in a nineteenth-century attic," Adams immersed himself in the Middle Ages because, he wrote in 1901, "I was tired and wanted quiet and solitude and absorption." Perhaps nothing was truer, in his vision of Mont-Saint-Michel, than the *chartrier*.[26]

In fact, his whole monastery was built on literary foundations. It belongs to the same order as the one pictured by Matthew Arnold in a fragment of a poem, never completed, "To Meta; the Cloister," and his "Stanzas from La Grande Chartreuse." In these, Chaunceer B. Tinker remarks, there is "something of Gothic romance and Italian opera . . . Arnold knew nothing of monasteries at first hand; and the glimpse that he gives us here is like no cloister that was or ever will be, save in the pages of fiction."[27] So it is, to be sure, with Adams as a guide when he flatly states: "the general motive of abbatial building was common to them all . . . the church was the centre."[28] Although quite exceptionally, and for obvious topographical reasons, this happens to be the case at the Mount, it is a measure of Adams' misconception of monastic life that he should imagine such a disposition to be the general rule.

Of course the heart of the monastery, as of all monastic life, is the cloister. Here, however, crowning the Merveille, in a fervent intimacy with the sky and the ocean, it stands out, "the most admirable and the most poetically beautiful of all the cloisters of the thirteenth century," much more moving as a piece of architecture than the great hall beneath. Adams alludes to its charm but curiously enough skips over all details, contenting himself with a rather vapid comment ("only the Abbey of the Mount was rich and splendid enough to build a cloister like this, all in granite"—

in fact, the local stone), and a quotation from Viollet-le-Duc, found ready-culled in Corroyer's book.[29] Why, we cannot help wondering, is Adams so reluctant to linger in this delightful spot? Perhaps once more the explanation is to be provided by the *Description*. For the part of the cloister over which the architect dwells most lengthily (pages 182–185) is the *lavatorium*, a fountain where, on certain ceremonial occasions, the monks ritually washed each other's feet; and there also, according to St. Benedict's rule, the bodies of the dead brethren were washed while all the friars, standing in the same order as in the choir, recited prayers. Adams' imagination must have shrunk away from such community life. His monastery was to remain a private demesne, ordered to his taste, if not to his fancy.

A rather paradoxical consequence ensues. A thorough egotist to all appearances, in surroundings wilfully made congenial, he is in fact much less tempted than Matthew Arnold was at La Grande Chartreuse to obtrude his own personality with a jarring: "And what am I, that I am here?" He essentially remains the adroit man of letters who, posturing as an uncle intent on "amusing" a "niece in wish," will give us valuable insights into the Middle Ages without ever suffering our interest to pall.

Indeed, seen as a literary composition, Adams' chapters on Mont-Saint-Michel are successful. For even if the guided tour is not altogether complete, is it not adequate to the purpose? However many errors or gaps we may point out, Adams' description of the Abbey will not, at any rate, seem impaired if we bear in mind, as we must, that never intent on writing an architectural study or a guidebook, he has been striving "to catch not a fact" (and still less facts) but a "feeling."[30] We are privileged not only with a heightened consciousness of the place but with a larger geography. It emerges through a wealth of comparisons and allusions, ranging from Saint Denis to Palermo and Byzantium, that suggest a whole world of architecture. A whole world and spacious times! All these references, architectural, literary, historical, skilfully woven together, tend to the same end which is to *translate* us, literally, into the Middle Ages. Adams' art precisely lies in this focusing our attention on multiple points at once in a period of history and a region of the world till everything is fused in one moment of recognition, and we become vitally concerned with a vision of the Middle Ages which is, of course, his own and personal vision.

And as the monastery has turned into a quiet estate where sixty monks are but faint shadows, so it is a privately held pageant with a rather exclusive cast that we now watch with absorbed interest, totally unaware that the door remains closed to the many peasant ancestors Adams also recalled to life in his preamble. Perhaps, after all, it was owing to this desire for privacy that we were directly transported to the abbey without having to jostle our way through the crowd, up the steep High Street lined with inns for pilgrims and covered stalls as it is today with hotels and souvenir shops. Not only do we feel quite at home but we may be also elated with a delightful sense, in modern jargon, of being *in*, for all the people we meet here, as nearly everywhere on our itinerary, are "interesting men," prominent members of a choice medieval society, in fact not unlike the select company Henry Adams himself used to keep in his Washington days. But, "of all our two hundred and fifty million arithmetical ancestors . . . the two who would probably most interest everyone . . . would be William the Conqueror and Harold the Saxon." For them "we have lain in wait" in the old refectory—and, as if by magic, here they come, with their retinue, to attend a performance of the *Chanson de Roland*.[31]

The analysis of the *Chanson* will come later. Let us only stress here how much the episode defies all probabilities. Supposing that such a visit really occurred and that by then the song had already been composed, one can hardly imagine a party, even royal, "assembled at supper" in a room "crowded with soldiers and monks," all listening to lay poetry, however magnificent, instead of the holy texts which were to be read during meals. This is Walter Scott, Alexander Dumas, or Matthew Arnold with his "Gothic romance and Italian opera." Indeed it is a costume play which is being staged under Adams' direction. He lays out the setting, prescribes the business, and interprets what he significantly calls the "libretto," without forgetting to comment upon the reactions of the audience. And the resulting fantasy is so catching that we readily effect a "suspension of disbelief." For there is a superior truth in literature that Adams has already led us to "absorb" here, as he will at Chartres: "For us the poetry is history and the facts are false. French art starts not from facts, but from certain assumptions as conventional as a legendary window . . . Frenchmen . . . looked on life as a drama—and on drama as a phase of life— in which the bystanders were bound to assume and accept the regular stage-plot. That the plot might be altogether untrue to real life affected in no way its interest."[32] Adams, who in a letter to Mrs. Cameron once described himself as "a sexagenarian Hamlet with architectural fancies,"[33] knows better than anyone that the world is a stage. And this is how he makes us visualize this "world of architecture." Mont-Saint-Michel reveals itself as a stage, and so Chartres in its turn appears to be. That the decors may be rather different from their actual prototypes does not affect in any way the interest of the personal drama enacted here, and whose study also belongs to another chapter: "The Meaning of *Mont-Saint-Michel and Chartres*."

CHARTRES

A "Synecdochist"?

In his introduction to an edition of *Mont-Saint-Michel and Chartres*, Lewis Mumford makes a significant observation: "It was only after visiting Chartres repeatedly that I discovered how many important aspects of the structure had actually been left out . . . Actually, he never skirts around the entire cathedral . . . and so, if one thinks of this essay as a purely architectural composition, Adams never fully embraces or comes to terms with the building as a whole."[34] Such a remark can be extended not only to Adams' description of Mont-Saint-Michel but to his poetic reconstructions of all buildings. Remembering what he said about his pursuing "poetry" only, it is rather easy to imagine "the uncle" adding, like Robert Frost: "If I must be classified as a poet, I might be called a Synecdochist; for I prefer the synecdoche in poetry—that figure of speech in which we use a part for the whole." To borrow Adams' own simile, there is before Chartres "an architectural *douane* to pass," where "one's architectural baggage must be opened." An inspection of this baggage should confirm how readily, in his interpretation of the Gothic, Adams applied the poet's precept: "All an artist needs is samples." The real question is the nature of these samples and the use he made of them.[35]

The illusion of completeness in Adams' treatment of architecture first comes from his choice of Mont-Saint-Michel as the starting point of our architectural journey. At once we are made aware of one of the architect's essential pleasures: his defiance of gravity with the maximum of daring commensurate with stability. For, "perched on the extreme point of this abrupt rock," the abbey seems to substantiate Nietzsche's conception of architecture as "a sort of oratory of power" (Adams actually speaks of *energy*), "man's pride, man's triumph over gravitation . . . assume visible form."[36] The uncle does not attempt any such definition of architecture, but the first structural elements he has made us notice on entering the church are the "four great triumphal piers or columns, at the intersection of the nave and transepts." Thus we have begun with the chief problems which confronted the architect, which were those of weight and equilibrium; this great heavy mass of stone "flung against the sky" had to be supported. The import of this lesson is reinforced by what we learn, all along the "journey," of the catastrophes which subsequently befell the Gothic, from the tumbling down of the towers on the west front of the abbey, "whose weight broke down the vaulting beneath," to the gigantic collapse of Beauvais. Here, in his feeling that the "repose" of architecture is "none too deep," that it is at best but a precarious equilibrium, Adams shows himself strikingly different from Ruskin, whose monuments seem to have been erected to last forever.[37]

The difference of attitudes between Ruskin and Adams in front of a monument not only stems from their already noted antithetical ways of approaching the monument; it lies in the very manner in which they apprehend architecture itself. According to John D. Rosenberg: "When [Ruskin] looked at a building, his eye was not caught by proportion, line or mass, for these were too abstract to gratify his visual demand for color and richly ornamental detail. It was surface, not structure, to which he instinctively turned."[38] By instinct, as has been proved by his first reaction to the Gothic in 1895, Adams, on the contrary, identifies himself with the builders of Coutances, while "the exterior magnificences of Amiens,

Chartres and Rouen" leave him cold. No wonder that he will one day express his distaste of Ruskin's "bad" (others would say "wedding-cake"—or Venetian) Gothic;[39] construction, not ornament, is for him the essence of architecture. In this can be traced the influence of Richardson, which he acknowledged;[40] but it is also a matter of temperament. "Austere," or, as Adams now prefers to say, "serious," the Normans please him even more owing to their "practical" side; they struggled, we read in chapter iv, "over the best solution of this particularly American problem of the twentieth century," which is of building higher and higher, and solidly. This reference to contemporary architecture helps Adams to sense the element of rivalry which often actuated medieval architects in their designs, just as their modern American counterparts would try to outvie each other with their skyscrapers. It also brings him to concern himself with the material used and to note how this material became of a cheaper quality in the thirteenth century, with the damaging consequences which ensued.[41] Ruskin, on the other hand, remains alien to such problems; he never realized —or at least cared to note—that behind their marble frontings Venetian buildings were rather cheaply made.

In reality, Adams' attitude toward "construction" soon proves ambivalent. For, when in "Roses and Apses" he asserts: "The expression concerns us; the construction concerns the Beaux Arts," not only the high "charges for repairs" are implied. The term is all-inclusive, as is made clear by the comment, a little farther, on the flying buttresses of Chartres: "If it were not *a matter of pure construction* it would be worth while to read what Viollet-le-Duc says about them (article 'Arc-boutants')."[42] Such a way of shelving a problem is in keeping with the program of a journey wherein we must "conscientiously try to keep as far away as we can from technique about which we know nothing." But how could we "feel" Gothic architecture without at least getting some notions about its chief characteristics? If it is possible to maintain, as Adams does, that: "flying buttresses were not a necessity. The Merveille had none," there are other fundamentals of the Gothic, exemplified both at Mont-Saint-Michel and at Chartres, which are less easy to dismiss.[43]

The first volume of *The Stones of Venice* deals with the structural principles of Gothic architecture; yet Ruskin scarcely mentions vaulting, which is a very basic element, and neither does Ruskin's foremost American disciple, Charles Eliot Norton, in his *Historical Studies of Church Building in the Middle Ages* (1880). Adams never seems to have taken an interest in the works of his one-time colleague (Norton had been appointed Professor of Fine Arts at Harvard in 1874), who concerned himself only with Italian churches and more precisely with the *moral* qualities of those who built them. A far more surprising gap in his documentation is the work of another Harvard professor of art, Charles Herbert Moore: *Development and Character of Gothic Architecture*, first published in 1890, with a second edition in 1899.[44] Applying the designation "pointed architecture" to other types hitherto "erroneously classed as Gothic," Moore insisted that the true recognition of the Gothic was to be based not on the substitution of pointed for round arches but rather on the use of a fundamental plan completely different from the Roman and the Romanesque: "a system of balanced thrusts in contra-distinction to the ancient system of inner stability . . . a logical adjustment of active parts whose opposing forces neutralize each other and produce a perfect equilibrium."[45] Adams did not avail himself of this up-to-date study by a fellow countryman. Even more revealingly, he never refers to Viollet-le-Duc's various articles on "the subject of vaulting." The subject itself, as we have already seen, was not to be touched.

There are two explanations for this apparently total lack of interest in an essential matter. One is the enduring influence, limited though it was, of Richardson and his neo-Romanesque architecture lessons. From his friend, Adams had learned to appreciate the round arch (one of the characteristic features used for the façade of his own house, on Lafayette Square) while gaining a distrust of the pointed arch. Such a bias is apparent in his September 8, 1895, letter to Brooks, in which he declares the pointed arch "cheap."[46] And there were also literary reasons to preclude his getting into the controversy about the origins of the Gothic. As he said at the beginning of "The Virgin of Chartres": "The Gothic gets away. No two men think alike about it, and no woman agrees with either man. The Church itself never agreed about it, and the architects agree even less than the priests." Why should one deal with such a slippery subject? Besides, it was beginning to be recognized by art critics that a modification of the

Armenian pointed arch, and the rib-vault of Arab invention, were in use in Europe from the end of the tenth century, in other words that the broken arch was already a component of Roman style. Admitting such a confusing truth would have detracted from Adams' *ensemble,* which rested on the clear-cut popular distinction between the round (or Romanesque) and the pointed (or Gothic) arch. Adams preferred to see it all in terms of literary symbolism, one arch becoming masculine and the other feminine. Nothing could seem happier to him than their marriage. This is what he called the Gothic Transition, his "corner of preference" in the field of art: "The quiet, restrained strength of the Romanesque married to the graceful curves and vaulting imagination of the Gothic makes a union nearer to the ideal than is often allowed in marriage. The French . . . never tired of its possibilities. Sometimes they put the pointed arch within the round, or above it; sometimes they put the round within the pointed. Sometimes a Roman arch covered a cluster of pointed windows as though protecting and caressing its children."[47]

This wilful reduction of the theme of vaulting to literary terms will be even less surprising once it has been noticed that before this passage Adams alluded only twice to the arch, first in a simile equating his own life with a broken arch and then in his comment upon the *Chanson de Roland,* where "the action of dying is felt like the dropping of a keystone into a vault." One could not be more resolutely untechnical. Even in "Roses and Apses," where he is to give the height of the vault of Chartres, Adams maintains the literary approach: "You may, if you like, figure it in a mathematical formula of infinity—the broken arch, or finite idea of space; the spire pointing with its converging lines, to unity beyond space; the sleepless, restless thrust of the vaults, telling the unsatisfied, uncomplete, everstrained effort of man to rival the energy, intelligence and purpose of God."[48] The "energy" to be sensed here, as in the powerful architecture of Mont-Saint-Michel, is purely spiritual.

What "sample" then did Adams select to give his reader, as he said, "a realizing sense"[49] of the problems of architecture? There is only one structural element on which he seems to have chosen to dwell in his description of all churches, whether on Mont-Saint-

Michel or at Chartres, or on the "architectural highway" which leads from one point to the other; it is the tower with its spire. The whole of chapter iv and the first half of chapter v (24 pages, out of a total of 422 for the "Mentor" edition) are devoted to the subject, and this estimate does not comprise the many allusions scattered throughout the other chapters. The importance Adams attached to the tower (a basic element also in the imagistic structure of *Mont-Saint-Michel and Chartres*) is obvious.

It is easy to understand this choice: "The spire is the simplest part of the Romanesque or Gothic architecture and needs less study in order to be felt," Adams remarks at the beginning of chapter v ("Towers and Portals"), and before passing on to the subject of portals, he emphasizes this point: "They are the least complicated part of church architecture." In "Roses and Apses," he also explains: "Towers and flèches are invariably more or less successful because they are more or less balanced, mathematical, calculable products of reason and thought." There is something Cartesian in this selection of the easiest and most rational element for an introduction to architecture; yet the reader who would consequently expect a lesson on the rudiments of art is bound to be disappointed. Whether we go hunting spires "like mushrooms" through Normandy and Île de France (chapter iv) or stand at the foot of the Chartres towers (chapter v), we will not learn much about the way they were constructed.[50]

Not that these pages do not make pleasant reading. Chapter iv is on a par with Proust's account of his motoring through Normandy in "En mémoire des églises assassinées" (*Pastiches et mélanges*). We participate in a regular "steeple-chase" party when, unlike what happens at Mont-Saint-Michel or at Chartres, we are allowed to feed our eyes "on the simplicity of the Norman flèche which pierces the line of our horizon." We even range far and wide in order to discover "the little church" at Fenioux on the Charente, with its conical steeple "that an infidel might adore." The verb last quoted is indicative of the tone of the whole section; everything is "delightful," "pretty," "charming"—very much as it must be to the eyes of a niece with no more critical acumen than a typical debutante. The only "technicalities" to be found in these twenty-four pages come by means of three long quotations of

Viollet-le-Duc; indeed, the uncle relies here so much on the French architect that he directly refers to him no less than twenty times, going to the extent of quoting others quoting him.[51]

All in all, however, we have here a good "sample" of Adams' interpretation of architecture, if not a sample of architecture itself; with two unmistakably personal touches. One is the wealth of allusions to other specimens of architecture, somewhat in the manner which had already provided its larger backdrop to Mont-Saint-Michel. Adams obviously delights in the "long list of spires," as he goes leafing through not only Viollet-le-Duc's *Dictionnaire* but his own collection of *Monuments historiques* photographs. By a clever subterfuge, instead of delving into the matter, he gets over it by extending it geographically. And he also translates it into romance. Ceasing to be masses of stone, the towers become *personae*, here (at Mont-Saint-Michel) the Archangel, there (the "new tower" at Chartres) Diane de Poitiers: "Its coiffure is elaborately arranged to cover the effects of age and its neck and shoulders are covered with lace and jewels to hide a certain sharpness of the skeleton." Before trying to identify the "old tower," Adams admits, "One cannot push these resemblances too far." Hesitating between Saint Bernard and Eleanor of Guienne, he launches into a comparison which remains quite labored, even though it was curtailed by six lines in the 1912 edition.[52] Were *Mont-Saint-Michel and Chartres* to be considered as a "purely architectural" essay (which it obviously is *not*), it would be difficult to account for such paragraphs.

Four doorways and an apse

From the two towers of Chartres, our eyes "drop down at last to the church itself." Before studying "Chartres to the ground," as we shall soon be assumed to have done, we must learn something about its history—and this résumé, spanning a period between "some time in the first half of the twelfth century" and the French Revolution (whose date is significantly made to coincide with the ill fate of Louis XVI in 1792), is an indication of the real limits of our visit.[53] No word is said of the ancient sanctuaries where "from time immemorial" the Virgin was venerated; no word of the crypt, still extant, but which, as we know, we shall not enter. Of the cathedral itself, what shall we see? "There seems to be a bit of clean carving here and there, a solid buttress or two, and perhaps a gleam through painted glass," wrote James Russell Lowell, in August 1869, of his own verses on Chartres.[54] Adams' description is more factual. Yet, if exception is made for the stained glass windows which are a world to themselves, all that we are made to see is four doorways (out of nine) and, once inside the nave, hardly more than the apse. Compared with all that Chartres has to offer, it is not much.

Here again a parallel with Ruskin would be tempting. Among the books the "Priest of Beauty" wished to write was one on Chartres, in the same vein as his *Bible of Amiens;* had he been able to fulfill this project, no doubt he would have given much space to the sculptural elements. In fact, such a "Bible of Chartres" exists; it is *La Cathédrale* by J. K. Huysmans, published in 1898. Adams possessed a copy of the book, to which he occasionally refers. "If you want to know what an enthusiast thinks of them," he says of the statue columns adorning the pilasters of the Royal Portal, "listen to Mr. Huysmans's 'Cathedral.' " But what he then quotes of Huysmans' rapturous description of the statue on the right of the central doorway is a very truncated, lifeless passage with none of the French novelist's graphic details. "I hope you can enter into the spirit of his enthusiasm," he adds a little further, in a tone which sounds rather diffident; it is clear that he does not react to this statuary in the same way.[55]

Even more so than it was with Ruskin, a difference not only in temperament but in formative background has to be called into account. In *L'évolution des idées esthétiques de J. K. Huysmans,* Helen Trudgian has shown how the novelist placed himself in the same romantic tradition which had made Victor Hugo write at the beginning of *Notre Dame de Paris:* "Inspirons s'il est possible l'amour de l'architecture nationale":

Huysmans' work is related to the *Monuments du Midi et du centre de la France* of Prosper Mérimée. Appointed inspector general of historical monuments under the Guizot movement, the short story writer readily joined the contemporary archeological movement. Like many romantics he is steeped in a definite kind of taste for architecture, a taste that will moreover be perpetuated by his literary successors. He owes this taste, as do Michelet and Victor Hugo, to the founding of the Museum of French Historical Monuments at the beginning of the century by Auguste Lenoir. In the diffusion of taste for Gothic during the first quarter of the century, the Museum of French Historical Monuments was more influential than the Benedictine excavations of the eighteenth century and had just as large an influence as the *Génie du christianisme*. In 1830 these memories are at work in people's minds, and committees are set up and commissions develop . . . After Mérimée and then Cahier come Martin, Viollet-le-Duc and Vitet, Daniel Ramée, Chapuy, Taylor and Guilhermy, and so many others. Huysmans is their immediate heir and in turn becomes an archeologist.[56]

Hence the loving attention which he devotes to minute details in his descriptions, whereas Adams, who has never been inspired with such a passion for old stones, will most often content himself with a cursory glance.

"The most colossal repertory of heaven and earth, of God and man," says Huysmans; as far as Adams is concerned, it seems rather as if "the sculpture inside and out," should be categorized in what he calls, at the beginning of "Roses and Apses," "the vast variety of bric-a-brac, useful or ornamental, belonging to the church." Bric-a-brac per se does not interest him. So, unlike his French forerunner, who heartily plunged into the "immense palimpseste" of the Royal (or West) Portal and tried to read as many of its 739 figures as he could, Adams simply reels off somewhat in the manner of Jacques Prévert, but without the humor, such pieces: "Then a prophet, then a saint next the doorway; then, on the southern jambshafts, another saint, a king, a queen, and another king." Even when he invites his companion to produce her camera (the only time in the whole journey) and photograph a certain queen "with utmost care to include the strange support on which she stands: a monkey, two dragons, a dog, a basilisk with a dog's head," we feel that the picturesqueness is for him less graphic than merely auditory, lying in this rigmarole of a list. Otherwise, why do we have to notice this one support, in the whole cathedral (our attention will never be called to any other pedestal, nor, as a matter of fact, to any particular capital), and not, for instance, the charming scene beneath St. Gregory's statue, in the embrasure of the right doorway of the south façade? The niece would have been "charmed" by the secretary at the pope's feet, crouching behind a curtain, peeping through a hole and apparently amazed at the sight of the dove speaking into his master's ear. It is true that on the south as well as on the north façades, only the central doorways will seem to hold any interest; of the Royal Porch itself whose study "covers all the rest," only the central and south doorways must retain our attention. We do not see any of the figures on the west façade such as the gigantic Christ towering above, the gallery of kings running between the two steeples, or the angel of the meridian. Twice, in a different context, Adams will allude to the *âne qui vielle;* we do not notice him now.[57]

Like Huysmans, Adams relies for much of his information on the Abbé Bulteau's *Monographie de la cathédrale de Chartres* (Chartres, 1887), a work about which he said, in a passage deleted from the 1904 edition, that it "makes authority for all matters connected with the dates of the cathedral."[58] He owes to this book not only his dates but nearly whatever he chooses to say about the sculpture. But, as he remarks about the statue columns, "the Abbé Bulteau has done his best to name these statues . . . The names would be only in your way." Rarely will he break from this attitude. An exception is made for the seven representatives of the liberal arts, carved on the arch of the central doorway of the Royal Porch: "Pythagoras, Aristotle, Cicero, Euclid, Nichomachus, Ptolemy and Priscian." Once again, in fact, the figures seem to be named merely for the sake of the sonorous roll. We are not made to see the crowns placed on their foreheads, which show that, clothed with the majesty of the Arts, the scholars have become kings as well as symbols. They testify to the renown which the school of the cathedral had from the end of the tenth century.[59] Adams does not point out such details, least of all minute details, like the *dais* above the statue columns, where an admiring Huysmans could perceive: "Tiny cottages and chapels, manor-houses and ports . . . a baby Sion, a celestial Jerusalem for dwarfs."[60] A fleeting reference is made to the signs of the Zodiac, and the works of the months also storied on the Royal Porch are not even mentioned. These are but instances of a general tendency. Indeed, in the crowded world of Chartres, only a few figures, a very few, attracted

Adams' attention; and what he saw in them, as will appear, was what he was himself bringing. In a sense, his Chartres resembled what the French call "a Spanish Inn," where the traveler must cater to his own needs.

"At Chartres," we are told," one sees everywhere the Virgin"[61] (were we to count all her pictures, we could find 175 of them); it is therefore natural that our attention should first fasten upon her and her son. For his interpretation of this major iconographical element, though, Adams does not avail himself (perhaps simply because he could not find a copy of the book on the market) of Didron's *Iconographie chrétienne, histoire de Dieu* (Paris, 1844), on which Huysmans so heavily relies. And it is worthy of notice how, from a purely iconographical point of view, his observations, whether for that reason or another, remain sketchy, not to say quite feeble. Let us see for instance what he does with the tympanum above the central doorway of the Royal Porch with which we are supposed to begin our study. Here is a typical "Majestas Domini." Surrounding Christ in Majesty, and placed according to the excellence of their natures—man, eagle, lion, and ox,—the four "Beasts of the Apocalypse" represent the four Evangelists; but on these we will not have a word. If Adams struggles for an approximation to describe the *amande mystique* (or Vesica Piscis) enclosing the central figure ("its long nimbus, or aureole, or glory"), he does not notice any of the other details: the throne on which Christ is seated, the cruciform nimbus behind his head, his right hand raised in blessing while his left holds the Book of the Law resting upright upon his knee. We must remain blind to the symbolic value of the scene: Christ, not Mary—even though the church is dedicated to the mother—is the real Lord here, to whom one must first pay homage.[62]

This feeling that the meaning of the religious iconography is either purposely ignored or at the very least misunderstood heightens as we pass on to the south doorway of the Royal Porch and see how the Nativity on the tympanum is described: "Mary lies on a low bed, beneath, or before, a sort of table or cradle on which lies the Infant, while Saint Joseph stands at the bed's head. Then the angel appears, directing three shepherds to the spot, filling the rest of the space." It little matters that the sheep accompanying the shepherds are left out of the account; we are concerned with the interpretation of a scene very often represented in thirteenth-century works. In the words of Emile Mâle:

> The thirteenth century, faithful in other respects to the tradition of previous centuries, represents the birth of Jesus after a fashion which could not fail to strike us as curious did we but take the trouble to observe it. This scene, so often reproduced in windows, has in it nothing tender, one might almost say nothing human. The Madonna of the Italian quattrocentists kneels before the child, gazing at Him with clasped hands, the personification of infinite love. In thirteenth-century art Mary, lying on her bed and regardless of her Son, looks intently before her at some invisible object. The child does not lie in a manger, but curiously enough on a raised altar, which occupies the whole central portion of the composition . . . . The scene appears to take place not in a stable but in a church. It is indeed to a church that the artist-theologian of the Middle Ages would direct men's minds, for it seems he would tell us that from the moment of birth Jesus must have the semblance of a victim . . . Before such a mystery even maternal love is stilled. Mary keeps a religious silence and ponders, say the commentators, the words of prophets and angels which had even now come to pass. Saint Joseph shares her silence, and motionless, with a fixed gaze, the two are wrapt in solemn contemplation.[63]

Such a theological conception is so far removed from Adams' own idea of the Virgin (as will appear when we come to this part of our study) that it was impossible for him to understand the scene, still less to describe it correctly; even once he had read Mâle's *Art religieux en France au XIIIᵉ siècle* (Adams, as we are going to see, had access to it before publishing his second edition of *Mont-Saint-Michel and Chartres*), he could not bring himself to revise his comments.

His own interpretation of Mary also colors his view of the South Porch when the Son's precedence over the Mother seems to be too graphically demonstrated for his liking. He treats of it but glancingly, betraying his misapprehension in one detail: his setting down the Last Judgment on the lintel of the central doorway as "bad taste" because it has been put there "without regards to Mary's feelings." Had he really cared to observe the Virgin's attitude, as she is represented on the tympanum above, seated to the right of Christ and lost in prayer, he would have sensed that she is very much concerned with it all. But the heart of the matter was that he found no *personal* interest in this porch. A short sentence which he added in the 1912 edition is revealing: "No figure on this porch suggests a portrait or recalls a memory." In other words, it offered no ground to his fancy.[64]

Except for this additional last line, Adams' description of the South Porch (like that of the Royal Porch) is the same in the 1904 and 1912 editions; on the other hand, he intensively revised the pages dealing with the North Porch. Here was the statuary which most securely captured his imagination, owing to reasons which had nothing to do with art, for nowhere in this chapter does he concern himself with the visual quality of sculpture or notice (as he will, when treating of the stained glass) a possible difference in technique, due to the fact that the porches were done at different stages and by different workshops. The grim beauty of the biblical scenes on this porch, which, in the words of a commentator, illustrates "the doctrine of the atonement and the Old Testament, so far as it was a preparation and a figure of the New Alliance" did not fascinate him.[65] In spite of his Protestant background, Adams shows little inclination to read the Bible in the stone book of Chartres; and if this porch especially appealed to his imagination because it was dedicated to the Virgin, his interest, in fact, took a lay direction, as is proved by his remarks in the 1912 edition:

Critics are doing their best to destroy the peculiar personal interest of this porch, but tourists and pilgrims may be excused for insisting on their traditional rights here, since the porch is singular, even in the thirteenth century, for belonging entirely to them and the royal family of France, subject only to the Virgin. True artists, turned critics, think also less of rules than of values, and no ignorant public can be trusted to join the critics in losing temper judiciously over the date or correctness of a portrait until they know something of its motives and merits. The public has always felt certain that some of the statues which stand against the outer piers of this porch are portraits, and they see no force in the objection that such decoration was not customary in the church. Many things at Chartres were not customary in the Church, although the Church now prefers not to dwell on them.[66]

For the first time in *Mont-Saint-Michel and Chartres,* the tone has become somewhat heated; it is because Adams has entered into a cryptic argument with Emile Mâle (only in a later chapter will he mention the French scholar's name), who maintains that "personal interpretation is out of place" when dealing with the subject of thirteenth-century iconography. In point of fact, when he wrote his study (published as early as 1898), Mâle could not have in mind the 1904 version of *Mont-Saint-Michel and Chartres*. His rebuke was specifically aimed at such French commentators who, like the Abbé Bulteau, identified "without the shadow of a proof" some statues on the North Porch with members of the thirteenth-century nobility. "There are in the cathedrals," Mâle said, "few works of art which can with certainty be said to represent figures in French history." Of these, he found none at Chartres. Where the Abbé Bulteau, in conformity with an old tradition, saw the portraits of Philip, Count of Boulogne, and his wife, Mahaut, we are thus invited to recognize Jesse, father of David, and his wife.[67] This new interpretation, however, did not suit Adams in the least.[68]

The figures of Philip and his wife actually appear to play at Chartres the same imaginative function as the Chartrier at Mont-Saint-Michel; here, too, in T. S. Eliot's phrase, is an "objective correlative" through which Adams can best express the particular quality of his emotions. Unlike the Chartrier, however, these statues owe their power not to physical characteristics, whether fancied or real (we have no descriptive details about them) but to the story they can conjure, in a way also reminiscent of the staging of *Chanson de Roland* in the old "refectory" of the Mount. Adams projects himself into the "rich and strongly connected" Comte de Boulogne who donated this portal, less out of faith than in order to outdo Pierre de Dreux, himself the donor of the South Porch, and his fellow conspirator against Queen Blanche. Thrilling at the romance of "an age when passions were real," Adams indulges in an imaginative flight, which is far less relevant to the reality of the cathedral than the "longues rêveries" which some figures aroused in Huysmans. No wonder he felt the need to justify himself after reading Mâle's book. In the 1912 edition, he added a lengthy passage of Viollet-le-Duc about the "personal character" of each statue, as well as a direct reference to a plate of the *Monographie;* he even indicated the paging of his sources. And should these precautions not be sufficient, hammering at what he had said, as early as 1904, in his chapters on Mont-Saint-

Michel, about the superiority of "poetry" over facts, he also vindicated "the first privilege of tourist ignorance," which is the right to look at architecture "with thirteenth-century eyes," or with associationist eyes.[69]

However, it is only once we have stepped inside the nave that "of a sudden, between the portal and the shrine, the infinite rises into a new expression; there and then, the process of reaching the inner truth of architecture through a fantasy well supported by means of authoritative (but not definitive) reference receives its best exemplification. Adams, in this particular case, did not feel any diffidence, and "Roses and Apses" could pass untouched into the 1912 edition. The title, however, is slightly misleading, for the frequent references to "the inevitable Viollet-le-Duc" (seventeen in this one chapter, including two paragraph-long quotations), as well as the ten diagrams of various churches and cathedrals, also taken from the *Dictionnaire*, all serve, in fact, to concentrate our attention on one part of the architecture, which is the apse; there Adams has found his ideal "sample."

"Architecture is applied geometry," said Gundisalvo (*circa* 1140–1150), and this definition found general assent among the medieval architects. In Friedrich Heer's words: "A Gothic Cathedral is a mathematical work of art constructed with numbers, lines of force and rays of light. The first essential was to enliven the inert mass of the walls."[70] At first sight, this might appear as a capsule of "Roses and Apses," but closer examination reveals that Adams does not really concern himself with the "architectonics" (as Huysmans would say) of the walls. A device often used by medieval architects in order to enliven this inert mass is the fourfold articulation of the masonry into arcade, gallery, triforium and clerestory, as, for example, in the Notre-Dame de Paris. The thirteenth-century builders of Chartres did without the gallery, thus reducing the division to three. Adams, for all his insisting on the visual presence of the Trinity in the cathedral, does not even as much as note this basic disposition. Neither does he, though he produces some measurements borrowed from the Abbé Bulteau, point out the rigorous purism of the architecture of Chartres. Writing some forty years later than Adams, Otto von Simson reveals conclusive evidence that Chartres is a unit bonded together by exact proportions. Compared, for example, with

Noyon, which has all the variety and richness characteristic of the twelfth century, Chartres is austere, impersonal; according to Von Simson: "The perfection of this great architectural system is the perfection of its proportions, proportions that the master developed not according to his personal intuition but by exact geometrical determination." On the contrary, Adams would have it that the "Chartres scheme is unorthodox, not to say heretical," and that here lies its greatness.[71]

At the origin of this statement is Viollet-le-Duc's remark, as translated by Adams, that "at Chartres the choir of the cathedral presents a plan which does no great honor to its architect." There exists, he asserts, a certain "want of accord" between the circular apse and the parallel sides of the sanctuary; the spacings of the columns are "loose (lâches)." "A severe, even unjust evaluation," has since commented Chanoine Delaporte. "On the contrary, one cannot but admire the designer's skill in so overcoming the difficulties of his task that the irregularities of the plan are visible only on paper."[72] For the master builder had not a free hand in the establishment of his plan; indeed, Adams himself notes (though without mentioning the presence of the crypt which determined the place and design of the apse), it was "imposed on him, like the twelfth-century portal." And it was a measure of the architect's mathematical genius, that despite all limitations he could build a piece of seemingly perfect proportions. Adams recognizes this success: "The Chartres apse, enormous in size and width, is exquisitely lighted." But if it is so, he adds, paraphrasing "Viollet-le-Duc's words into a more or less emotional or twelfth-century form," it is because "it overrides the architect"; it was built under the influence of the Virgin, who "herself saw to the lighting of her own boudoir."[73] No doubt this is a very "unorthodox" explanation. But one fact is clear: by translating architecture into emotion, instead of technical terms, Adams has reached a truth: that the apse was a work of inspired genius, which Viollet-le-Duc was unable to perceive.

"A Delirium of Colour and Light"

"Notre Dame de Chartres! It was a world to explore, as if one explored the entire Middle Age." These words of Walter Pater in *Gaston de Latour* could have been said by Adams. At the beginning of "The Legendary Windows" he compares "one's first visit to a cathedral" to "one's first visit to the British Museum"; both places are "stored" with "chaotic" wealth.[74] It is clear that our visit has proceeded up till now at double step; we have had but a digest (quite minimal at that) of the architectural and sculptural wealth. Now our pace slackens; we pause to drink in the beauty of the stained glass windows: "Sitting here in the subdued afternoon light of the apse one goes on for hours reading the open volumes of colour."[75] The difference between the two stages of our visit is made patent by the change of verbs in Adams' opening remark: "If this imperial presence [that of the Virgin] is stamped on the architecture and the sculpture with an energy not to be mistaken it radiates through the glass with a light and colour that actually blind the true servant of Mary." What had been a mere *stamp* (cold, inert) thus transforms itself into a *radiation* (warm, animated); and our guide, who had some pains to enter into the spirit of Huysmans' enthusiasm, will become "the true enthusiast in glass," to the point of waxing "a little incoherent when talking about it," and even quite "extravagant."[76] Whereas Huysmans devotes but a few pages to the stained glass windows,[77] for Adams three full chapters will not suffice; his enthusiasm for glass suffuses the whole book. One of the clues to this change of attitude can be found in a letter to Mrs. Cameron, dated February 13, 1891. Then in Tahiti, Adams was, as we know, going through his artistic "rebirth," thanks to his discovery of the world of colors: "La Farge has settled down to painting, varied by his usual mania for collecting photographs. I call it a mania because with me it has become a phobia; and he is almost afraid of telling me about his photographs because I detest them so much . . . I hate photography abstractly, because they have given me more ideas perversely and immoveably wrong, than I ever should get by imagination. They are almost as bad as an ordinary book of travels . . ."[78]

Such hatred of photographs is no doubt connected with the memory of Marian Adams' suicide;[79] it has apparently subsided when, a few years later, Adams "immersing" himself in the Gothic finds it useful to collect reproductions of *Monuments historiques* by the score. Yet it is a fact that through their use, and that of "ordinary books of travels" (or guide books), he gets some "perverse" (or erroneous) notions; only on the chapter dealing with the apse, and even though most of it is literally "cribbed" from Viollet-le-Duc's *Dictionnaire,* do his comments achieve the quality of true perception. He is then reacting, not to photographs and diagrams, not to what he has been able to read about the subject, not even to what he has seen of the stone work, but to the world of colors this architecture encases; as in the South Seas, he is reacting to what he calls "the fun of life."

Adams had made only one visit to Mont-Saint-Michel, several years earlier, when he wrote his description of the abbey; much more familiar with Chartres, he can go back there while at work on his book. We must, however, wait until "at last we are face to face with the crowning glory of Chartres" to sense that we have really deserted the "attic" on the Avenue du Bois de Boulogne to *live* in the cathedral. For the first time autobiographical warmth penetrates the journey; we circulate physically as well as spiritually. Although Adams has read "all that is readable" (a point on which we shall have to come back) he is aware that: "Even the learning of Viollet-le-Duc was at fault when dealing with a building so personal." So, even if he relies on his "schoolmaster's" work, advising us to "read it here in the church, the Dictionary in one hand, and binocle in the other," the binocle, he avers, is "more important than the Dictionary."[80] In one of the most deeply felt passages of *The Education,* he will tell of his happy hours when, after buying a Mercedes in the summer of 1904, he could go "wooing" the Virgin through all her demesne:

For years past, incited by John La Farge, Adams had devoted his summer schooling to the study of her glass at Chartres and elsewhere, and if the automobile had one *vitesse* more useful than another, it was that of a century a minute; that of passing from one century to another without break. The centuries dropped like autumn leaves in one's road, and one was not fined for running over them too fast. When the thirteenth lost breath, the fourteenth caught on, and the sixteenth ran close ahead. The hunt for the Virgin's glass opened rich preserves. Especially the sixteenth century ran riot in sensuous worship. Then the ocean of religion, which had flooded France, broke into Shelley's light dissolved in star-showers thrown, which had left every remote village strewn with fragments that flashed like jewels, and were tossed into hidden clefts of peace and forgetfulness . . . One dared not pass a parish church in Champagne or Touraine without stopping to look for its windows of fragments, where one's glass discovered the Christ-child in his manger, nursed by the head of a fragmentary donkey, with a Cupid playing into its long ears from the balustrade of a Venetian palace, guarded by a legless Flemish *leibwache*, standing on his head with a broken halbert; all invoked in prayer by remnants of the donors and their children that might have been drawn by Fouquet or Pinturicchio in colors as fresh and living as the day they were burned in, and with feeling that still consoled the faithful for the paradise they had paid for and lost.[81]

Here too he paints himself with his "glass" (or "binocle") indulging in the "amusement" which, he says in *Mont-Saint-Michel and Chartres*, can take "many days." The window he describes is probably imaginary—a composite of details which, here or there, have caught his fancy—but the humor of his description, in the sense of Thackeray's definition, "wit and love," is genuine. Adams is really "amused"; the adjectives "pretty," "charming," "graceful," and "droll," as well as "uncanny," which he uses in *Mont-Saint-Michel and Chartres*, are typical of his reaction to many windows. Mrs. Mary Ward, Charles Milnes Gaskell's daughter, whom I had occasion to interview at Much Wenlock, could still remember with delight the time when, many years earlier, "Uncle Henry" took her to a church in Paris (it can be identified as St. Etienne du Mont) and showed her the figure of Christ issuing out a wine press. The same delight in picturesque, or apparently incongruous, details informs his comment on the number of lady friends with whom the Prodigal Son disports himself on his Chartres window: "No one has offered to explain why Chartres should consider two ladies theologically more correct than one; or why Sens should fix on three, or why Bourges should require six."[82] Such details bear the stamp of personal observation. In one case at least Adams is even making an original contribution to our knowledge of the cathedral by noting how the southern lancet, on the west front, slightly narrower than the other lancets owing to a disparity of width between the towers, nonetheless balances the color values of the other windows:

When you search with the binocle for the outside border, you see its pattern only at the top and bottom. On the sides at intervals of about two feet, the medallions cover and interrupt it; but this is partly corrected by making the border, where it is seen, so rich as to surpass any other in the cathedral, even that of the Tree of Jesse. Whether the artist has succeeded or not is a question for other artists—or for you, if you please—to decide; but apparently he did succeed, since no one has ever noticed the difficulty or the device.[83]

This lived-in quality of the observation has to be traced to what Adams called, in a letter to Henry Osborn Taylor, on May 4, 1901, "the many years of La Farge's closest instruction to me, on the use of eyes, not to say feet."[84] Undistinguishable from the "binocle," even if not on all occasions physically present in the cathedral, is the "animated prism" or "spectacled" La Farge of the South Sea years who, we are told in *The Education*, "not only felt at home but felt a sort of ownership" at Chartres, "while Adams, though near sixty years old before he knew anything either of glass or of Chartres, asked no better than to learn, and only La Farge could help him, for he knew enough at least to see that La Farge alone could use glass like a thirteenth-century artist." Here was, besides, the only mentor Adams had at Chartres. "Poor Richardson" was dead, and if we learn from a letter sent to John Hay on August 20, 1899, "that once in a while, St. Gaudens drops in to dinner," there is no evidence that the sculptor ever accompanied his friend to Chartres or any other cathedral. At any rate, he would have proved a poor teacher, judging from his portrait in *The Education:* "Of all the American artists who gave to American art whatever life it breathed in the seventies, St. Gaudens was perhaps the most sympathetic, but certainly the most inarticulate."[85] La Farge, on the contrary, was anything but inarticulate, and "pupil" Adams profited by his teaching. This explains the awareness he evinced of the problems of glass and which he never had when sculpture was concerned. He can visualize the draftsman "chalking out the designs on the whitened table that served for his sketch-board"; he recognizes the difference of workshops ("you see at a glance that it is quite differently treated"); he dates, as often as he can, the windows and even tries to give a notion of the price they cost to their donors, calculating "that the 'miles montatus super equum suum' in glass was equivalent to fifteen oxen." It is evident that he is himself feeling at home on the subject.[86]

How and to what extent does Adams make us share this familiarity with glass? As with all other subjects, he begins his discussion with a quotation of authorities, stating in the 1904 edition:

Therefore let us plod on . . . using such material as the books furnish for help. It is not much. The French have been shockingly negligent of their greatest artistic glory. One knows not even where to seek. One must go to the National Library and beg as a special favour permission to look at the monumental work of M. Lasteyrie, if one wishes to make even a beginning of the study of French glass. Fortunately there exists a fragment of a great work which the Government began, but never completed, upon Chartres; and another, quite indispensable, but not official, upon Bourges; while Viollet-le-Duc's article "vitrail" serves as guide to the whole.[87]

In the 1912 edition, the list is thus completed: "Ottin's book 'Le Vitrail' is convenient. Mâle's volume 'L'Art Religieux' is essential. In English, Westlake's 'History of Design' is helpful."[88] A comparison between the two editions reveals that Adams made no use of the authorities quoted in this additional sentence; the only one he mentions again is Mâle's study (it was, as we know, under its influence that he revised his comments on the North Porch statues, but without changing his basic position), and his reference comes by way of a mere addition, inserted in his description of the Charlemagne window: "The most elaborate account of this window can be found in Mâle's 'Art Religieux' (pp. 440-450)." We look in vain for any sign that he has availed himself of this information; the fruitlessness of the search is surprising, considering what he wrote to A. S. Cook, who had lent him a copy of the book in early 1911: "Curiously enough, it was a new book when I was working up the subject, and I never saw it. This autumn a friend of mine [Ward Thoron], who is passing the winter at Chartres for the sake of the Cathedral alarmed me by quoting his account of the Charlemagne window, which made me fear I had betrayed some unpardonable ignorance."[89]

The exaggeration of the tone is sufficient proof that in reality Adams did not attach much importance to the discrepancies between his own account of the window and Mâle's new version; there is only one major difference of interpretation, and it concerns but one panel (the fifteenth, starting from the bottom of the window) out of a total of twenty-one. Mâle's version reads:

Here the artist has interpolated an incident taken from the "Life of St. Gilles." Charlemagne had committed so grave a sin that he dared not confess it, but one day, as St. Gilles said mass in the emperor's presence, an angel brought the hermit-saint a scroll on which the sin was written. Charlemagne repented, and God pardoned him. This is the subject which the artist represents in the panel where the Abbé Bulteau and Father Durand thought to see Bishop Turpin saying mass. They did not notice that the officiating priest is a monk, not an archbishop, that he has a saint's nimbus, that an angel from heaven brings him a scroll, and that the emperor is seated apart with his head on his hands.

Like the Abbés Bulteau and Durand, Adams has simply noted: "You see the Archbishop Turpin celebrating mass when an angel appears to warn him of Roland's fate." His interpretation of the other panels appears not only correct, but much more graphic than Mâle's: here is panel 3:

Mâle: A battle. Charlemagne delivers Jerusalem.

Adams: Charlemagne has advanced with his knights and attacks the Saracens; the Franks wear coats-of-mail, and carry long pointed shields; the infidels carry round shields; Charlemagne, wearing a crown, strikes off with one blow of his sword the head of a Saracen emir; but the battle is desperate; the chargers are at full gallop, and a Saracen is striking at Charlemagne with his battle-axe.[90]

To make the comparison wholly valid, we must also bring into parallel the corresponding passage in Paul Durand's *Monographie,* which Adams closely followed:

A battle between the French and the Saracens. The slightly flattened shape of the helmets of the French, their long shields pointed at the bottom, and their coats of mail should be noticed, in contrast to the infidels' conical helmets, round shields, and lamellated armour. The fighting is fierce. The king of the Franks, distinguished by the crown he wears with his helmet, cuts off the head of the enemy king, while a Saracen is swinging his battle-axe at Charlemagne, who is defended by his comrades. The horses' swift movement is well caught; they are at full gallop.[91]

Adams, it appears, is a little less "technical" than the learned abbé; what he is after is the movement of "the story of adventure," to quote a phrase he used in connection with another window. And unlike what happened with the North Porch statues (he directly referred to them in 1912, after mentioning Mâle's account of this window: "Its feeling or motive is quite another matter, as it is with the statuary of the North Porch"), his basic stand was not destroyed by the French scholar's discoveries. Here was by general consensus a legend, "a roman, not in verse but in colour." And as Adams remarked, squarely departing from his model:

Of the colour and its relation with that of the Saint James [another legendary window which has just been depicted], one needs time and long acquaintance to learn the value. In the feeling, compared with that of the twelfth century, one needs no time in order to see a change. These two windows are as French and as modern as a picture of Lancret; they are pure art, as simply decorative ⸺s the decorations of the Grand Opera. The thirteenth century knew more about religion and decoration than the twentieth century will ever learn. The windows were neither symbolic nor mystical, nor more religious than they pretended to be.[92]

The last two sentences are also 1912 adjuncts; they merely confirm that his real aim in his study of the window was to seize the color or *fun* of life.

Thus, with the help of Paul Durand's *Monographie,* Adams recounts the stories of several "legendary windows"—four, including that of Charlemagne. The other three deal with Saint Eustache, the Prodigal Son, and Saint James. There is nothing particularly religious about any of these windows either. Full of "droll" little demons, "the Saint James window is a tale of magic told with the vivacity of a fabliau." The details, at least most of them, may come from the *Monographie,* but the "amusement," which Adams makes us share, is personal. In the same way, he has his fun in "making amusing digressions" about the "romance" of the donors; he conjures up the "very great men" belonging to "all these great ruling families" as well—and here is the power of Chartres—as the less aristocratic crowd of the merchants: "You can see, with a glass, the Pastry-cooks and Turners looking across the Weavers and Curriers and Money-Changers, and the 'Men of Tours.' "[93] Already at Mont-Saint-Michel, he had called up our millions of arithmetical ancestors; but these, as we saw, were excluded from the *sanctus sanctorum.* Here they are present in "the glory of the glass."

The longer one looks into it, the more overpowering it becomes, until one begins almost to feel an echo of what our two hundred and fifty million arithmetical ancestors, drunk with the passion of youth and the splendor of the Virgin had been calling to us from Mont-Saint-

Michel and Chartres. No words and no wine could revive their emotions so vividly as they glow in the purity of the colours; the limpidity of the blues; the depth of the red; the intensity of the green; the complicated harmonies; the sparkle and splendour of the light; and the quiet and certain strength of the mass.

For our ancestors had "a natural colour-sense, primitive like the scent of a dog," and which governed their vision: "So we laugh to seen a knight with a blue face, on a green horse, that looks as drawn by a four-year-old-child, and probably the artist laughed, too; but he was a colourist, and never sacrificed his colour for a laugh."[94] This feeling for color which Adams, with all the intensity he is able to summon, tries to revive not only in himself but in his reader is his most personal contribution to the study of Chartres.

It is paradoxical—but in appearances only—that Adams should reveal himself at his best precisely when he is leaning most on Viollet-le-Duc. In part, this is due to the very quality of the text he extensively quoted. Many other studies have since been published on the subject, but nearly all authors have paid homage to Viollet-le-Duc for his article on "Vitrail." Charles Connick, in *Adventures in Light and Color* (1937) translated its most important passages. They are also reproduced by L. Grodecki in *Vitraux de France* (1953). In a symposium on the problems of color, held in Paris in 1954, the latter of these two art critics insisted on its excellence: "All our ideas on the fundamental problems of colour in medieval stained glass are still based upon the admirable article 'Vitrail' [Stained Glass] in the *Dictionnaire raisonné d'Architecture* of Viollet-le-Duc. His study is an account, or rather a rationalist and positivist interpretation, of medieval art. Whatever reservations one may have as to Viollet-le-Duc's general thesis, it cannot be denied that his remarks on the art of stained glass are remarkably penetrating. His main ideas are taken up by all the authors previously mentioned."[95] Adams resorted the more readily to his favorite "sacred source" as he found the architect's explanations "not very technical"; he could easily blend them with his own text. We pass very smoothly from his own comments to Viollet-le-Duc's on the essential subject of blue:

Adams: —A tourist never should study, or he ceases to be a tourist; and it is enough for us if we know that, to get the value they wanted, the artists hatched their blues with lines, covered their surface with figures as though with screens, and tied their blue within its own field with narrow circlets of white or yellow, which, in their turn, were beaded to fasten the blue still more firmly in its place. We have chiefly to remember the law that blue is light.

Viollet-le-Duc: But also it is that luminous colour which gives value to all others. If you compose a window in which there shall be no blue, you will get a dirty or dull (*blafard*) or crude surface which the eye will instantly avoid; but if you put a few touches of blue among all these tones, you will immediately get striking effects if not skilfully conceived harmony. So the composition of blue glass singularly preoccupied the glassworkers of the twelfth and thirteenth centuries. If there is only one red, two yellows, two or three purples, and two or three greens at the most, there are infinite shades of blue . . . and these blues are placed with a very delicate observation of the effects they should produce on other tones, and other tones on them.[96]

By Adams' own admission, his translation is "very free"; he plays with the text, seizes on a simile (for instance Viollet-le-Duc's remark that the artist had to exert his talent "according to a given harmonic scheme on a single plane, like a rug"), and develops the idea in very accessible terms: "The thing seems simpler still when it appears that perspective is forbidden, and that these glass windows of the twelfth and thirteenth centuries, like Oriental rugs, imply a flat surface, a wall which must not be treated as open. The twelfth-century glassworker would sooner have worn a landscape on his back than have costumed his church with it; he would as soon have decorated his floors with painted holes as his walls. He wanted to keep the coloured window flat, like a rug hung on the wall."[97] This is but a piece of fantasy, but it is illuminating. Nowhere in the book shall we get a more convincing or a more pleasant lesson.

The interest of the lesson is further enhanced by our guide's communicative excitement; it is an excitement which has literary sources. Like Adams' vision of the Chartrier at Mont St. Michel, it might be traced as far back as Milton's *Il Penseroso*, with its

> Storied windows richly dight
> Casting a dim religious light.

In her study of "Mediaeval Windows in Romantic Light," Erika von Erhardt-Siebold has shown how Milton's dim religious light acquires a definite tint of color as medieval glass windows become a frequently used motif in English romantic literature: "Poets, such as Beckford and Shelley, discover on their journeys to Italy windows gleaming in saffron light, that product of a fourteenth-century invention when a thin veneer of yellow color applied on glass left it delicately stained and highly translucent. Filtering light appears pale and visionary, imparting a hue of sanctity. Beckford thus experiences a church in Florence as 'breathing Divinity.' For Shelley this yellow light in the Cathedral of Milan is an inspiration to read Dante."[98] The "light dissolved in star-showers thrown," in the passage from *The Education* we have quoted earlier, when Adams went hunting for the Virgin's glass, comes from Shelley's *Adonais*. For it must be realized that, just as Huysmans adhered to the French romantic tradition when he chiefly reacted to the sculptures of Chartres, Adams, in his emotional response to this "delirium of colour and light," plainly places himself in the English romantic tradition. "The lovely moon des Anglais" of which the Marquis de Girardin spoke, when in 1775 he tried to introduce and explain the English word *romantic* to his French compatriots, is also the chiaroscuro of Chartres; it is no accident that the very first reference in *Mont-Saint-Michel and Chartres* is to Wordsworth. Indeed, on the "architectural highway" we have been following with Adams, we must also situate Tintern Abbey as well as Keats' "casement high and triple-arch'd" in the *Eve of St. Agnes,*

> ... diamonded with panes of quaint device
> Innumerable of stains and splendid dyes[99]

Where lovely Madeline kneels in prayer, illuminated in red, rose, purple and gold.

These panes have their pendants, for instance, in the "five long windows" beneath the Chartres southern rose, all ablaze with red, because their makers have "discarded blue in order to crush us under the earthly majesty of red."

The dominant color-note of "Gothic" literature, red is not only a medium of mystery; it brings a vision of warmth and love into Keats' otherwise cold, lonely interior. In Adams' cathedral, colors

—the effulgent hues of the Romantics' rainbow—play the same part. They restore the Virgin's presence in a sanctuary where, according to Adams, she could otherwise no longer dwell. This is why the splendor of polychrome effects is much more important than the actual designs. Adams recounts but a few legends; he mostly concerns himself with the sensuous wealth of the color schemes, whether it be in the Tree of Jesse, or in the lancets, or in the roses. This is also a typical romantic attitude. In all the many descriptions of medieval windows in English romantic literature, there is, we are told, one common factor: "The poets are not interested in the pictorial values; to them painted windows merely represent impressions of colored light . . . The mediaeval window, once designed to present a story in the language of religious symbolism or armorial emblems, now turns into a medium of impressionism."[100] This truly characterizes Adams' response to medieval glass, particularly if we consider that when he is attracted by the stories told in some windows, these stories are never "in the language of religious symbolism"; behind the legends and behind the colors, there is, as in the apse, "a woman's presence," synonymous in his impressionistic construct of "the fun of life." The truth of which we must by now be aware is that Adams turned the windows of Chartres—and not only them but indeed all the architecture of Chartres and all of *Mont-Saint-Michel and Chartres* itself into a "medium of impressionism." This is, as he said, what "one must be content to feel," even if one cannot properly, at least in such a study, "let the rest go."[101]

6

"La Cathédrale Litteraire"

A LESSON IN FEELINGS

"The best essay"

Four chapters out of sixteen, or, if one prefers Max Baym's "conservative estimate," 27 percent of *Mont-Saint-Michel and Chartres,* deals with French medieval literature, an impressive proportion in what purports to be the tale of an architectural journey. Of course these hundred pages or so can hardly be expected to cover all the aspects of a field described by their author as *enormous,* but their very number justifies our assumption that this is a journey with a distinct literary coloring.[1] Besides, their originality is certain. In the words of F. B. Luquiens, professor of Romance languages at Yale University, who came across the book in "June of 1910 . . . in the Yale Library": "It seemed to me that its chapters on mediaeval literature constituted the best essay I had ever read on the subject or ever could read for that matter." Luquiens' enthusiasm is warranted by what we know of the American context in which these chapters were read.[2]

Adams was no lone pioneer when he began to study Old French, in that summer of 1897. As had been noted in the review *Romania*, some twelve years earlier: "The Romance languages are now the object of scientific study at universities in the United States. Serious courses on the Romance languages and literatures during the Middle Ages are assured of an audience. The universities of the United States have advanced a good deal further in these studies than have their elder sisters in England."[3] With the appointment, it so happened, in 1884, of A. S. Sheldon as professor of Romance philology, Old French, which had not been taught at Harvard since Lowell's departure in 1877, had come there into its own. This was in conformity with a general tendency. At the origin of this academic interest may be traced the influence of a former Harvard student, Aaron Marshall Elliott, now the mainstay of a department of Romance languages at Johns Hopkins University which was destined, George B. Watts notes in his history of "The Teaching of French in the United States," to serve as "a model of scholarship for many an American University."[4] After graduating from Harvard in 1869, Elliott had attended lectures in Paris at the Collège de France and Ecole des Hautes Etudes (1868–1871), then proceeded to Florence (1871–1872) and Madrid (1872), before finally putting in three more years of studies at the Universities of Munich, Tübingen, and Vienna. During his first two years at Johns Hopkins, his classes were "only" in Italian, Spanish, and Persian. In 1878, however, he started giving courses in Old French and Provençal as well; by the time another scholar, H. A. Todd, fresh from a circuit of romance studies in Paris, Berlin, and Madrid, joined the staff in 1883, French medieval literature had become a subject of exhaustive attention.

The year 1883 was also marked with the founding of the Modern Language Association. Elliott, who had played a leading part in its formation, was elected its first secretary, thus gaining a position in which he could give an even greater impetus to the study of romance philology in the United States. It was therefore fitting that in his address delivered before the seventh annual convention of the association, held at Cambridge in December 1889, James Russell Lowell should dwell on the outstanding progress made in this particular field: "Old French is now one of the regular courses of instruction and not only is the language taught, but its literature as well. Remembering what I remember, it seems to me a wonderful thing that I should have lived to see a poem in old French edited by a young American scholar."[5]

The young American scholar happened to be H. A. Todd, who, in a 153-page supplement to the last *Proceedings* of the association, had presented a French poem of the twelfth century, *La Naissance du chevalier au cygne*, "published for the first time together with an inedited prose version from the mss. of the National and Arsenal libraries in Paris, with Introduction, notes and vocabulary." Less bulky, but edited with the same painstaking care, several similar contributions were also to find their way over the years into the *Proceedings*. Such publications may well have been prepared in seminars like those initiated by Elliott at Johns Hopkins in 1881 and "which concentrated on an exhaustive analysis of single documents, the students using facsimiles of manuscripts."[6] How striking is the contrast between those seminars and the small "hand-picked" classes in which James Russell Lowell would go ramblingly and charmingly over old French and Italian poems. Germanic seriousness had superseded Harvard dilettantism, but not to the advantage of literature itself.

Indeed, admirable for their patience, seriousness, and learning as scholars of Elliott's school and their disciples were, they seemed hardly equipped for an imaginative reconstruction of the Middle Ages. Not only were all flights of fancy, as might be expected, impossible to them, but it is also a fact that whatever feeling for literature they naturally had must have been dulled by their very love of sheer erudition. At least this is the feeling one gathers from such articles in the *P.M.L.A.* as J. H. Hanford's "Mediaeval Debate between Wine and Water" (1913), or, in the same volume, "Personal Relationship in Mediaeval France," by William H. Sitwell, author of *Old French Titles of Respect in Direct Address* (Baltimore, 1908).

The first general study of early French literature done by an American was to appear in 1920 only; it is but a section in Barrett Wendell's *Tradition of European Literature,* an immense survey "from Homer to Dante," and the author, emeritus professor of English at Harvard, and one of J. R. Lowell's former students, renders so willingly and glowingly homage to *Mont-Saint-Michel and Chartres,* quotes it so often that, in fact, his medieval chapters look not deceptively like a reflection of Adams'. The work of an enlightened amateur, yet covering a much larger area than any scholarly study done not only at the time but for many years to come,[7] Adams' chapters thus enjoy a unique position in American literature. Indeed, they are akin to one work only, Walter Pater's essay "On Two Early French Tales," but it is doubtful whether Adams ever read this particular piece, and no direct influence can be traced. At any rate, unlike all other contemporary American medievalists, and quite in Walter Pater's manner, Adams proved the perfect essayist. F. B. Luquiens' judgment after reading *Mont-Saint-Michel and Chartres* still holds true today.

Samuel Johnson's definition of the essay, "an irregular undigested piece," provides a convenient starting point for a broad analysis of these chapters before we go over them in detail. For the first question concerns the value of Adams' scholarship: was it really digested? It is now quite apparent that whatever knowledge he had of his subject was acquired in a dilettantish fashion; even more than in the domain of architecture, he had to depend on the notions he could garner by himself, nearly haphazardly, from his own library. As an appendix to *The French Education of Henry Adams,* we have a catalogue of the "philological items" owned by the author and now entrusted to the Massachusetts Historical Society; "most of them," according to Max Baym, "contain his scorings."[8] Hunting for these scorings, for there are hardly any annotations, is a disappointing experience, since nearly all volumes are virgin; a few pages even remain uncut. One may, for a contrast, turn to James Russell Lowell's own Old French collection in the Harvard Library. The student having recourse to these books, Horace E. Scudder observes, "is constantly reminded of the care with which Lowell read them, pencil or pen in hand going over the text as if it were proof-sheets requiring revision and jotting down, now textual criticism, now ingenious comparisons with words and phrases in other languages. Sometimes he had two texts by him and revised one by the other; sometimes his better knowledge or his mother wit enabled him to supply emendations to some careless editor's work."[9] Nothing of the kind could be expected from Adams.

A good instance is the *Chanson de Roland;* his only copy was Léon Gautier's "Critical text with a new translation and an historic introduction," which, the year of its appearance, 1872, had been highly praised in the *North American Review.* Such an enormous amount of scholarly labor had since been expended in France and in Germany on the *Chanson* that at the turn of the century, Gautier's work, though at its twenty-fifth edition, looked somewhat antiquated. Among newer works were notably Léon Clédat's *Nouvelle édition classique* (1887), Gaston Paris' *Extraits* (1887) and Edmund Stengel's *Kritische Ausgabe* (1900). Adams consulted none of them and, just as it was given in his copy, he faithfully transcribed the third line of the poem: "conquist la tere tresque en la mer altaigne," whereas the correct reading adopted by Gautier himself in later editions appears to be: "tresque en la mer conquist la tere altaigne."

This feeling of trust in a text—such as it offered itself to his eyes—is even more manifest in the other chapters. There, his chief source was Karl Bartsch's *Chrestomathie,* a time-hallowed anthology which, as early as 1872, Lowell was using in his classes at Harvard. Adams made it, as it were, his holy book, even giving at times, though not on all occasions, chapter and verse for some quotation, that is, mentioning which edition (the contents somewhat vary from one to the other) he had been using. Little inclined, not to say hardly qualified, to do any personal research work in such an arduous field, he was only too willing to trust scholars whose prominence seemed to him undisputed.

As he thoroughly depended on Bartsch, not only for a number of his texts but for their very form, their spelling, and even the acceptance of some words, he likewise turned for literary judgments on the authors, to Gaston Paris, "the highest academic authority in the world," whose *Littérature française au Moyen Age* (1888) he had read carefully, scoring many passages. He borrowed liberally from it, bringing in a whole paragraph, for instance, with as little an excuse as "Gaston Paris has something to say which is worth quoting." For it serves here the same function which Viollet-le-Duc's *Dictionnaire* has for the chapters on architecture. Relying on such authorities, Adams dispensed with all encumbering scholarly apparatus. As he said of *Aucassin et*

Nicolette: "Indeed few poems, old or new, have, in the last few years, been more reprinted, translated and discussed . . . yet the discussion lacks interest to the idle tourist and tells him little."[10] Thus he could concentrate on what really interested him and which was literature itself, or rather whichever part of it suited his purpose.

"Even a summer tourist," Adams held, "may without offence visit his churches" (and why not his literature?) "in the order that suits him best." Should we find his "essays" therefore "irregular," or to quote Samuel Johnson again, "loose sallies of the mind"? Loose, to an admitted extent, all essays are, since their essence lies in the liberty with which a writer, starting from any standpoint of his choice, may in a wholly personal way treat only of such aspects of a subject as please his fancy; yet this liberty does not necessarily imply a desultory pace. A good example is Walter Pater's essay "On Two Early French Tales," whose similarity with Adams' work has already been noted. At the heart of medieval literature Pater chooses to see a certain element of sweetness, of "early passion" savoring already of the Spirit of the Renaissance, and it is this element which he pursues consistently through the tragedy of Aucassin and Nicolette. In the same manner Adams adheres to a single theme: "It is the art we have been chasing through the French forest, like Aucassins hunting for Nicolette, and the art always leads to the woman."[11] At least it does so in the three chapters where three faces of eternal Eve are revealed, while in the other, which is wedged into the description of Mont-Saint-Michel, the very absence of the woman in eleventh-century literature is represented as a chief motive.

One of Samuel Johnson's terms proves particularly apposite here, since these chapters really *sally* from two points which are localized. The *Chansons de geste* first of all appear in their connection with the Mount; the north portal at Chartres also proves to be a direct gate to Queen Blanche's and Queen Aliénor's literary courts, where poetry is seen entwined round a royal family tree. Then Adams' interest centers on a group of heroines of fiction before finally shifting to the Virgin herself, as she is painted in the tale of her miracles. Though he is here pushing on to literary domains which lie rather apart, no sense of sequence is lost, since he always follows the same direction. Indeed, it is, one feels, as journeys into a picturesque world of belles lettres that such essays were essentially devised, not as learned disquisitions. How otherwise could the reader, like a leisurely traveler delighting in the landscape, so thoroughly enjoy medieval literature?

One must be grateful to Adams, as F. B. Luquiens was, "for his general appreciation of the value of that literature as literature, a value which has been but dimly perceived, strange to say, by specialists in the field of romance scholarship." For him poems were living, companionable entities and not dead bodies one could dissect. "There seems to be a tendency of late," complained James Russel Lowell in his address to the Modern Language Association convention in 1889, "to value literature and even poetry for their usefulness as exercises to put and keep the mental muscles in training . . . To give pleasure merely is one, and not the lowest function of whatever deserves to be called literature. . . . In my weaker moments, I revert . . . to the old notion of literature as a holiday."[12]

Thus, far more than he anticipated a modern school of criticism, Adams himself reverted to his old master's formula. Considering "literature as a holiday" was all the easier for him since his excursion through medieval literature did happen, as we know, to originate with a summer amusement when, in the midst of birthday parties, he set about giving the finishing touch to the "Hooper girls' " education. Like all amusements, he took it seriously. There is something sedate, or if one prefers, gently pedagogic, in this way of rambling from one point of delight to another, according to a prearranged itinerary. In his treatment of literature, Adams' method remains the same as when he deals with architecture; it came naturally to him, for this was a technique to which he also had recourse in his earlier historical works. He recommended it to Sarah Hewitt in January 1904: "Your task is only to give a running commentary on the documents in order to explain their relation."[13] Here also he selected samples, arranged them, introduced them with a minimum of pertinent data, and then let them breathe with their own life. He showed himself at his best with the *Chanson de Roland*.

"The prayer is granite"

"The second chapter of Adams' book discusses the Song of Roland so compactly and yet so fully that whoever would approach the story may best do so there," Barrett Wendell states;[14] and, at least for an original approach to the *Chanson de Roland,* it is true that Adams remains unequaled. Rather abruptly we start from a quotation of the first twenty lines of the *Roman du Mont-Saint-Michel.* Their author, William of Saint-Pair, though said to "come in here out of place," is in fact, by way of his own introduction, given credentials to serve for an instant as a master of ceremonies; these ceremonies are the annual pilgrimage to the abbey, of which we now read "his pretty description." For "to feel the art of Mont-Saint-Michel and Chartres," and of the *Chanson de Roland* as well, "we have got to become pilgrims again." To our help, so that we may take part in a pilgrimage "as historically exact as the battle of Hastings, and as artistically true as the abbey church," above all, as interesting as possible, there also comes Wace with two passages from his *Roman de Rou,* bringing in the two most fascinating pilgrims whose company we might have wished to have, William the Norman and Harold the Saxon. They are presented together on their way to Brittany and also later, pitted against each other at Hastings, where, according to the poet Taillefer, the brave *jongleur* rode, singing "de Karlemaigne et de Rollant" at the head of the Duke's warriors.

"All this preamble" leads only to unite the "Chanson with the architecture of the Mount by means of Duke William and his Breton campaign of 1058." The two men are visualized stopping together at the Mount and dining with the abbot in the old refectory. At a nod from his duke, Taillefer rises and sings of Roland's high deeds and noble death: "One must imagine the voice and the acting. Doubtless Taillefer acted each motive . . . the verse gave room for great acting . . ." Thus it is a regular dramatic representation of the Chanson, or at least of its most pathetic passages, that we are privileged to watch. No doubt, like William's barons, Adams, when the climax approached, saw "the scene itself"; for him the Chanson was intensely vivid and stirring, and this is how he wanted his own companions to *see* and *experience* it.[15]

Such an approach is unorthodox—not to say highly artificial —but no more engaging way could have been devised to make the reader immediately aware of the life with which the *Chanson* is instinct. Resolutely brushing aside the dusty volumes of "Roland scholarship"—already a formidable array[16]—Adams invites us to take the poem at its face value, that is, as a very part of medieval life. We must plunge not only into the *Chanson* but into the Middle Ages themselves. This is why, before entering the abbey, we were bidden to grow eight centuries old and thus "learn to feel" what this mass of architecture meant to its builders: "The poem and the church are akin; they go together and explain each other." Only a poet not a scholar can perceive such kinship. In the introduction to his rhymed translation of the *Chanson,* Maurice Bouchor draws a simile which might serve here as a motto: "For a comparison with the *Song of Roland* I should certainly not turn to ogival art, least of all to the florid or flamboyant period of that style, with its stone lacework, vertiginous spires and walls of polychrome stone. The old poem rather suggests a Romanesque church, set solidly on the ground, sparely decorated, severe and chaste, with a grandeur that does not exclude sombre elegance, and strongly affecting through its very simplicity." It is this simplicity which also stirs Adams: "The Chanson in the refectory actually reflected, repeated, echoed the piers and arches of the Abbey Church just rising above. The verse is built up. The qualities of the architecture reproduce themselves in the song; the same directness, simplicity, absence of self-consciousness; the same intensity of purpose; even the same material; the prayer is granite."[17] There is no place for love or dalliance in the poem; Alda, Roland's betrothed, the only Christian woman who is so much as mentioned, appears at the very end, in one stanza which "looks exceedingly like a later insertion." Even in a most moving passage, quoted at length, where Oliver, blinded by wounds, strikes Roland unawares and is not rebuked, "the sentiment is monosyllabic and curt." Little is made here of Roland's and Oliver's emotional ties, on which critics like to dwell. The two friends are merely said to display "the singular courtesy of knighthood and dignity of soldiers." Probably feeling what has recently been demonstrated by G. F. Jones, namely, that even in such a pathetic passage the passion of honor—and not friendship—remains paramount for Roland, Adams chose to go no further in his comments.[18]

Concluding a review in 1958 of Alfred Junker's new *Roland* bibliography, F. Whitehead deplored that "the most important problem—that of the relation between the *Roland* and the cultural and ideological background—is receiving the least attention."[19] This relation Adams perceives clearly. No poem "has ever expressed with anything like the same completeness the society that produced it," he asserts, anticipating Edmond Faral's statement that it is perhaps the most impressive depiction we possess of the "physionomie morale" of the century in which it appeared. Steeped in the most vital notions of a feudal society—sentiments of patriotism, honor, and duty—it is the quintessence of the eleventh century.[20] Such a view would probably pass nowadays as obvious, but for the scholars who linked the *Chanson* to a remote and more or less Germanic past, its evidence was less compelling. Even as fine a critic as Gaston Paris admitted having to make efforts not to find the coming of the Archangel Gabriel to Roland at the moment of his death "surtout bizarre." Served in good stead by his teaching experience at Harvard, Adams knew enough of the moral climate of the age to understand the meaning of this passage: "The naiveté of the poetry is that of the society. God the father was the feudal seigneur . . . To this seigneur, Roland in dying, preferred (puroffrit) his right-hand gauntlet. Death was an act of homage. God sent down his archangel Gabriel as his representative to accept the homage and accept the glove. To Duke William and his barons nothing could seem more natural and correct. God was not farther away than Charlemagne."[21]

Adams' originality, however, lies less in the instinct he thus reveals for the historical truth, or even the "local color" of the details, than in his feeling for the language in which they are told. Contrary to Gaston Paris, who deplores the lack of brilliancy of the form, he admires "the simplicity of the verse" which repeats "the naiveté of the thought." There entered more than a poet's license in his comparison of the material of the *Chanson* with the granite of the abbey. Really matching the solid stones, the words are clear like pebbles lifted from a brook, endowed with a visual quality.[22] And they fit perfectly: "Not a syllable is lost, and always the strongest syllable is chosen." It would be impossible, Adams says, to recover all the music of these lines, since "our age has lost so much of its ear for poetry; but any one who will take the trouble to catch the metre . . . can follow the feeling of the poetry as well as though it were a Greek hexameter. He will feel the simple force of the words. It is the grand style—the eleventh century." One has but to think here of F. Brunetière's remarks of the *étrange cacophonie* of the *Chanson:* "Unequalled for shambling monotony, these ill-paired leashes, these assonanced couplets jerk along, the consonants strike and clash together sounding like bad German, and the very number of lines seems to have been determined simply by the length of time the minstrel's breath lasted."[23]

How much more perceptive the foreign amateur was! Standing apart from the other chapters on medieval literature Adams' "essay" on the *Chanson* proves exceptional in other ways; it was the one which could most easily and most glowingly be commended by specialists in the field, because of this very sympathy with the subject. Loudest in his approval, F. B. Luquiens thanked Adams for pointing out "what all the German and Germanic scholars who had been studying the 'Roland' for fifty years had failed to see, and what is worse had prevented others from seeing: that the Song is beautiful in exactly the same way that the Abbey of Mont-Saint-Michel is beautiful; that it possesses the beauty of *sheer structure* and possesses it to a greater extent than any other poem written before or since."[24] The partisan tone of this judgment calls for an explanation. If the controversy about the origin of the poem had more or less subsided, vital differences of opinion remained concerning the text itself. Editors had to opt for one or the other of two radically different positions. Either they swore allegiance to the Oxford "original" version discovered in 1832, and which was still proclaimed by Bédier to be the best, or, placing criticism purely on the basis of linguistics, they drew upon all versions so as to patch up a text consonant with their scientific philological tenets. It was against such "monstrous" architecture, as exemplified by Edmund Stengel's edition, that Luquiens revolted in 1909. Appealing throughout, in his "reconstruction of the original *Chanson de Roland*," to aesthetic considerations, he insisted on the "wonderful structure" revealed by the author of the Oxford version, whose "outstanding technical excellence" should serve for a key to all the textual problems of the *Chanson*. That on this technical issue Luquiens should have considered Adams, if not as a forerunner, at least as a ready ally, may at first appear rather surprising. Not only had Adams shown very little concern for which or whose version he was using but in his own analysis of the Song, far from bringing out, as Luquiens did, "the perfect unity, coherence and emphasis of the poem," he had not gone any further than Roland's death, thus omitting the very episodes (Charlemagne's campaign against Baligant, Ganelon's trial) usually held as adventitious. It nevertheless was a fact that in his appreciation of the *Chanson*, he anticipated F. B. Luquiens, for to both men the poem was first and foremost a work of art standing on its own account and which had to be judged from an aesthetic point of view. Such an attitude of utter sympathy with the text and the spirit breathing through it does not, one may add, fundamentally differ from the attitude urged on the reader today by Menéndez Pidal: "It is for us to approach this age and place ourselves in sympathy with the feeling proper to this art form, without making the anachronistic claim that men at this time experienced poetry with feelings similar to our own."[25] In this necessary effort of adjustment, Adams succeeded quite well—at least as far as the *Chanson* was concerned. Unconventional as his treatment might be, he truly recaptured the spirit of the age. For what reason would he prove less equal to his task in the other "essays"?

THE PROPER STUDY OF MANKIND

The elusive pursuit of "courteous love"

The twelfth and thirteenth centuries were a period of great literary creation; following the robustly masculine epics, many works of a variegated inspiration were produced—allegorical poems, narrative romances in verse, religious dramas—a rich literature whose main characteristic appears to be the increasing part that the woman came to play in it. It is possible to link, as Adams does, this emergence of the literary heroine with the worship of the Virgin, then at its highest emotional peak. At any rate, there is an historical concordance, justifying Adams' inclusion of new chapters of literature after a tour of the Virgin's sanctuary at Chartres: "The great period of Gothic architecture begins with the coming of Eleanor (1137), and ends with the passing of Blanche (1252)." Together with Countess Mary of Champagne, who was "certainly a queen in social influence,"[26] Queens Eleanor and Blanche form the glorious trinity dominating Adams' chapter xi, wherein he deals with *courtois* poetry.

The literary prominence these three women are given is in no wise fanciful. In the introduction of *Troubadours et cours d'amour*, Jacques Lafitte-Houssat makes the point perfectly clear:

Of the four or five centuries that make up the Middle Ages we will only consider the greatest of all, the twelfth, and we will further confine our attention to the second half of this century, as we consider that courtliness then reached its apogee. Before 1150 refined manners or courtly behavior had not yet found favor. In the thirteenth century courtly love, like the chivalry to which it is related, became ridiculous by degenerating into that kind of knight-errantry which was to be caricatured in *Don Quixote*.

Our study is therefore limited approximately to the reign of Louis VII, called the Younger. It is relevant to recall here that Louis VII had married Aliénor or Eléonore, only daughter of the Duke of Aquitaine, the greatest lord in the South of France . . . Aliénor brought with her . . . a taste for poetry that had developed from contact with the troubadours in the south of France. Further, Queen Aliénor had two daughters, one of whom, Marie, was later to marry the powerful Count of Champagne. The Queen of France and the Countess of Champagne are two famous names that we will come across time and again.[27]

And Queen Blanche, let us not forget, was Aliénor's granddaughter. Accordingly, the whole chapter is going to be built round Aliénor, or Eleanor, as Adams prefers to call her. The first part, where she already repeatedly appears, leads up to her portrait, and from this portrait stems the second half of the chapter, since nearly all the poets mentioned there have a connection of a sort with her, either directly or through some descendant. Moreover, in the following chapter, she will still be part of the structure. For the author of *Aucassin et Nicolette* was perhaps a companion of her crusading son, Coeur de Lion, and "passed the rest of his life singing to the old queen"; at least, "we can take the liberty of supposing so." And Adam de la Halle wrote *Marion* for Robert de Artois, one of Queen Blanche's nephews.[28] This kind of link—especially when it becomes so tenuous—leaves a greater impression of artifice than the introduction to the *Chanson* through the abbey on Mont-Saint-Michel. Indeed, laboring with what he calls himself, a "paradox" instead of resting secure on the rock of the Mount, Adams appears here less at ease than in any other part of the book.

"The proper study of mankind is woman, and by common agreement since the time of Adam it is the most complex and the most arduous." The reader is thus warned, in the very first paragraph of "The Three Queens" that the study of "feminine" literature will present almost insuperable difficulties. That Adams in fact refuses to grapple with these difficulties is made obvious by the syllogistic development which immediately follows. It is introduced by a paragraph-long quotation, which, although it is still too lengthy to be reproduced here, is exceedingly truncated, representing several pages from Garreau's *Etat social de la France au temps des croisades*. Advancing the thesis that the women were "distinctly superior" in the age of Queens Aliénor and Blanche, whose names have been brought together by means of this ruthless cutting, it merely serves as a premise which Adams undertakes to support with a double argument, historical and literary. First it is a fact, he states, that Duchess Mathilda "got more than even" with her husband, William the Conqueror, even though the latter in a fit of exasperation "dragged her by the hair tied to his horse's tail as far as the suburb of Vaucelles." Saint Louis stood in still greater awe of his mother to the extent of hiding away from her behind a bed. And if such strong-willed ladies seem rather too exceptional to prove a rule, literature demonstrates, Adams insists, that it was then a custom for all wives to consider their husbands as nincompoops. Hence it apparently follows that all French women were great; and "Eleanor d'Aquitaine was the greatest of all," great not only because of the numberless legends that grew about her but also owing to her progeny of two French daughters and eight English children. "The relations thus created proves fantastic." All this leading to the final remark: "We are concerned with the artistic and social side of life and have only to notice the coincidence that, while the Virgin was miraculously using the power of spiritual love to elevate and purify the people, Eleanor and her daughter were using the power of earthly love to discipline and refine the courts."[29] Nothing indeed has been proved by this syllogistic approach, which only tends to make *courtoisie* appear as a special, well-nigh miraculous dispensation of an extraordinary, fascinating family.

Although *courtois* poetry flourished almost by definition in princely courts, it never was, never could have been, a mere off-shoot, so to speak, of a royal family tree. It is somewhat surprising for an historian to so flatly ignore the sociological and economical background which made the flowering of *courtoisie* possible. Nowhere does Adams allude to the transformations brought about by the Truce of God, now nearly permanently observed in the provinces of France, nor the economic impetus given by the crusades. Neither does he stress how powerful the civilizing influence of the South was on Aliénor's France—from there came a very heightened sense of luxury, which only a prosperous society could have invented, or at least imported. Edmond Faral gives a good account of its development:

From the end of the eleventh century material prosperity accompanied by a new culture had brought about the devel'opment in courts of a social life in which luxury, festivals, and the play of mind naturally required the participation of women. It appears that the practice originated in the south of France and spread northward through allied military expeditions and matrimonial alliances. Women then assumed a place in society that progressively rose in status and was increasingly better defended. Men realized instinctively that women could no longer be won simply by the law of the stronger. Inventing a fiction that was to be in fashion for more than a century, they represented their chosen lady as a feudal suzerain whose favors they aspired to win through obedience, through faithful and ardent service as liege-men. The concept, the feeling that will be called courtly love is born . . . it is a new mysticism, exalting the soul that out of love for a lady dreams only of attaining the perfections of chivalric virtue and purity of heart, the means whereby the lover will merit his reward. And thus at the same time women assume the role of judge.[30]

This seems a clear and logical explanation. But Adams preferred to approach his subject in a rather "complex and arduous" way. Accordingly the woman is pictured as an impenetrable goddess:

"We do not and never can know the twelfth-century woman, or for that matter any other woman, but we do know the literature she created." And through this literature we are invited to try as best as we can to unravel part of her mystery.[31]

"Mary of Champagne created the literature of courteous love." We shall quarrel no more with Adams for his way of bringing in the subject. The countess is here by her own right, as the patroness of Chrétien de Troyes, whose work will serve for an introduction to the study of this literature. Little is known of the poet's life, except that he spent many years at Marie de Champagne's court, a small refined circle, devoted to the arts, and that there he received, in Adams' words, "the subject of Lancelot with the request or order to make it a lesson of 'courteous love,' which he obeyed." In lines 26–27 of *Lancelot* or *Le Chevalier à la charrette* (for it is one and the same poem), Chrétien freely acknowledged this debt; to the countess he owed *matière et san*, that is, not only the plot, but the meaning, the psychological and moral *frame* of the *roman*. The actual extent of such a collaboration between the hired poet and his dame is impossible to determine, but one fact is certain; he grew so surfeited with his work that he could not bring it to completion. Since another poet, Godefroy de Lagny, did the work, one cannot really maintain, as Adams does, that "Lancelot was never finished." Later on, we are told, "Christian wrote a Perceval, or conte du Graal which must have been intended to please Mary." It could not have been so, for the poet was then no longer in Champagne, but at the court of Philippe d'Alsace, count of Flanders. As stated in Gaston Paris' *Manuel* (p. 99) it was under this new patronage that Chrétien de Troyes undertook his last and most celebrated work. Death caught him before he could finish it, about 1185, some ten years later than the date mentioned in *Mont-Saint-Michel and Chartres*, but such minor inaccuracies are immaterial, since at any rate we get but a nodding acquaintance with the man himself. From Gaston Paris' *Manuel*, which he mentions twice, Adams does not really draw details, but a mere pretext for stylistic variations:

Son grand mérite est dans la forme. Il passa sans conteste aux	The quality of this verse is something like the quality of the

yeux de son époque et de celle qui suivit pour le meilleur poète français; "Il prenait" dit un auteur du XIIè siècle "le beau français à pleines mains, et n'a laissé après lui qu'à glaner." Ses oeuvres nous offrent en effet le meilleur spécimen de l'excellente langue du XIIè siècle. Quant au style il a souvent les défauts habituels au moyen âge, la banalité, la monotonie, la minutie, l'absence de souffle, d'éclat et d'ampleur; mais on y trouve une grande délicatesse d'expression, une grâce simple, et ça et là un véritable sentiment (pp. 95–96).

glass window—conventional decoration; colors in conventional harmonies, refinement, restraint and feminine delicacy of taste. Christian has not the grand manner of the XIth century.

His is poet-laureate's work, says Gaston Paris; the flower of a twelfth century court and of twelfth century French; the best example of an admirable language; but not lyric; neither strong nor deep, nor deeply felt. What we call tragedy is unknown to it. Christian's world is sky-blue and rose, with only enough red to give it warmth, and so flooded with light that even its mysteries count only by the clearness with which they are shown.[32]

There is, one must admit, only a faint resemblance between the alleged original and this gossamer of words into which Adams manages to weave some of his most familiar themes. Apparently he takes very little real interest in *matière et san;* the rest of his comments will confirm that impression.

Indeed, not the least allusion to the Celtic or Arthurian elements of this poetry will be found in the few paragraphs devoted to Chrétien de Troyes. Yet no medieval subject, as Professor Holmes remarks, has since aroused more interest among American scholars. It was, it seems, through Marie de Champagne herself that the poet had become acquainted with the *matière de Bretagne;* casting aside the national, bellicose element so important in old Celtic tales, he chose to retell in his own French way the adventures of some personages, using these episodes to air, at the Countess' suggestion, the theories of love then in fashion at her court. Thus, enchanted gardens, fairies, wonders of all kinds, became rather incongruously united with the dialectic subtleties of *courtoisie*. The poet and his audience, who only sought amusement, never bethought themselves of conjecturing in such pleasant marvels the remnants of some obscure mythology. As a modern critic warns us: "We must so bear ourselves in the company of these twelfth-century people as not to spoil with our Arthurian problems their Arthurian entertainment. For them as for us . . . the Grail story was something of a problem, but keeping its mystery, it remained charming in its form, evocative and stimulating in its symbolism. It never was, in the Middle Ages, ground up with the grit of erudition."[33] Neither is it so with Adams—and for one good reason: he starkly disregards the subject. To his eyes the *Chevalier à la charrette* is "unintelligible" as well as "tiresome"; and if he finds any interest in *Perceval,* it is not on account of its "symbolism" but for its "practical" side. As a matter of fact, like all the poet's romances, this work remains permeated with the life of twelfth-century France; the feasts, tournaments described as taking place in mysterious castles are for a good part made of truth. Adams is right when he points out how essential this concrete, vivid quality is in Chrétien de Troyes' work. With him, we partake of Perceval's "solid meal in the style of the twelfth century," as we did of the imaginary supper with William and his retinue at Mont-Saint-Michel. It is significant that the one trait selected and offered to our admiration should be the factual "simplicity" of the narration, a simplicity not unlike that of the *Chanson de Roland.* Though a knight of romance, Perceval is earth-bound: "He slept the sound and healthy sleep of youth, and when he woke the next morning, he felt only a mild surprise to find that his host and household had disappeared, leaving him to ride away without farewell, breakfast or Graal."[34] One could not better turn one's back to all form of mystery, including the mystery of love in its *courtois* avatar, or in any other guise.

Strange to say, no more than Chrétien de Troyes in all the quoted excerpts, can the next two poets presented as exemplars of "courteous" literature be taken to sing of love, even in a mock way. Richard Coeur de Lion certainly does not do so in his "Prison Song." Few poems seem to have been more precious to Adams. In the first edition of his book, he quoted its last lines:

> Countess sister! your supreme renown
> May he save and guard to whom I appeal

And for whom I am captive.
I do not speak of her of Chartres
Mother of Louis.

Lovingly, in 1912, he came back to the poem, bettering its translation, and adding all the other stanzas. It did not even then occur
to him that he could also improve on his first comment, which
was glaringly irrelevant. Nothing indeed could be farther from
"a true cry of the heart" than this graceful, accomplished piece
with which the royal prisoner whiles away the tedium of the jail,
complaining of friends who allow him to remain so long unran-
somed, while the King of France ravages his lands. Twelfth-century poets, whether princes or commoners, were far less intent,
Jean Frappier notes, on creating a subjective poetry than on con-
forming to certain well-defined patterns. Chief among their ideals
was "a refined and learned technique, a preoccupation with perfect form," all of these exemplified in Richard's particularly clever
song. No doubt it was this royal skill which impressed Adams, to
the point of making him try to emulate it in English. Much more
than his heart was moved; his wits were challenged, and with
Thibaut de Champagne his reaction was the same.[35]

At first sight, however, Adams appears to have been more fascinated by the latter. It is because Thibaut's life provides him with
more material for an imaginative development. Richard may
have proved, as Adams asserts, "a far greater king than any Louis
ever was," and may also have "composed better poetry than any
other king known to tourists." Nearly all the years of his reign,
however, were spent in faraway countries, and besides the prison
song none of his poems has come to us. The grandson of Marie
de Champagne, Count Thibaut IV "was a great prince and great
poet who did in both characters whatever he pleased," and he
too, Adams might have added, became a king in 1234, when he
inherited the kingdom of Navarre. Great as he was, his worldly
affairs did not run as smoothly as his quill. He involved himself
in many difficulties, now among Queen Blanche's enemies, now
on her side; it was even (falsely) rumored that he had an intimate
liaison with her. Adams fastens with eager interest on this alleged
love affair, which he endows with the superior truth of poetry:
"Whatever they were off the stage, they were lovers on it." Their

love, he maintains, was after all "as real and as reasonable as the worship of the Virgin."[36]

Our imagination is severely taxed if we try to follow Adams in his visualizing this man of the world as a "Tristan," the lover *par excellence*. Sixty-nine of Thibaut de Champagne's poems have been preserved; thirty-six are *chansons d'amour*. In nearly all, there runs a vein of lightheartedness and subtle persiflage which seems to prove that their author was never more than half in earnest. Sometimes his banter becomes so irrepressible that Jean Frappier calls him *le pince-sans-rire de l'émotion courtoise* (the tongue-in-cheek poet of courtly love). Though it is quite true that the man "is still alive in his poems," we would not go as far as Adams does in stating that these pieces all "vibrate with life"; Thibaut was too much of a "précieux," a "cérébral," to quiver with emotion except on rare occasions.[37] We may try a few verses to see what he meant by courtesy, but they will be chiefly interesting for what they reveal about Adams.

Supposedly addressed to Queen Blanche, the first lyric offered by Adams to our examination is no. xiii in A. Wallensköld's definitive edition. A glance discloses that Adams purposely left out not only the third and the fifth stanzas, but the *envoi*:

> Chançon, va t'en à Nanteuil sanz faillance!
> Phelipe di que, s'il ne fust de France,
> Trop puet valoir.*

After turning out, no doubt by way of recreation, this piece of elegant trifling, Thibaut dedicates it not to a lady but to his friend Philippe de Nanteuil; and in these lines he reproves him, says Wallensköld, for being "de France," that is, one of the Queen's allies.[38] A very likely reproach, had Thibaut really been Blanche's lover! No wonder Adams preferred to excise the passage. His comments on the deceptive "simplicity" of the poem "so refined and complicated" like "the simplicity of the thirteenth-century glass" are however brilliantly to the point: "The verses are as perfect as the colors and the versification as elaborate." The last adjective is fitting. An aristocratic virtuoso, the poet is

---

* Song, go to Nanteuil without fault!
Tell Philip that, were he not of France,
He could be worth much.

exquisitely toying with some time-approved clichés and conceits. As is normal with this kind of poetry, he will not disclose the name of his dame, but whether he has no liege-lady, or several, matters very little.

"Now see," Adams goes on," how Thibaut kept the same tone of courteous love in addressing the Queen of Heaven."[39] It so happened that, on the eve of his departure for the Holy Land, the King of Navarre did pray very fervently to the *Vierge bienheureuse* that no misfortune might befall him (*mescheoir*) during his journey:

> Douce Dame, roine coronée,
> Priez pour nos, Vierge bone euree!
> Et puis après ne nos puet mescheoir!*

Never was he more sincere and moving than in this poem, but it is not the one that Adams selects. *De grant travail et de petit esploit* (no. lx, in Wallensköld's edition), which we have instead, is one of the pious pieces composed by Thibaut toward the end of his life. A troubadour, Perre Guilhen, then made fun of the old king (he was only fifty, but one aged quickly in those times) who, being no longer able to pay homage to his Dame, could only sing Psalms and Penance. "Ces pièces où Thibaut transpose du profane au sacré les éloges qu'il avait adressés autrefois à sa dame sont plutôt froides et artificielles," Jean Frappier remarks. "L'une (no. lvii) est un commentaire laborieusement laudatif des cinq lettres du nom de Maria; les autres tournent au sermon en vers, mais on a de la difficulté à y relever quelques rares passages d'effusion religieuse."[40] There does not seem to be any "effusion" at all in no. lx, which Adams quotes but in part, and without the slightest attempt at analysis. Of love, whether profane or religious, we still have not heard.

It was only years after writing *Mont-Saint-Michel and Chartres* that Adams learned a fundamental truth: *troubadours* and *trouvères* were musicians as well as poets. They could unweariedly sing the same eternal themes because words counted less than the melody; in the musical composition lay the greater part of

---

* Sweet Lady, Crowned Queen,
  Pray for us, Blessed Virgin!
  That no misfortune may henceforth befall us.

their originality. The alliance of music and twelfth-century poetry was not the only element that had escaped his notice. In "The Three Queens," he fails to recapture the essence of *courtoisie,* though it is a notion supposedly central to the whole chapter. Hence it is that the chapter, though so elaborately constructed, lacks inner balance. In it, Adams twice uses the term *bric-a-brac,* and though it is true that these pages are replete with a medley of literary references ranging from Partenopeus of Blois to Scheherazade and Bluebeard, among such a bric-a-brac love remains an item which, we now realize, will not be found.

Indeed, the fruitlessness of the search is made apparent at the very outset, when Adams refuses to deal with the "cour d'amour" over which Marie de Champagne presided and whose laws were codified by André le Chapelain: "With her theories of courteous love every one is more or less familiar if only from the ridicule of Cervantes and the follies of Quixote, who though four hundred years younger, was Lancelot's child, but we never can know how far she took herself and her laws of love seriously, and to speculate on so deep a subject as her seriousness is worse than useless since she would herself have been as uncertain as her lovers were." Such a flippant way of dismissing the subject reveals how little stock he actually takes in the literature of love "created" by the countess. Of Chrétien de Troyes we have seen him praising the "practical side" to the exclusion of all others. Yet Adams can also assert in the same chapter: "If the Middle Ages had only reflected what was practical, nothing would have survived for us."[41] What prompts this contradictory remark is an extended comparison between Blanche's alleged love affair with Thibaut de Champagne and Tristan's story.

Few heroes of romance have suffered harsher treatment than Tristan now does in Adams' hands. Originally a caveman armed with "bow and stone knife," and who "never saw a horse or a spear," Tristan even when decently accoutered by French poets will always remain, we are told, "a comparatively poor figure," overshadowed by a domineering Isolde. In proof thereof we are offered ten lines from *La Folie Tristan* (Oxford version) written by an Anglo-Saxon poet at the close of the twelfth century. A single episode narrating how, one day, during his exile, Tristan, disguised as a madman, gains access to his paramour, this *Folie* appears as a distinctly minor piece. Adams, who does not even give his source, nevertheless turns to it as if it were the only extant version. The one author he cares to mention is Chrétien de Troyes, whose *Tristan* is lost, a loss, he exclaims, which "makes a terrible gap in art, for Christian's poem would have given the first and best idea of what led to courteous love." Once more the overemphasis of the tone is revealing. It is obvious that Adams is not attracted by the legend under whatever form. Significantly Barrett Wendell will have the same attitude, refusing like him to enter its "world of passion and mystery." The theme of the inevitability of love and its victory over fate held perhaps little "charm" for a New England mind. We may also think that, for very deep-seated personal reasons, Adams revolted against its poetic fallacy, since Tristan and Iseult dying epitomize the sublimity of reunion which even in death transcends the tragedy of separation. At any rate he speaks of the lover's adventure—and of love in general—in strangely inadequate terms: "Perhaps the passion of love was more serious than that of religion. Love was certainly a passion; and even more certainly it was . . . complicated beyond modern conception." So complicated was it indeed that Adams seems to have thought that even speculating on it would be "worse than useless."[42]

"The Woman's Greater Intelligence"

The pursuit of *courtois* love has proved disappointing, because there was nothing to be chased. Far from being what Shakespeare in *Venus and Adonis* calls "a spirit all compact of fire," love, if we believe Adams, is in reality but a form of the woman's dictatorship over the witless male; this is how it clearly reveals itself in "Nicolette and Marion." The difference of title—as compared with the preceding chapter—is revealing. No longer are we to be interested in "personalities," whether of poets or of their patronesses; characters of romances, or rather heroines, come to the fore and will engross our attention.

Of "the woman's greater intelligence," we are given proof, and it is always not only at the expense of man but, so it appears, with Adams' connivance. The theme was already illustrated in

"The Three Queens" by means of two works which did not pertain to *courtois* literature, "La Belle Jehanne," a thirteenth-century short story, and "Le Mistère d'Adam," the first "drama" ever written in French. The latter is of particular interest because Adams' handling of the hero already betrays his bias: "Adam, as the Devil truly said, was a dull animal, hardly worth the trouble of deceiving. Adam was disloyal, too, untrue to his wife after being untrue to his Creator . . . The audience accepted this as natural and proper. They recognised the man as, of course, stupid, cowardly and traitorous."[43] The tone is forced, the characterization exaggerated. An English critic will, within a few years, find words much more appropriate: "Adam, upright in principle but somewhat careless and inconsistent, above all timid and the reverse of the heroic, discerns right and wrong readily enough when tempted by Satan, but moral courage forsakes him as soon as he succumbs to the charms of Eve." Even after the Fall, he will appear "much more humane than in the Bible."[44] Adams does not feel the need to bring out this more engaging aspect of the hero's personality; on the contrary, he readily accepts the judgment of the medieval audience, which he seems to extend to all heroes. As a matter of fact, in his interpretation of both *Aucassin et Nicolette* and *Le Jeu de Robin et Marion,* he obviously delights in proving how man is essentially "stupid," or at least, as he says of Aucassin, "not very bright."[45]

One is at a loss how to classify *Aucassin et Nicolette,* since no other work quite like this *chantefable* has come down to us, but it is generally agreed that, as Walter Pater puts it: "The piece was probably intended to be recited by a company of trained performers, many of whom, at least for the lesser parts, were probably children."[46] Hence the life as well as the freshness and naiveté of a tale which captivates Adams; he concerns himself only with the early part of the story, when Aucassin, the son of the Count of Beaucaire, and Nicolette, the converted Saracen slave he is in love with, are both imprisoned in order to be kept apart; Nicolette escapes and he is released, and we can follow him in his search for his paramour. A very sweet figure, "so stamped is she with nobility and courtesy and high-breeding and all good qualities," Nicolette is portrayed with glowing sympathy; but it is to Aucassin that Adams nearly all the time directs our attention; the boors the young man meets in the forest "play him as if he were a trout," and how ridiculous he appears in his meeting with the ungainly "villain" who has lost his ox! Adams says, "The little episode was thrown in without rhyme or reason, . . . as though the jongleur were showing his own cleverness and humour at the expense of the hero." Adams' prejudice leads him into error. A more sympathetic critic would feel the rich human value of this episode, where Aucassin's own grief helps him to understand, and even share, the distress of a "brother." Besides, does not the surge of pity which mounts in him carry its own reward, since, almost at once, the poor man's blessing is going to bring him luck? But Adams does not attach much importance to the hero's feelings. His only attempt at an analysis of the scene consists in a quotation from a German editor (Herman Suchier); it is not very profound: "The old poet sings and smiles to his audience as though he wished them to understand that Aucassins, a foolish boy, must not be judged quite seriously." We shall in time deal with Adams' curious way of spelling the name of Aucassin; the immediate interest of the passage is in the word *foolish,* a word all the more worth stressing since the poem has just been presented as "the most exquisite expression of courteous love."[47]

Is it not as though the notions "courteous love" and "foolishness" went together in Adams' mind? The truth is that, scattered amid many traits of sly humour in the description of the hero, there are, as Walter Pater more perceptively remarks, "morsels of a different quality, touches of some intenser sentiment." Aucassin is not dull and slightly spineless, but paralyzed: "It is the very image of the Provençal love god, no longer a child, but grown to pensive youth . . . He rode on through the gates into the open plain beyond. But as he went, that great malady of his love came upon him. The bridle fell from his hands; and like one who sleeps walking, he was carried on into the midst of his enemies, and heard them talking together how they might most conveniently kill him." The scene is not retold in *Mont-Saint-Michel and Chartres,* and if Aucassin's "charming tirade against Paradise," in which he does not care to go without his Nicolette, is duly introduced, it is only followed by pointless generalizations. Aucassin's portrait is not fully sketched, just as not all of his story is told. "There," we are told, after the lovers have met in the forest, "we will leave them, for their further adventures have not much to do with our matter. Like all the romans, or nearly all, 'Aucassins' is singularly pure and refined."[48] Though never really coarse, the burlesque interlude which then takes place in the country of Torrelore where men lie in bed and say they are pregnant while women fight wars in their stead, hurling cheese and baked apples at their opponents, is certainly much less refined than the preceding scenes and looks rather, as Andrew Lang says in the introduction to his own translation, "like a page of Rabelais stitched into the cantefable by mistake."[49] Yet, if we were to believe Adams, not only all of *Aucassin et Nicolette* but practically all of thirteenth-century literature is pervaded with the same punctilious refinement; even works "avowedly bourgeois" like those of Adam de la Halle are stamped throughout with decency.[50] The reader somewhat familiar with *Le Jeu de la feuillée,* and its author's ungallant description of his wife, with and without chemise, is likely to be a little skeptical.

Let us at any rate accept Adams' bringing together of the "Idyll of Beaucaire" with the "Idyll of Arras," or *Jeu de Robin et Marion,* Adam de la Halle's dramatized *pastourelle*: "Robin and Marion were a pendant to Aucassins and Nicolette; Robin was almost a burlesque on Aucassins, while Marion was a Northern, energetic, intelligent, pastoral Nicolette." At the very start, the scales are tipped by the sheer weight of the adjectives. Unlike Aucassin, however, Robin will not need to be made a butt for ridicule, since the "chevalier," who, in the first part, makes advances to the pretty sheperdess, represents a much better target: "Bête the knight certainly was, and was meant to be, in order to give the necessary colour to Marion's charms." Adams dwells at length on this *bêtise,* showing how the man, not very "intellectually brilliant," and with repulsive manners, is mocked by Marion, who prefers her Robin; but he quotes much less of the second part, which he sums up in a rather surprising way:

Adam de la Halle, who felt no great love for chevaliers, was not satisfied with ridiculing them in order to exalt Marion; his second act was devoted to exalting Marion at the expense of her own boors.

The first act was given up to song; the second, to games and dances. The games prove not to be wholly a success; Marion is bored by them, and wants to dance. The dialogue shows Marion trying constantly to control her clowns and make them decent, as Blanche of Castille had been all her life trying to control her princes, and Mary of Chartres her kings.[51]

Conceived as a skit on *courtoisie*, the piece was in fact, Jessie Crosland observes, "obviously cultivated to tickle the fancy of members of the upper classes" with the frolics of earthy, colorful lovers.[52] No doubt the audience little thought of Queen Blanche, nor sensed the innate ridiculousness of man, when, in mirth, they watched Marion pulling a piece of cheese (a real *tarte à la crême* in the play) out of her breast and poking it back:

Dieus! con chis froumages est cras! (1. 150)*

or indulging in such rough embraces with Robin that the latter bites her cheek:

Je cuidai tenir un fromage,
Si te senti je tenre et mole. (lines 551–552)†

"Marion is in her way as charming as Nicolette," Adams simply remarks, without noting the racy flavor of this charm. His comments on her relationship with Robin are no doubt substantially true: "Marion loves him much as she would her child; she makes only a little fun of him; defends him from the others; laughs at his jealousy; scolds him on occasion." But how can he say that love "turns Robin into a champion of decency"? Indeed, such decency, mockingly affected, is part of the jollity itself, when, in the game of the King, Robin bandies words with Baudoin:

LI ROIS
Robin, quant une beste naist,
A coi cès tu qu'elle est femele?
ROBINS
Chest demand est boine et bele!
LI ROIS
Dont i respon

---

* God! Is this cheese greasy!
† I thought I was holding a cheese,
You felt so soft and tender!

ROBINS

    Non ferai voir;
Mais se vous le voles savoir,
Sire rois, au cul li wardés.
El de moi vous n'en porterés.
N'en cuidiés vous chi faire honte? (lines 533–540)*

A vivacious, sprightly spirit, delightfully smart in her answers to the knight, for a country girl, Marion is certainly endowed with a great natural distinction; it does not however follow that she is the Queen Blanche of the fields, and even less that her sweetheart should be held as a "rustic counterpart of Thibaut." With only a small, ludicrous pretence of *courtois* nicety about him, and "just enough intelligence to think well of himself," he remains essentially a booby.[53] In this loutish side of his character Adams is no more interested than in the countrified charms of Marion. Both likenesses are hit off pleasantly enough but only inasmuch as it is "to our purpose," and this purpose, when it is not an overlabored comparison, is an unabating championship of feminine superiority. Even when fair heroines like Nicolette and Marion needed least help, Adams could not help slightly manipulating the evidence in their favor.

The suppressed evidence

The quotation from Garreau at the beginning of "The Three Queens" is not only truncated but practically Bowdlerized. One of the omitted passages, dealing with the picture of domestic life in medieval *romans*, proves of particular interest: "Girls are generally represented in them as both shameless and heartless. They have one idea: to win a handsome husband, and all means are

* *The King:*

    Robin, when a beast it born,
    How do you know it's a female?

Robin:

    That's a very good question.

The King:

    So, answer it!

Robin:

    I'm not going to show you;
    But if Your Majesty wants to know,
    Look at the beast's behind!
    You won't get any more from me.
    You thought this one would embarrass me?

fit to achieve their end. The picture is unrelieved by any touch of filial attachment or devotion." Italo Siciliano has also remarked how, in many *romans courtois,* the heroines "are often downright hussies: voluptuous, brazen, even brutal," their acts of deceit are countless.[54] Indeed, "amour courtois" and adultery seem to be of one and the same essence. Even for Marie de Champagne, feminine frailty remained a fact of nature; André le Chapelain, who codified for her the laws of courtly love, concluded *De Arte Amandi* with a list of Eve's shortcomings. Yet Adams will have little of it. There is but one allusion, in all of *Mont-Saint-Michel and Chartres,* to the somewhat promiscuous quality of *courtoisie;* it comes in a "charming" passage, which makes it appear innocent. Hell, Aucassin says, is a pleasant place because "there go the fair courteous ladies, whether they have two or three friends besides their lords." Otherwise the subject is carefully eschewed; the cunning stratagems Iseult uses to "hoodwink" her own lord are not allowed to illustrate "the woman's greater intelligence." In Adams' selections of medieval literature, Eve, whether married or still "jeune fille," can appear high-handed and even cruel to a very unconventional degree, but not *sans vergogne.*[55]

"Woman is an imperfect animal," maintained Aristotle—a theory which went echoing down the centuries until it was voiced again in still stronger terms by Boccaccio: *La femina è animale imperfetto, passionato da mille passioni spiacevoli e abbominevoli.*[56] Of all commonplaces, satire against women is probably the most enduring; but it seems to have never been more scathing than during the Middle Ages. As Italo Siciliano points out:

> Woman was never treated kindly; the creation of the world was no sooner conceived than woman was made the guilty cause of its loss. The ancient world, however, managed to retain the cult of feminine beauty and give woman a certain tragic grandeur; but the Middle Ages showed neither pity nor justice. They dragged woman through the mud, heaped abuse and contempt on her, laid all kinds of crimes at her door. Woman—rather than the Lady—was truly their creature and victim. The Fathers of the Church pronounced her anathema, and the people jeered noisily at her.[57]

Sculptures on church portals, carved during the twelfth century, represent her loaded with snakes and being devoured by toads. Together with a jongleur, the Devil is playing on her, as if she were a musical instrument. For she is, Emile Mâle comments, "la lyre de Satan."[58] The notion of woman's frailty, already at the heart of *courtois* poetry, was blithely exploited in popular literature and particularly in the *Fabliaux*. On page 113 of Gaston Paris' *Manuel,* two short sentences have been scored by Adams: "Ils [Les Fabliaux] ne sont pas écrits pour les femmes," and a little further on: "Ce sont des écrits destinés aux hommes." Accordingly they will have no place in *Mont-Saint-Michel and Chartres.* "Invented to amuse the gross taste of the coarser class," they are dismissed as soon as mentioned. Yet, they offered Adams—had he cared to use them—many examples of wives getting "more than even" with their husbands. "Our chroniclers," says Bédier, "ceaselessly elaborated in their tales an actual saga of feminine ruses." Such portraits, Bédier insists, should not be taken too seriously; they are *amusettes,* and their broad jokes do not belong specially to the thirteenth century. Yet one may feel, and this is peculiar to the age, the growth of a kind of anger, of sardonic scorn, directed against all womankind: "It is no longer a matter of the latent resentment that men always harbor against women but a doctrine that is clearly defined and deeply rooted: women are inferior and evil beings."[59] The bitterness of this attack is in close relationship with what then seemed to be the exaggerated idealisation of woman. "Never," Blanche H. Dow notes, "has woman been so attacked, and never has she been so exalted." The church was partly responsible for this rising tide of satire: "Its efforts to require celibacy on the part of its clergy gave an additional motive to some mocking spirits for the discrediting of marriage and the consequent denigration of woman. *En rabaissant le mariage, on rabaissait la femme.* In 1205 the Synod of Latran issued its decretal forbidding the marriage of its clerics." Immediately, the roaming students, the *Goliards* as they were called, caught up the subject for their songs. Though we are to go with Adams to the Latin Quarter of Abélard—himself a cleric barred from matrimony— we shall never hear the students' ungallant description of Eve: "Dregs of a cesspool, vicious viper, handsome rot, lecherous slipway, Devil's Common, ravenous prey; horrible nightbird, public entrance, sweet venom, angelic faced hussy, flexible, hardened, a vessel of pestilence; unspliceable, cleavable, litigious."[60] No doubt such a rollicking jingle of adjectives is essentially a piece of sophomoric humor, but it nonetheless expresses a deeply rooted prejudice; it is the prejudice sensed by Bédier in the *Fabliaux* and which is going to be vented by Jean de Meung in the second part of the *Roman de la Rose*.

At the end of his chapter on "Nicolette and Marion," Adams quotes two passages from the *Roman de la Rose*. There was no more fitting work with which to conclude a literary study of the place of women in medieval times: "The long poem epitomizes the two contradictory attitudes of the thirteenth century in that respect. We are here in the presence of two manners of thinking, of two concepts of life, of two ethical codes."[61] Under the deceptive appearance of an identical form, two works more antithetic could not be imagined; they were written by two different hands at a generation's interval; the first part by Guillaume de Lorris is a poem of romantic love. Adams' *résumé* is accurate: "The scene is the Court of Love and the action is avowedly in a dream, without time or place. The poet's tone is very pure; a little subdued; at times sad; and the poem ends sadly." Properly speaking, however, it does not end at all. The slender thread of the action simply breaks off while the lover, expelled from the Garden of Love, is exhaling his grief. Perhaps to Adams' eyes this is a very appropriate conclusion, since true love always comes to naught; at any rate, the action "owes its charm chiefly to the constant disappointment and final defeat" of the lover.[62] Such an interpretation is wholly personal, in contradiction with the views expressed by Gaston Paris in his *Manuel:* "The author doubtless intended the romance to be as long again; Guillaume assures us that the end of the dream was the most beautiful part." Such as it has come to us, his poem represents one of the most "delectable" pieces in medieval literature: "Written for the brilliant circles of high society during the regency of Blanche of Castille, his work bears throughout the stamp of the public to which it is addressed; consequently the morality is not at all severe."[63] Is it not really a little shocking for a young man in love with a pure maiden, Gaston Paris asks, that the idea of marriage never occurs to him? Honest or not, his ends would certainly have been achieved; and so they are, in Jean de Meung's sequel, though this second part could hardly pass for a happy ending.

A clerk who lived in the Latin Quarter, Jean Clopinel, called De Meung, did not, like Guillaume de Lorris, write for the entertainment of an aristocratic circle; no votary of courtly love himself, he not only brought into the *roman* the torrent of his plebeian verve but appears in Gaston Paris' phrase as "the Voltaire of the Middle Ages, with all the reservations implied by such a compliment."[64] Encyclopedic in scope, permeated with the author's bold, cynical spirit, the second part of the *Roman de la Rose* represents one of the most trenchant satires ever unleashed against women:

> Toutes estes, sereiz et futes
> De fait et de volonté putes*[65]

Needless to say, Adams does not quote such lines. Nor could he allude to the central part—a long monologue which amounts to a complete course in licentiousness. The only part he quotes is Jean de Meung's "picture of Time which foreshadows the end of Love —the Rose—and her court, and with it the end of Love"; except for these lines, all the rest of the work must remain "beyond our horizon." Yet, distasteful as one may find the second half of the *Roman de la Rose*, it could not really play the fiendish role which Adams describes in melodramatic terms: "Between the death of William of Lorris and the advent of John of Meung, a short half-century (1250–1300), the woman and the Rose became bankrupt. Satire took the place of worship. Man, with his usual monkey-like malice, took pleasure in pulling down what he had built up. The Frenchman had made what he called 'fausse route' . . . The world had still a long march to make from the Rose of Queen Blanche to the guillotine of Madame du Barry; but the 'Roman de la Rose' made epoch."[66]

Satire has always existed, and the pendulum will long keep swinging backward and forward in the endless controversy about Eve's virtues and imperfections. The truth is that, with chivalry on the wane, the robust philosophy of the *fabliaux* has, with Jean de Meung, found its way into poetry. There are but two ways to

---

* You all are, always were, and always will be,
  In fact and in desire, whores.

deal with a woman, we could have learned from the *Fabliaux:* either beat her, like the "Vilain Mire," or flee, as the poet exclaims:

> Fuiez, fuiez, fuiez, fuiez,
> Fuiez, enfant, fuiez tel beste.*

Adams does not quote these lines either. "It is the cry of Jean de Meung," Italo Siciliano says, "a cry of terror—in fact centuries old."[67] Here is the explanation of the "despair" which Adams senses and to which he alludes at the end of chapter xii. It is the voice of eternal anti-feminism, not of some metaphysical despair. If it sounds only at the very end of the chapter—and if even then we do not perceive what it says—it is because Adams does not really wish us to hear it. Never has any advocate better succeeded in suppressing the hostile evidence. For these chapters on medieval literature—it is now obvious—are a plea, a clever, biased, impassioned plea, not a tableau.

OF THE EVIL OF TRANSLATION

"Translation is an evil," Adams declares, after presenting his first effort at rendering old French into English.[68] He had already voiced this feeling, a quarter of a century earlier, when dealing with Gallatin's correspondence.[69] In *Mont-Saint-Michel and Chartres* he gives it an even more forcible expression when he exclaims, after quoting Dante's and Petrarch's prayers to the Virgin: "He who will may undertake to translate either; not I! The Virgin, in whom is united whatever goodness is in created being, might possibly, in her infinite grace, forgive the sacrilege; but her power has limits, if not her grace; and the whole Trinity, with the Virgin to aid, had not the power to pardon him who should translate Dante and Petrarch."[70] No doubt, in *Esther,* he himself was guilty of the sacrilege toward some of Petrarch's sonnets, but that was in a work of fiction and under the cloak of anonymity. Although there is probably no lack of posturing in this attitude, Adams, when Old French is concerned, now really seems to be the diffident amateur who will one day profess to F. B. Luquiens: "With us *outsiders* who study things historically and as sequences, our efforts to

---

* Flee, flee, flee, flee,
  Flee, child, flee like a beast.

translate are only meant to give us a little habit of thinking in the thought of our period. We want to get at the atmosphere of the art, so we translate; but, *once we feel at home there, we throw away our scaffolding.*[71] Throw away his scaffolding, that is, dispense with translation, he gladly does in *Mont-Saint-Michel and Chartres,* not only with the two prayers quoted in Italian and some Latin verse but with a whole paragraph from Joinville.

Joinville is rather easy, and a "niece" should have no great difficulty in puzzling out his French, but she would probably be quite embarrassed if all texts went similarly untranslated. In some cases Adams chooses to help with a loose paraphrase ("one may translate to suit oneself"); most often, however, he feels compelled to attempt a proper rendering, but not without warning his reader, as he does before bringing in his own version of William of Saint-Pair's tableau of the Archangel's Day: "The supreme blunder is that of translating at all when one is trying to catch not a fact but a feeling. If translate one must, we had best begin by trying to be literal, under protest that it matters not a straw whether we succeed." No sooner has he gone through this attempt than he apologizes: "If you are not satisfied with this translation, any scholar of French will easily help to make a better, for we are not studying grammar or archaeology, and would rather be inaccurate in such matters than not, if at that price a freer feeling of the art could be caught."[72] These parallel statements reveal an ambivalence in Adams' aims which will become more and more apparent as he gets further engaged in translating. For how can literalness and inaccuracies even wilfully committed be reconciled in a transcription from one language into another? Much less than an aesthetic essay dealing with architecture, a translation which is supposed to adhere to a set pattern will allow sheer flights of fancy.

Familiar since his early youth with modern French, Adams could ably translate contemporary texts. When dealing with Old French he was much more handicapped. Apart from the few pages at the end of Karl Bartsch's *Chrestomathie,* he does not seem to have had a proper syntax he could resort to in his solitary vigils, when he immersed himself in medieval literature. We may even doubt whether he actually mastered these rudiments of grammar—a supposition which a particularly striking detail seems to support. In Old French, Latin declensions are exceedingly simplified; only two cases remain: the nominative, or *cas sujet* (e.g., *li murs* in the singular, and *le mur* in the plural, which will eventually disappear, and the objective or *cas régime,* the only form to survive—*le mur, les murs*). Adams mistakes the "s" of the nominative singular in *Aucassins* for an integral part of the name of Nicolette's lover, a blunder all the more amazing since this is a well-known cognomen used in its proper form, not only by Bourdillon and Lang in their translations of the *chantefable,* but by Walter Pater and Gaston Paris. Giving further proof that his notions are in that matter sadly blurred, he conversely makes the young man address a group of shepherds as if they were only one "fair child," because, quite normally, they are called *bel enfant.* In the face of such evidence we would expect many such grammatical errors, but these remain notably few: here the subjunctive is used to translate the future; and in another line the perfect seems to have been mistaken for the present; there the failure to recognize the real subjunctive form empties a verb of its meaning.[73]

With the help of Frédéric Godefroy's *Dictionnaire de l'ancienne langue française et de tous ses dialectes du IXe au XVe siècle,* as well as Karl Bartsch's glossaries, Adams somehow managed to plod through all texts, now and then stumbling on the sense of a substantive or an adjective, rather more often than on grammatical forms. Not unlike Longfellow in his relish for the color, the "sensual" glow of words, he sometimes stops to play with one, such as *bataille, caitif,* or *heron,* making comments which unfortunately are not quite apposite, or giving weak approximations.[74] Indeed his mistranslations are frequent, offering a whole range of wrong shades of meaning, from the very minor to the rather shocking or at least ludicrous. We may start from his easily forgivable confusion with modern French. Roland's valor has not made the emperor "rich," but powerful (*riches*); when Eve calls Adam *franks,* she does not mean "frank" but "noble," as is made clear by the Devil's retort that he is much of a serf (and not merely "low").[75] "Faux amis" of all kinds deceive him. Like any schoolboy, he automatically equates *ennui* with "annoy"; what is worse, *fox* (or *fols*, that is to say, foolish), somewhat confused perhaps with its homonym in English, is rendered by "traitor" or "felon." Such confusions reach a dismaying level when *deport du vieil caitif* (entertainment of the old captive) is construed as "captive from o'er seas," or when Adams marvels at Chrétien de Troyes' "curious similes" in his homage to Marie de Champagne: "As much as a gem would buy of straws and sardines is the Countess worth in queens." Actually the poet was referring to his dame in terms of pearls and sards![76] These are, however, mere accidents.

We must not take advantage of these accidents and hold up Adams to ridicule. Most often his slips are simply run of the mill. One need quote only a few: Roland's sword fails to "shatter," instead of getting dented (*fruisset*); the shepherd tells Aucassin of his wheat field (*froment*), not of his close; the *mervellex* peasant is strange to look at, not "menacing."[77] Two good excuses can be proposed in Adams' favor. One is that Godefroy's *Dictionnaire* was still incomplete without its supplements; translating obscure technical terms remained a matter of *flair*, of pure luck. And, of course, some misconstructions must be imputed not to Adams but to the editors of the texts he used. It is on the strength of Bartsch's judgment that he described Tristan and Iseult's grotto as spacious (*geräumig*) instead of vaulted.[78] Likewise we cannot reproach him with failing to translate, in the description of Nicolette's bower, *erbe du garris* by grass of the moor when the learned Herman Suchier explains in a footnote that since *garris* is masculine it surely designates some Mediterranean shrub tree. Adams, in his case, copes with the difficulty more aptly even than a competent translator like F. W. Bourdillon:

> Ele prist des flors de lis
> Et de l'erbe du garris
> Et de la foille autresi,
> Et une belle loge en fist,
> Ainsques tant gente ne vi.

Henry Adams:
So she twined the lilies flower
Roofed with leafy branches o'er
Made of it a lovely bower
With the fresh grass for floor,
Such as never mortal saw.

F. W. Bourdillon:
She took many a lily head
With the bushy kernes offshoot,
And of leafy boughs to boot,
And a bower so fair made she,—
Daintier did I never see![79]

If we compare the two versions, no doubt Adams', with a word left out (*autresi*) and a rather gratuitous fourth line, appears not only less scholarly, but looser. Yet it is more likely to pass muster. The reason lies, as we are going to realize, in the genuineness of his efforts to "catch a feeling."

Although there could already be found, at the turn of the century, a good many translations in English and still more in modern French, it is obvious that Adams was not interested in such help, preferring to reach an understanding of the texts in a strictly personal way. We see from his letter to Luquiens that he kept to this method until the last years of his life, even when he was, as he said, "passed printing." And this "honesty" is also evidenced by the language he chose, fluent, matter-of-fact, with no quaint turn of phrase. The old-world taste redolent of Malory which was the prevailing fashion of the day must have seemed spurious to him. It is interesting to bring into parallel his own version of a passage from "La Belle Jehanne" with William Morris' translation.

Henry Adams:
Much was Sir Robert grieved when he came to Marseilles and found that there was no talk of anything doing in the country; and he said to John: "What shall we do? You have lent me your money; I thank you, and will repay you, for I will sell my palfrey and discharge the debt to you."

"Sir," said John, "trust to me, if you please, I will tell you what we will do; I have still a hundred sous; if you please I will sell our two horses and turn them into money; and I am the best baker you ever knew; I will make French bread, and I've no doubt I shall pay my expenses well and make money."

"John," said Sir Robert, "I agree wholly to do whatever you like."

William Morris:
Much was sorry Sir Robin when he came to Marseilles, whereas he heard tell of nought toward in the country so he said to John "What do we? Thou has lent me of thy moneys, whereof I thank thee; I will give them back to thee, for I will sell my palfrey and quit me toward thee."

"Sir," said John, "if it please thee, believe me, and I shall tell thee what we shall do. I have yet well an hundred sols of Tournay, and if it please thee, I will sell our two horses and make money thereby; for I am the best of bakers that ye may wot of; and will make French bread, and I doubt me not but I shall earn my spending well and bountifully."

"John," said Sir Robin, "I grant it thee to do all as thou wilt."[80]

We can admire William Morris' command of archaic idioms and still doubt whether his use, however skillful, of *thee* and *wilt* and *wot* enables him better than Adams' colloquial phrasing to recapture the essential simplicity of the twelfth-century tale. There is even the risk of the translator's dexterity intruding upon the reader's attention, to the detriment of the original text. When considered in such light, Adams' apparently less talented version reveals itself to be much truer, for, as Longfellow maintained, "a translator, like a witness on the stand, should hold up his right hand and swear to 'tell the truth, the whole truth and nothing but the truth.' "[81] And in what words shall a witness tell the truth, if not in his everyday words? Yet the whole truth, particularly in a poem, remains, as Adams says of old French assonances, "beyond recovering." Time and again, when dealing with the *Chanson de Roland,* he pauses to mourn the loss by our age "of its ear for poetry," and our inability to render "into English—or indeed into modern French," such admirable verse where "words bubble like a stream in the woods."[82] This unfeigned humility before the text appears all the more worthy of note since the feeling is not shared by all translators. It proves rewarding to compare Adams' rendering of the *Chanson* with two rhymed English versions, composed in the following decade, one in 1913 by Arthur S. Way, D. Lit., who proudly styled himself "Author of Translations into English Verse of Homer's Iliad and Odyssey, the Tragedies of Aeschylus, Sophocles and Euripides, the Georgics of Virgil, etc.", the other in 1914 by Leonard Bacon, then assistant professor of English at Berkeley. Here is, for instance, the end of the scene, as rendered by Adams, when, grown blind with loss of blood, Oliver has struck out at his friend:

Dist Oliviers: "Or vus oi jo parler
Io ne vus vei. Veied vus damnedeus!
Ferut vus ai. Kar le me pardunez!"
Rollanz respunt: "Jo n'ai nient de mel.
Jol vus parduins ici e devant deu."

Says Oliver: "Indeed I hear you speak,
I do not see you. May God see and save you!
Strike you I did. I pray you pardon me."
Roland replies: "I have no harm at all.
I pardon you here and before God!"

A icel mot l'uns al altre
ad clinet.
Par tel amur as les vus
desevrez!

At this word, one to the other
bends himself.
With such affection, there
they separate.

Arthur S. Way
"I hear thee speak," said his comrade, "but thy face I cannot see.
God look upon thee! I have smitten thee — O forgive it to me!"
"No hurt have I gotten," said Roland: "I forgive thee before God's face."
On each other's necks then fell they in love's long last embrace.

Leonard Bacon
Said Olivier: "I hear thee speak. I got no sight of thee.
God keep thee! If I smote thee thy pardon will I cry."
And Roland spoke this in answer: "No hurt I have thereby.
Here I give thee my pardon, and before our God on high."
And at the word each champion bowed his head before his peer.
And thus it was they parted that each other held so dear.[83]

Do not these heroic hexameters sound forced and even ungainly compared with Adams' limpid flow? The amateur alone has infused himself with the true feeling of the passage, "the simple force of the words and action." "It is the grand style," he comments, having probably in mind Matthew Arnold's celebrated definition of Homer's "grand style in simplicity." As a matter of fact, he seems to have taken his lesson from Arnold's lectures "On Translating Homer" and approaches the original "in the simplest frame of mind possible," encumbered with no "special vocabulary," no preconceived ideas. The result is a translation, cleaving to its model and retaining its essential movement, if not its music. Nothing better can be offered in English, as far as the Chanson is concerned. Only in one instance does it fall amiss—and it is very significant that it should be on the one occasion when Adams departs from this rule of strict adherence to the truth: Here Oliver bids his friend draw near; in great dolor today they will be separated:

Munjoie escriet e haltement e
cler.
Rollant apelet sun ami e sun per;
"Sire compainz a mei kar vus
justez.
A grant dulur ermes hoi deser-
veret." Aoi.

"Montjoie!" he cries, loud and
clear.
Roland he calls, his friend
and peer;
"Sir Friend! ride now to help
me here!
Parted today, great pity were."

Because two rhymes were lying ready for his pen, Adams finds himself lured into devising another pair—not even real ones—to match, and he falls into sheer nonsense. Yet be it left to his credit that he does not reach the height of ridicule attained by Arthur S. Way, who, for the sake of a rhyme, pads out the most preposterous line:

> Sundered in sorrow exceeding this day must we be, o brother!
> Then brake they forth into sudden weeping, each for other.[84]

It is now obvious that for Adams the greatest danger lay in the rhymes. By his own admission, "any blunderer in verse, who will merely look at" Thibaut de Champagne's rhymes is bound to realize how intricate their pattern is; he all the same ventures not only to translate two poems but to duplicate the exceedingly elaborate structure of their *coblas unissonans* or isometrical stanzas (10a, 10b, 10a, 10b, 10c 10c, 4d, plus the burden: 10c, 4d). In neither poem does he actually prove equal to the five stanzas. Though in his truncated adaptations he somehow manages, at least within the scope of each stanza, to reproduce the rhyme scheme as well as something of the metrical pattern, it is not without taking liberties with the text.

Adams was aware of his comparative failure, as is evidenced by his comments to F. B. Luquiens, in March 1911, about his similar attempt with Richard's Song:

The task attracted me greatly because, as literature, it is so difficult . . . On the *laisse* I broke down altogether. With the rhyme *free*, I would have made perhaps one stanza, but not on *captive* or *prisoner*, or any equivalent for *pris*. My failure in this respect is total and abject, but is only a repetition of my failure with the Chanson de Roland. The next failure is with the rhymes. The rhyme obliged me to translate *por avoir* as *for gain*, meaning *for economy* or *for meanness* or *greed;* but I could invent no rhyme for *want of money* and am regularly blocked by the difficulty . . . The *encombreis* is still worse. I had there to depart entirely from the text in order to get a rhyme, and I think it the worst case of mistranslation I am guilty of; but I boggled over it long before submitting to the defeat . . .[85]

Of course his judgment over his defeat with the *Chanson de Roland* cannot be accepted, were it only for the reason that, in his rendering of a text all in assonances, he rarely betrays the fascination with the jingle of the rhymes which now seems to possess him. But neither will we share his assumed severity toward his "poor attempts at verse," such as this stanza of Richard's song:

> No prisoner can tell his honest thought
> Unless he speaks as one who suffers wrong;
> But for his comfort he may make a song.
> My friends are many, but their gifts are nought.
> Shame will be theirs, if, for my ransom, here
> I lie another year.[86]

The translation sounds a little awkward, but it is neither wooden nor ridiculous, and it even remains "literal" enough. "If the translator is a good poet," George Moore says, in his *Confessions of a Young Man*," "he substitutes his verse for that of the original . . . if he is a bad poet, he gives us bad verse, which is intolerable."[87] Calling these lines "bad," "intolerable," would be unfair. Never meant to be great literature and built we are told, "upon a foundation of several weeks of patient drudgery," they are pleasantly readable. None of the poems which Adams chose to translate is very emotional. The count, the king who wrote them, took an intellectual pleasure in thus beguiling the tedium of a court or of a prison; there is an unmistakable echo of this intellectual delight in Adams' own versions. He too, in his "nineteenth-century garret," liked poetry as a noble pastime. This is why even when, as in the last instance, he sounds artificial, he is in reality remarkably alert and sincere. We must look upon his translations in the summer light bathing this whole journey into the heart of the Middle Ages. Adams is not trying to convey "anything that can possibly be useful or instructive, but only a sense of what these centuries" (or these poets) "had to say and a sympathy with their ways of saying it."[88] We will then easily forget the few slips and, in sympathy with the spirit of the venture, we will pronounce this "amusement" to be, all in all, a success.

7

The Meaning of
Mont-Saint-Michel and Chartres

What did "these centuries" have to say? Adams conveys the answer through two *personae*, used metaphorically; "The Virgin and St. Thomas are my vehicles of anarchism," he writes to Gaskell on December 20, 1904, but, he adds, "nobody knows enough to see what they mean."[1] What these two figures symbolize is the conflict at the heart, not only of *Mont-Saint-Michel and Chartres* but of all of Adams' work during the second part of his life. For the relationship of faith and reason emerges as the central philosophical premise in what he called "the series: from the thirteenth-century unity to twentieth-century multiplicity." As R. Spiller says of both *Mont-Saint-Michel and Chartres* and *The Education*, they are "a testament of faith urgently needed rather than of faith achieved."[2] The replacing of Saint Thomas by the image of the dynamo in the latter book does not alter the basic symbolism of the struggle: faith or instinct versus reason or science.

Of the Virgin and Saint Thomas, the Virgin is the more prominent symbol, as is natural in a book sometimes referred to as *Les Miracles de la Vierge*. Such a prominence, however, is not to be accounted for by theological reasons. Indeed there can be no greater mistake than to see Mary of Chartres in a religious light, as Hugh F. Blunt did in "The Mal-Education of Henry Adams," to find out that it "left a kind of bad taste in [his] Catholic mouth." John P. McIntyre, S. J., has a much wiser approach, which we shall adopt: "Adams' representation of the Virgin as irrational, perverse, illogical, arbitrary and even heretical, certainly does not coincide with the role of the Blessed Mother in Catholic theology or in Catholic devotion, whether medieval or modern. However, Adams is careful to insist that he is not interested in orthodox theology. *His Virgin is a fiction and should be treated as such.*"[3] To borrow Adams' very words on Queen Eleanor, the "real na-ture" of Mary "in no way concerns us; it is only the "fiction," the figure alive in the writer's imagination, that counts. That she is in reality intimately connected with her lay creator is not sur-prising. "One sees what one brings," Adams remarks in *The Edu-cation*, about Gibbon darting his celebrated "contemptuous look" on the Gothic cathedrals of Rome. At Chartres, when he himself admiringly looks at the Virgin, he too sees nothing but "what he brings," that is, his own conception of Eternal Eve. Indeed it is because of the highly personal quality of this vision that the figure is so fraught with meaning. "No one means all he says, and yet very few say all they mean, for words are slippery and thought is viscous," he also says in *The Education*. The gist of *Mont-Saint-Michel and Chartres* is to be found in the image of Mary.[4]

MARY OF CHARTRES

"If I were beginning again as a writer," Adams tells George Cabot Lodge on April 27, 1903, "I think I should drop the man, except as an accessory, and study the woman of the future." We have already learned from *Mont-Saint-Michel and Chartres* that the "proper study'" of mankind is woman. "What will the woman turn out to be?" Adams now asks young Lodge. "Read me that riddle aright and art will conform to the answer." This is not the first time he uses the word with reference to the woman; the riddle itself has been central to his preoccupations for many years.[5] We find an interesting contradiction in two letters he sent in 1910, one dated May 19, addressed to Raphael Pumpelly, and in which he asserts: "The only book I ever wrote and that was worth writing was the first volume of the series—the *Mont-Saint-Michel*." In the other letter, dated August 6 and addressed to Gaskell, he describes that self-same volume as "the second in the series."[6] What could then antedate *Mont-Saint-Michel and Chartres* in his mind? If a probable guess is *Tahiti*, we should perhaps rather see a composite work which would include not only Queen Marau's "Memoirs" but Adams' two novels as well, in which he already concerns himself with the workings of the feminine soul. For if *Democracy* and *Esther* deal with two of the most vital problems in human experience, the one with political, the other with religious faith, their interest springs less out of their subjects than out of the personality of the seeker for truth, in both a woman. "Both novels," R. Spiller comments, "become in their closing theses *studies of the inability of woman to accept faith as man formulates it*." The study is particularly poignant in *Esther,* an intensely personal book, since Adams puts in it so much of his married life; no doubt, to quote R. Spiller: "The trail from Esther to the Virgin of Chartres is a long and intricate one, but it is straight." Of course, it is possible to start the trail earlier. By and large, the image of the Virgin of Chartres, Samuels once observed, reflects: "the heroic virago of Teutonic tradition as [Adams] had studied her for his Lowell Institute lecture of 1876."[7] We may even begin with Adams' first real experience of "the eternal woman," when, in 1859, he joined his sister, Mrs. Kuhn, for the summer: "She was the first young woman he was ever intimate with—quick, sensitive, wilful, or full of will, energetic, sympathetic and intelligent enough to supply a score of men with ideas—and he was delighted to give her the reins—to let her drive him where she would. It was his first experiment in giving the reins to a woman and he was so much pleased with the results that he never wanted to take them back. In after life he made a general law of experience—no woman had ever driven him wrong; no man had ever driven him right."[8]

In reality, much of Adams' education, concerning the higher reaches of feminine character, can be traced back to his married years. "[Henry] James knows almost nothing of women but the mere outside; he never had a wife," Adams wrote in September 1883, thus dismissing him as the possible author of the anonymous novel, *The Breadwinners.* "This new writer" (none other than John Hay, to whom he happened to be writing) "not only knows women, but knows *ladies,* the rarest of literary gifts." Unlike James, Adams was a married man, and, as he had said with facetious understatement some eleven years earlier (to Robert Cunliffe, on July 25, 1872): "From the start [I] have felt as though my wife was my oldest furniture."[9] His bantering comments to John Hay confirm how much, indeed, he genuinely felt indebted to his wife. He owed her the "sea of happiness" (their thirteen years of married life until her suicide in 1885) which he would refuse to touch in *The Education,* and also a model for his greatest heroines of fiction, not only Esther Dudley, but Mary of Chartres. Though in the portrait of the latter heroine there also could enter, to be sure, something of Elizabeth Cameron, who had by then come to occupy a dominant position in Adams' life, not unlike the position formerly held by Marian Adams.

"She was a queen, a woman and a mother," Adams says of the Virgin. When in March 1872, he describes his "fiancée" to Gaskell, she also appears as a sovereign: "She rules me as only American women rule men and I cower before her."[10] He had at once let her take command of their social life, submitting, E. Samuels says, "with affectionate docility to her management"; according to Henry James, he was much "improved" by this management. A later comment of James is also worth quoting: "We never knew how delightful Henry was till he lost her; he was so proud of her that he let her shine as he sat back and enjoyed listening to what she said and what others let her say."[11] At Chartres, Joseph the husband similarly hugs the shadow, while Mary shines in regal splendor. Consequently, theirs appears to be a purely feminine household: "The wants of man, beyond a mere roof-cover, and perhaps space to some degree, enter to no very great extent into the problem of Chartres. Man came to render homage and to ask favours. The Queen received him in her palace, where she alone was at home, and alone gave commands." Mary has seen to it that her "private apartments" are according to her wishes, ordering the artist about, as Marian Adams may have done, when the Adamses were building their Washington house. She insisted on having the best ("the Virgin was never cheap"), that is, the most "refined."

Much is said about Mary's feminine delight in decoration, which can be transposed in nineteenth-century terms and acquire an autobiographical relevance. "At least one can still sometimes feel a woman's taste," Adams observes, after deploring the congenital "feebleness of our fancy"; "and in the apse of Chartres one feels nothing else." In the Adams house, the same taste prevailed.[12]

"Still you know that the ladies are essentially feminine and will do anything they d[amn] p[lease]," Adams was to remark to Royal Cortissoz.[13] Mary's attitude and expression are always "calm and commanding; she never calls for sympathy by hysterical appeals to our feelings."[14] Outwardly, she is a model of Anglo-Saxon composure. "The woman as I have known her," we read in the April 27, 1903, letter to George Cabot Lodge, "is by no means the woman of sentiment." This does not prevent her from having strong feelings, prejudices, fancies, in other words from being quite vivacious, just as Marian or "Clover" Hooper-Adams seems to have been. Henry James, who liked her profoundly, saw in her, he once said, "the perfect incarnation of my native land" (a compliment, she felt, "most equivocal" coming from him). Writing to his brother in 1870 James compared her with the stiff dowdy Englishwomen he was then among: "I revolt from their dreary, deathly want of—what shall I call it?—Clover Hooper has it—intellectual grace—Minnie Temple has it—moral spontaneity."[15] In this description the emphasis bears upon the terms *grace* or *spontaneity* rather than on the adjective *intellectual*. In a footnote to *Henry Adams: The Major Phase*, E. Samuels quotes from a letter which John Hay wrote to Mrs. Cameron, in the midst of a cabinet meeting, in 1899: "There is something unreal, something tant soit peu divine about all my knowledge of you. That you should be the most beautiful and fascinating woman of your generation, the most attractive in wit and grace and charm and yet be so good to me is a thing I never realize and find it hard to believe when I am away from you."[16] This fascinating "grace," this liveliness characterized Marian Adams, as they characterize Mary of Chartres; the charm which one feels in the court of the Queen of Heaven is also that of the "Five of Hearts" when it was enlivened by Marian's humor, a charm which Adams subsequently managed at least partly to recover in his *faux ménage* with Elizabeth Cameron.

Mary "was not above being amused"; she was even fond of a *faux pas* when it was done on purpose. "Never sympathetic to the Curia " (neither was Mrs. Adams for the Washington dignitaries), Mary "exasperated" even the devils by her sheer disregard for conventions. "Irreverence was her most natural state," E. Samuels says of Marian Adams;[17] we can establish a parallel between her handling, for instance, of Freeman when she was inquiring about his raw-meat-eating ancestors, and many of the scenes described in chapter xiii, "Les Miracles de Notre Dame." Adams fastens on this trait, in which he finds an explanation for the decline of Mary's power: "Mary's treatment of respectable and law-abiding people, who had no favours to ask, and were reasonably confident of getting to Heaven by the regular judgment, without expense, rankled so deeply that three hundred years later the Puritan reformers were not satisfied with abolishing her, but sought to abolish the woman altogether as the cause of evil in heaven and earth. The Puritans abandoned the New Testament and the Virgin in order to go back to the beginning, and renew the quarrel with Eve."[18] Such an explanation is highly confusing, since it apparently isolates the unconventional side of Mary's character, making her in effect a sexless entity different from Eve. Yet, is she not also Eve herself—or Venus? E. Samuels' contention that "the Virgin and Venus and the Eternal Feminine are interchangeable symbols" is at any rate supported by Adams' equating of Mary, in *The Education*, with "Diana of the Ephesians" or "any of the Oriental Goddesses": "She was Goddess because of her force. She was the animated dynamo; she was reproduction—the greatest and most mysterious of all energies; all she needed was to be fecund."[19] For the Virgin was not only "a Queen" and "a woman" but first of all, as Adams said, *a mother;* all religious imagery bears proof of it.

It is in this last side of her personality—the mother—that Adams' "fiction," Mary of Chartres, is puzzling. Must one really think that she was inspired by "the outcry in France over depopulation," ringing in Adams' ears during his semiannual residences in this country? In "Vis Inertiae," one of the last chapters of *The Education*, Adams, to be sure, dwells on the importance of the birthrate. "An elderly man, trying only to learn the law of social inertia and the limits of social divergence could not compel the

Superintendent of the Census to ask every young woman whether she wanted children, and how many; he could not even require of an octogenarian Senate the passage of a law obliging every woman, married or not to bear one baby—at the expense of the Treasury—before she was thirty years old under penalty of solitary confinement for life; yet, these were vital statistics in more senses than all that bore the name, and tended more directly to the foundation of a serious society in the future." As he has a little earlier explained: "Of all the movements of inertia, maternity and reproduction are the most typical. . . . Whatever else stops, the woman must go on reproducing."[20] There is "a dynamics of sex" or, to use another phrase, a "biological energy"—a mechanism, in fact, with a perpetual movement ("the woman's force . . . as inertia of rotation . . . and her axis of rotation . . . the cradle and the family")—which accounts, among other instances, for the increasing weight of Russia and China such as they are foreseen at the end of *The Education*.[21] In that sense, Adams' use of the notion of *energy* in connection with the Eternal Feminine appears perfectly to the point as well as convincing. But when Adams grieves over the failure of the American woman, it is the failure not of the *genitrix* but of the *mater familias;* the theme is already put forth in a letter he wrote not long after the publication of *Mont-Saint-Michel and Chartres*, when he was beginning to work on *The Education:* "I admit that the American woman is a failure; that she has held nothing together, neither State nor Church, nor Society nor Family . . . Our fascinating old 12th-century friends had a job that could be handled. There were never enough of them to fill a good-sized church, and the only force they controlled was a horse, without roads even for him. America has nearly a hundred million people running at least five-and-twenty million horse-power equivalent to the power of the whole animal world since Eve. It worries me to see our women run away from the job."[22] Such a job, obviously, is not to increase the population ratio but to "hold the family" [or twentieth-century society] "together," just as Mary held, at least for a blessed time, the society of the Middle Ages, and, we may add, Marian Adams held the "Five of Hearts." The energy needed to that end is of a spiritual, not of a biological, nature. Adams' explanation in *The Education* thus proves equivocal and contradictory, and it confuses the critical interpretation of Mary of Chartres. For it is as much a mistake to examine this heroine in an anthropological or biological light as it is to assess her from the theological point of view. The preface to Havelock Ellis' *Studies in the Psychology of Sex* in 1897 ("I regard sex as the central problem of life . . . the question of sex—with the racial questions that rest on it—stands before the coming generations as the chief problem for solution"), from which E. Samuels quotes, has no more relevance to Adams' Virgin than Pope Pius IX's bull *Ineffabilis* proclaiming the dogma of the Immaculate Conception in 1854.[23]

Indeed, it scarcely seems that Mary's energy could be identified with that of "the rotation of the cradle." Her maternity is so to speak, *figée*, that is, unique and for all ages; and if in Adams' private hagiography, the image of Elizabeth Cameron and her daughter Martha may have somehow become superimposed to that of the Holy Mother, it still was the vision of a Madonna with an only child. At any rate, Mary of Chartres hardly appears in her role as a mother; when she is maternal, it is to adults whom she mothers much more than to her own son. And how could she behave differently, since there is so much in her of Marian Adams, who never had a child? Of all the Adams' heroines, as a matter of fact, only one, besides the Virgin, has ever been a mother—Madeleine Lee, in *Democracy*, whose son is dead. And not only are these, as a rule, childless, not to say barren, but there is a certain disquieting element about them which we cannot but designate as their frigidity. "As for conjugal love," E. Saveth remarks, "the women of the thirteenth century, as Adams describes them, seemed, like Madeleine and Esther of another era, rather uninterested in it."[24] Indeed, if at the beginning of *The Education* Adams bemoans the disappearance of the religious emotion ("the most powerful next to the sexual"), as far as he and his heroines are concerned, this is not the only emotion which seems to be extinct. For the world of Chartres, even when it extends and covers most of medieval literature, remains not unlike young Henry Adams' Boston: "From women the boy got the domestic virtues and nothing else. He might not even catch the idea that woman had more to give. The Garden of Eden was hardly more primitive."[25] As if the flesh did not exist for Adam and Eve!

The total absence of the "sexual" emotion (as a physiological phenomenon) in Adams' world can find its explanation in the fact that he is writing "genteel" literature. Of no book does this seem truer than of *Mont-Saint-Michel and Chartres,* expressly intended for young female readers. The "Madonna" whom H. H. Boyesen denounced in 1894 is no doubt cousin to Mary of Chartres: "She is the Iron Madonna who strangles in her fond embrace the American novelist; the Moloch upon whose altar he sacrifices, willingly or unwillingly, his chances of greatness . . . When, however, we read a novel like Tolstoi's *Anna Karenina* or Daudet's *Le Nabab,* we appreciate perhaps the difference between a literature addressed to girls and a literature intended for men and women."[26] We do not, however, feel that Adams was in any way deflected, in the present instance, from what was his own personal truth. The very nature of the subject genuinely precluded a "naturalistic" treatment; this was not only due to a feeling of private reverence, because, even more than Esther, Mary of Chartres, in R. P. Blackmur's words, was "the result of his cultivated and endeared meditation upon the image of Marian Adams,"[27] or because any treatment of the Virgin, even fictionized, required delicacy, a delicacy which extended to the treatment of all women. The thoughts of the man who wrote *Mont-Saint-Michel and Chartres* were naturally sublimated. He had long since been adjusted to his platonic relationship with Mrs. Cameron. Even when, years before, during his South Sea journey, he was, to quote Samuels' phrase again, "swept off his Puritan feet," there is not the least evidence that he enjoyed, or wished he could have enjoyed—like Melville's hero, in *Typee*—the companionship of some Fayaway. For the reawakening of the senses which then took place in him was a reawakening of the senses of *perception;* he then learned to enjoy the *color* of life. And fittingly enough, his companion was an artist.

If Leslie Fiedler has been able to feel a rather dubious quality in the relationship between Huck Finn and Nigger Jim, no such suspicion can certainly come to our mind, concerning Henry Adams and his artist friends. It is nonetheless a fact that, to a still greater degree than Elizabeth Cameron, Adams' real "helpmates" during the later part of his life were the two men with whom he traveled most often, Clarence King and John LaFarge. Let us remember how he described them in *The Education:* King, perfectly irresistible with his "bubbling energy," and "his personal charm of youth and manners . . . as though he were Nature herself," in fact a "true bird of paradise," and La Farge who "alone owned a mind complex enough to contrast against the commonplaces of American uniformity." How fittingly they match the portrait of the American woman which Adams draws in his letter to George Cabot Lodge, in April 1903: "If I understand her, she is apt to turn up in a number of unexpected lights . . . The American man is a very simple and cheap mechanism. The American woman I find a complicated and expensive one. Contrasts of feminine types are possible. I am not absolutely sure that there is more than one American man. The American man is one-sided to deformity." But both King and La Farge are many-sided; both are governed by instinct, which is the only safe guide. This was the lesson which Adams finally perceived in the Pacific: "Even a contradiction was to [La Farge] only a shade of difference, a complementary color, about which no intelligent artist would dispute. Constantly he repulsed argument: 'Adams, you reason too much!' was one of his standing reproaches even in the mild discussion of rice and mangoes in the warm night of Tahiti dinners. He should have blamed Adams for being born in Boston. The mind resorts to reason for want of training, and Adams had never met a perfectly trained mind."[28]

It is by this lesson that he wants us now to benefit. When Oscar Cargill writes that *Mont-Saint-Michel and Chartres* should be looked upon "as a cathedral of words . . . various, complex and beautiful, yet designed to give a single impression—a cathedral erected by Henry Adams to the glory of womankind,"[29] the statement acquires its full meaning only if, by womankind, one understands a woman's power of perception (Marian's) which is also that of an artist like La Farge or King. Richard P. Blackmur, in "The Expense of Greatness," thus gives the best possible definition of the Eternal Feminine, according to Adams: "Women, for Adams, had instinct and emotion and could move from the promptings of the one to the actualities of the other without becoming lost or distraught in the midway bog of logic and fact. Impulse proceeded immediately to form without loss of character or movement. More than that, women had taste; taste was what held things together, showing each at its best, and making each contribute to a single effect. Thus the argument of a woman's taste dissipated every objection of logic, and at its highest moments made illogicality itself part of its natural charm. Taste was the only form of energy sure enough of itself—as all non-human energies may—to afford beauty; elsewhere the rashest extravagance."[30] *Mont-Saint-Michel and Chartres* is the study of the rise and fall of that now "lost" energy which was once best symbolized by Mary of Chartres.

A PSYCHOLOGICAL ALLEGORY OR DIAGRAM

One must read *Mont-Saint-Michel and Chartres* as an allegory, translating into intensely felt images Adams' interpretation of human (that is, masculine as well as feminine) psychology, within the framework of the Middle Ages. The basic theme of the book, as it has been analyzed by Robert Spiller, consists in a psychological preparation—that of the "medieval mind" (but is the term *mind* quite apposite?) bracing itself "for its gigantic effort of synthesis in terms of emotion and faith,—and the attempted translation of this emotional unity into the rational terms of scholastic philosophy." In its broadest statement, this theme is how eleventh-century "instinct" flowered into twelfth-century "will," which in turn thirteenth-century "logic" degraded.[31]

The beginning represents the time of instinct, when the world of the Middle Ages was young and full of exuberance. Symbolized by the towering figure of the Archangel, masculine energy is high and seems bound to keep increasing. A key to this first phase is provided in a marginal note appended by Adams to William James' chapter on instinct in *Principles of Psychology* (p. 441). Adams had read this book very carefully and critically. Here he took issue with James' interpretation of instinct, and offered instead his own definition: "Instinct ought to be habits founded on appetites incident to self-preservation. Other habits would be mere tricks or incidental vices."[32]

Since Adams defines instinct as those "habits founded on appetites incident to self-preservation," it is accordingly not surprising that his discussion of Norman society focuses on architecture and arms. Saint Michael the Archangel easily becomes the patron saint of self-preservation, not only on the supernatural order but on the natural level as well. His inspiration unifies and solidifies Norman society, so that "our two hundred and fifty million arithmetical ancestors" can explain: "We have little logic here, and simple faith, but we have energy. We cannot do many things which are done in the centre of civilization, at Byzantium, but we can fight, and we can build a church." The church militant with Saint Michael as its leader instinctively repels its foes, whether they be diabolical spirits or Englishmen. It is the reflex action proper to self-preservation which accounts not only for the masculine and military passions but also for the "grand style" of the eleventh century.[33]

The two salient characteristics of instinct that Adams develops in his discussion of the masculine church and the heroic epic are its practicality and its spontaneity. Their practical sense impelled the Normans to unite in order to build the abbey church at Mont-Saint-Michel. For as long as the Normans were in danger, the Archangel was their protector and intercessor: "He is the conqueror of Satan, the mightiest of all created spirits, the nearest to God. His place was where the danger was greatest, therefore you find him here. For the same reason he was, while the pagan danger lasted, the patron saint of France. So the Normans, when they were converted to Christianity, put themselves under his powerful protection." The spontaneity which characterizes medieval devotion properly belongs to instinct, as the Normans themselves proclaim: "No doubt we think first of the church, and next of our temporal lord; only in the last instance do we think of our private affairs, and our private affairs suffer for it; but we reckon the affairs of Church and State to be ours, too, and we carry this idea very far." Although, thanks to this instinctual energy, society can already appear as a unified whole, something is lacking to its ultimate perfection. The missing element is going to be provided under the form of the twelfth-century worship of Mary. Then for an all too short time society can know its highest point of development; masculine energy is made to serve feminine sensibility.[34]

In the world of Chartres, the wars are over; the heroes have been relegated to stone and glass; the church militant is succeeded by the church triumphant. Feminine will dominates. Adams borrows his concept of will from Schopenhauer, as is made clear in his "Letter to American Teachers of History": "Schopenhauer held that all energy in nature, latent or active, is identical with Will. Before his time—he claimed—the concept of Will was included in the concept of Force; he reversed the order on the ground that the unknown should be referred to the known, and that therefore the whole universe or energy, known or unknown, of whatever intensity or volume, should be brought into the category of intuition." Like instinct, will manifests active and kinetic energy. And like instinct, will is not rational, but a natural inborn inclination which Adams refers to variously as intuition, will, or emotion. The quality and intensity of this will or feeling is reflected in art and is measured by taste. According to Adams' reasoning, the Gothic exhibits the finest quality of taste, which argues for the highest intensity of will. Because her will dominates and rules the age as well as her church, the Virgin of Chartres rightly assumes a psychological importance rather than a theological significance.[35]

As an emblem of will, the Virgin shows that subtlety of sense which must always be felt rather than reasoned; it is the same infallible capacity for intuition which distinguishes all of Adams' heroines beginning with the enthusiastic Madeleine Lee and the skeptical Esther Dudley. The immediacy and spontaneity of intuition precludes logical judgment; the Virgin never offers a reason for her activity other than the cryptic but forceful "I will it!" No wonder it can be felt that "the church at Chartres belonged not to the people, not to the priesthood, and not even to Rome; it belonged to the Virgin." Any surprises or irregularities the tourist may find at Chartres, such as the irregular apse, the hidden window of the Last Judgment, the irreligious window of Roland, the isolated window of the Prodigal Son, illustrate the Virgin's predilection for her own amusement. Only the Virgin and her taste explain the aesthetic unity of Chartres. "Some controlling hand has given more or less identical taste to all." It is this controlling harmony of the Virgin's taste that Adams has set out to feel, if not to understand.[36]

A final corollary of the Virgin as energy or motive is her irrationality: "The fact, conspicuous above all other historical certainties about religion, that the Virgin was by essence illogical, unreasonable and feminine, is the only fact of any ultimate value worth studying, and starts a number of questions that history has shown itself clearly afraid to touch." The rational discipline of mathematics displeases Mary; political economy disturbs her no less. Her spontaneity transcends the Trinity, which stood for law and judgment: "She was above criticism. She made manners. Her acts were laws. No one thought of criticizing, in the style of a normal school, the will of such a queen; but one might treat her with a degree of familiarity, under great provocation, which would startle easier critics than the French." Consequently, her miracles need no explanation; they indicate another fact of feminine will. In Adams' psychological dialectic, will is infinitely superior and diametrically opposed to reason. Adams clarifies this dualism: "God was Justice, Order, Unity, Perfection. He could not be human and imperfect, nor could the Son or the Holy Ghost be other than the Father. The Mother alone was human, imperfect, and could love; she alone was Favour, Duality, Diversity." Because love represents a higher value of energy than reason and law, the Virgin either absorbs or excludes the Trinity: "The Virgin indeed, made all easy, for it was little enough she cared for reason or logic . . . The Trinity has its source in her—totius Trinitatis nobile Triclinium—and she was maternity. She was also poetry and art. In the bankruptcy of reason, she alone was real."[37] Such is the character of Adams' symbol, the Virgin as energy, force, will, capable of unifying man and society through her harmonious taste and spontaneous love.

To this attractive ideal, the twelfth and thirteenth centuries respond: "Men were, after all, not wholly inconsequent; their attachment to Mary rested on an instinct of self-preservation." They reared churches in her honor, begged for her favor, fought battles under her banner. As an amateur financier, Adams calculates their devotion in terms of economics: "According to statistics, in the single century between 1170 and 1270, the French built eighty cathedrals and nearly five hundred churches of the cathedral class, which would have cost, according to an estimate made in 1840, more than five thousand millions to replace. Five thousand million francs is a thousand million dollars, and this covered only the great churches of a single century." Although Adams admits that "the twelfth and thirteenth centuries, studied in the pure light of political economy, are insane," this side of life nonetheless reveals the practical intensity of the social instincts: "The thirteenth century could not afford to admit a doubt. Society had staked its existence, in this world and the next, on the reality and power of the Virgin; it had invested in her care nearly its whole capital, spiritual, artistic, and economical, even to the bulk of its real and personal estate; and her overthrow would have been the most appalling disaster the Western world had ever known. Without her the Trinity itself could not stand; the Church must fall; the future world must dissolve. Not even the collapse of the Roman Empire compared with a calamity so serious; for that had created, not destroyed a faith."[38]

Man's instinct for the Virgin impelled him to enormous energy, which from one vantage may be tantamount to a business investment but from another represents man's highest achievement. For if the medieval architect and craftsman designed and executed splendid monuments in the Virgin's honor, he submitted to the refining influence of feminine taste. To that degree he participated in the Virgin's energy. The Virgin conditioned man's attitude toward woman, rendering him as docile as a child and transforming military passions into knightly courtesy. This is what we see in "The Three Queens" and "Nicolette et Marion," where Adams parallels man's service of women and man's service of Mary. For the Virgin's presence refined the instinctive passions of the eleventh-century soldier, enabling him to feel her power and to respond to her love: "Mary concentrated in herself the whole rebellion of man against fate; the whole protest against divine law; the whole contempt for human law as its outcome; the whole unutterable fury of human nature beating itself against the walls of its prison-house, and suddenly seized by a hope that in the Virgin man had found a door of escape." Whatever else this period of the flowering of the Gothic, which coincided with the highest point of the worship of Mary, may suggest from man's point of view it is a moment of hope—and according to Adams the greatest moment in the history of mankind. Then, as R. Spiller sums up: "Intuition is above reason; love may triumph over logic; art can speak deeper truths than science." Mary is sovereign, and all is right in the world.[39]

THE VEERING POINT

"All is in the spire," Adams held. Similarly, if we keep figuring *Mont-Saint-Michel and Chartres* as a diagram, all is in the apex. The curve veers down the moment scholasticism (man's attempt to substitute a rational unity for the emotional unity which had come to prevail) becomes a dominant cultural force. Thus, the true apex of the book is to be found at the end of the chapter on "Les Miracles de Notre-Dame," where Adams exalts the Virgin's perverse irrationality as the greatest unifying element the world ever knew; then he turns to the passionate, yet dryly technical debate between Abélard and William of Champeaux over the problem of universals. The emotional contrast between the two chapters makes Adams' point perfectly clear; as Michael Cola- curcio puts it: "Unity, while it existed, was prerational; it simply was. Action, will, faith, these are all unifying principles; logic is divisive. As long as man could simply believe; and believing, love; and loving, act out the simple tasks of worship, all was well. The minute they began to reason on the basis for their believing, the journey to multiplicity had begun."[40] The catastrophe anticipated at the end of "Nicolette and Marion" now got under way while "man, with his usual monkey-like malice, took pleasure in pulling down what he had built up."[41] Questioning the natural hierarchy (that is, the superiority of the female over the male principle, whose recognition had made this marvelous moment of unity pos- sible) masculine energy tried to assert itself again, this time as logic; and it was the beginning of a long, long fall—only the be- ginning, however, since for some time yet, there remained enough feminine energy to save man from his own folly.

Adams' theme is clear, but it is deceptively simple. In reality, as J. C. Levenson observes, the denouement proved "Adams' greatest difficulty": "In the feminine triad of chapters, he had shown the medieval imagination defying facts and transcending reason through the active idea of love and its embodiment in the Virgin and this he could do mostly in words which were already set down for him. In the masculine chapters, he had to present the paths of thought and act as they radically diverged, only to be brought together at the end in the precarious unity of the scholastic synthesis; and for the most part, he had to make his action out of the meager dramatic possibilities of philosophic texts."[42] Understandably, as has been already noted, the "metaphysical" chapters were longest in preparation; they required most labor. No doubt, it was owing to the challenge they represented, because their completion taxed the utmost of Adams' intellectual capacity, that he so prided himself on the result. We have his comment in a letter to William James dated December 9, 1907: "Weary of my own imbecility, I tried to clean off a bit of the surface of my mind, in 1904, by printing a volume on the twelfth century, where I could hide, in the last hundred pages, a sort of anchor in history. I knew that not a hundred people in America would understand what I meant."[43]

The challenge which he thus, in his turn, issued to all critics has been taken up, for whereas his chapters on architecture and literature have until now never been the object of a detailed analysis, there are remarkable studies on his interpretation of medieval metaphysics.[44] Among these, R. P. Blackmur's "The Harmony of True Liberalism" is quite sympathetic; others are more severe, such as John P. McIntyre's *"Mont-Saint-Michel and Chartres:* Structure and Meaning,"[45] or Michael Colacurcio's article, "The Dynamo and the Angelic Doctor; the Bias of Henry Adams' Medievalism," which, to all appearances, is "definitive." Yet there is at least one point on which we disagree with Colacurcio, not his conclusion but his assumption, when he asserts: "In his more or less scholarly investigation of the Middle Ages—outside the dramatized world of *Mont-Saint-Michel*—[Adams] was no doubt quite concerned to read St. Thomas accurately and judge him fairly, but the close reading and judicious estimation are not part of his book."[46] We do not find that Adams ever really read Saint Thomas or any of the medieval philosophers he deals with in *Mont-Saint-Michel and Chartres*. He may well have been studying Saint Thomas "all day long," in July 1900, or sitting "in a corner with St. Thomas," during his stay at Inverlochy Castle in July 1902, but he certainly did not have in hand the *Summa Theologiae,* whose title, as a matter of fact, is never cited in the correspondence. Saint Thomas' works had been lately reprinted (*St. Thomae Aquinatis Opera Omnia* (Paris, 1871–1881). We find none of the thirty-four volumes in Adams' library, nor is there any evidence that he ever tried to borrow one. In all likelihood, then, the book he had in hand was one of the "authorities" we have earlier mentioned, such as Barthélémy Haureau's *Philosophie scholastique* (Paris, 1850), which stood him in as good stead here as Gaston Paris' *Manuel* for the chapters on literature. Two other books which he also profusely scored, and occasionally annotated, were Rev. Elizée Vincent Maumus' *St. Thomas d'Aquin et la philosophie cartésienne* (Paris, 1890) and Charles de Rémusat's *Abélard* (Paris, 1845). There he found extracts and analyses on which he could build his own interpretations.[47] Indeed, the one medieval work from which he quoted directly in his last chapters was Adam de Saint-Victor's *Oeuvres poétiques* (Paris, 1894), of which he owned a copy; this was a book of poems, not a treatise. Otherwise, if for his description of the "Church Intellectual," exactly as when dealing with architectural or literary monuments, he heavily relied on guidebooks, there appears to have been a major difference; he never actually visited the church.

Adams' protestations that he cared more for his theology than for his architecture "and should be much mortified if detected in an error about Thomas Aquinas, or the doctrine of universals," will not, therefore, alter a basic fact: his "digest" of medieval metaphysics could not be very serious from a scholarly point of view. After all, as he wrote to Gaskell, in July 1900, he found the subject "as amusing as *Punch*, and about as sensible. St. Thomas is frankly droll, but I think I like his ideas better than those of Descartes or Leibnitz or Kant or the Scotchmen, just as I like better a child of ten that tells lies, than a young man of twenty who not only lies but cheats knowingly. St. Thomas was afraid of being whipped."[48] It is scarcely surprising that his interpretation of medieval metaphysics should be pronounced "not at all reliable." John P. McIntyre has pointed out that his "Thomistic Cathedral" is "an imaginative construct rather than an historical or philosophical accuracy,"[49] an observation which can apply to all of his metaphysical chapters. The truth is that, out of the body of medieval metaphysics, Adams takes only what suits his literary purpose and best helps him to phrase his own "meaning."

For there is no need to "debunk" Adams, even when he is glaringly inaccurate; indeed no undertaking could prove more off the point, whether applied to the last chapters of *Mont-Saint-Michel and Chartres* or those of *The Education*, where he also professes to have hid his meaning. As E. Saveth remarks in his introduction to *The Education of Henry Adams and Other Selected Writings:* "Rather than poke at the carcass of Adams' scientific theory, which was inadequate for the first decade of the twentieth century and is a fossil to-day, it is perhaps more fruitful to examine why Adams felt impelled to draw the conclusions that he did."[50] It is a fact not only that Lord Kelvin's theories of thermodynamics, which Adams used with such gusto in *The Education*, were outdated but that he did not even digest them thoroughly; acting as a literary executor, Henry Cabot Lodge did not hesitate to use his blue pencil and re-work some of Adams' calculations. Yet, such as they are, they very adequately translate Adams' confusion and dismay in a world rolling toward catastrophe. As for *Mont-Saint-Michel and Chartres*, churchmen have wisely refused to attach any controversial value to his "theology"; far from treating him as "a hell-born scorpion," John P. McIntyre (though one of these critics "taught in Jesuit schools" whom Adams feared), indulgently admits that "this confused garble really or imaginatively represents the helplessness of modern reason."[51] And this is the right stand to take. Rather than assessing these chapters from a theological or "technical" point of view, one must examine them in a broad continuum, as part of the one and same psychological allegory or imaginative diagram, translating Adams' thoughts, or rather his "feelings."

"As the west portal of Chartres is the door through which one must of necessity enter the Gothic architecture of the thirteenth century, so Abélard is the portal of approach to the Gothic thought and philosophy within."[52] There are two reasons for the pride of place thus given to Abélard—one historical, because Abélard was the first famous great "adventurer" who early in the twelfth century began to contest the established theological order, the other personal, owing to the fascination he exerts on Adams' imagination. To be sure, nowhere in the book is the departure from "facts," that is, verifiable history, more evident than in the imaginary debate, which, eight pages long, opposes Abélard and William of Champeaux. Adams takes obvious delight in the clash of arguments which he has himself contrived out of his metaphysical readings, but his interest springs not only from the excitement of the debate ("the subject is as amusing as a comedy; so amusing that ten minutes may well be given to playing the scene between William and Abélard"),[53] it springs also from the eternal drama of the mind present behind it all:

> In these scholastic tournaments the two champions started from opposite points:—one, from the ultimate substance, God—the universal, the ideal, the type;—the other from the individual, Socrates, the concrete, the observed fact of experience, the object of sensual perception. The first champion—William in this instance— assumed that the universal was only nominally real; and on that account he was called a nominalist . . . "I start from the universe," said William. "I start from the atom," said Abélard; and, once having started, they necessarily came into collision at some point between the two.[54]

Using the syllogism as a weapon, Abélard won. Yet the exact terms of his victory matter little, since it could at best prove but a very momentary one. The conflict was as old as Plato and Aristotle, and it continued to echo through all the schools. As Adams notes in the following chapter: "The schools argued according to their tastes, from unity to multiplicity, or from multiplicity to unity; but what they wanted was to connect the two. They tried realism and found that it led to pantheism. They tried nominalism and found that it ended in materialism. They attempted a compromise in conceptualism which begged the whole question. Then they lay down exhausted."[55] Whatever these solutions meant, they all in the end appeared equally void and absurd, owing to the powerlessness of man's reason to understand the universe. Reading Charles de Rémusat's *Abélard*, Adams felt impelled to argue in a marginal note on page 140:

> God is a substance (p. 98)
> There is no substance without essence (p. 140)
> Then God conceived and willed himself?
> or existed from eternity?
> Is not the most singular trait of Abélard's dialectics

the absence of treatment of the infinite?
Is the infinite a universal?
Is it subject to the senses?
Is it real or nominal?
Is the infinite the finite? (p. 114)
or the finite the infinite? (pp. 114–115)
or are both concepts?

Already in such "pugnacious marginalia,"[56] Adams tends toward the Pascalian attitude, which is to "doubt" logic itself. In *Mont-Saint-Michel and Chartres* he is going to invoke Pascal, "tortured by the impossibility of rejecting man's reason by reason," and to quote Pascal's famous "outcry of despair," when in the seventeenth century the same violent struggle which had agitated the medieval schools broke out again:

When I consider man's misery and blindness and the astonishing conflicts in his nature; when I consider the entire silent universe and man without light and abandoned, lost as it were in this remote corner of the universe, not knowing who has placed him here, what he has come to do, what will happen to him after death, I am seized with terror like a man who has been lulled asleep on a desert and fearful island and who wakes up without any idea where he is and with no means of escape.[57]

On such a "desert and fearful island" we also are; it is the desert island of the modern world "ruled" by reason which has replaced faith. For, Adams maintains, when twelfth-century schoolmen substituted reason for faith, rhetoric for spontaneity, and dialectic for emotion, they initiated a psychological phase which could only end in futile abstractions: "Time has settled few or none of the essential points of dispute. Science hesitates, more visibly than the church ever did, to decide once for all whether unity or diversity is ultimate law; whether order or chaos is the governing rule of the universe, if universe there is; whether anything except phenomena exists." Finally, there is only one possible solution; "and science only repeats what the church said to Abélard, that when we know so little, we had better hold our tongue."[58]

So Abélard was silenced. Yet, if we consider *Mont-Saint-Michel and Chartres* from a purely dramatic point of view (did not Adams plan to write a "drama" of the Middle Ages?) Abélard will certainly not appear as the villain of the play; indeed he rather seems to act the part of a hero, not unlike Hamlet, who makes *catharsis* possible. It is easy to understand how Adams could—more or less consciously—identify himself with this man "well-born," whose chief crime was to be more intelligent than his contemporaries, and whose long, nerve-racking struggle (he had by the end of his life become "a nervous invalid") eventuated in his condemnation by a "carefully packed and overawed" council,[59] not unlike an American Senate sitting to pass judgment over an Adams.

To be sure, Abélard had engineered his own fate by making religion the playground of human dialectics. As R. P. Blackmur says: "Abélard made anarchic hash of official theology by introducing the human concept into the irreconcilable conflict between Realism and Nominalism."[60] In other words, he introduced into religion all the contradictions of the mind—its eternal tug-of-war, its irresolvable problems; in so doing, he jeopardized the emotional unity on which medieval society had until then, according to Adams, rested secure. The real trouble with Abélard's venture, as we are made to realize, is that in effect he was dehumanizing religion as well as rendering it unintelligible. To the Holy Mother who had been a "human symbol" accessible to all ("no human being was so stupid as not to understand that the father, mother and child made a trinity,") he substituted the Holy Ghost, of which "he became a sort of apostle." And even though he and his followers feebly tried to give the Holy Ghost the Mother's attributes —Love, Charity, Grace—the Holy Ghost remained but a cold concept, shorn of all emotional appeal. "Castrated," Blackmur explains, Abélard "had become a lover of the abstract; the mystery disappeared because he could no longer feel it."[61] Such a physiological explanation, however, is nowhere implied by Adams, and even appears totally irrelevant in the light of his psychological allegory.

"To this day," Adams remarks, "Abélard remains a problem as perplexing as he must have been to Héloïse, and almost as fascinating." Assuredly he is the most complicated hero in *Mont-Saint-Michel and Chartres* as well as the one "lover" distinctly superior to his "lady"; Adams has created a character existing at least on two levels, and the conflict between these contradictory aspects of his creation reflects a very basic tension in his own mind.

When he wrote his marginal comments on William James' *Principles of Psychology,* he did not content himself with offering his own definition of instinct, which I have quoted; "but," he went on, "is my habit of mind—reasoning by analysis or synthesis—an instinct incident to self-preservation? Reason is an instinct."[62] This is why Abélard's faith in logic can now appear to match the masculine militancy of the Norman builders of Mont St. Michel. Indeed he had come up from Brittany to Paris, "with as much faith in logic as [Saint] Bernard had in prayer or Godfrey of Bouillon had in arms," and he led "an equal or even a greater number of combatants." What he and his followers attempted was "the conquest of heaven by force of pure reason." Using architectural similes, which already prepare the extended metaphor of the "Thomistic cathedral," Adams shows how the intensity of the scholastic disputations between Abélard and William of Champeaux truly rivaled the architecture of the abbey on the mount. "Realism was the Roman arch—the only possible foundation for any church; because it assumed unity." Like a Gothic architect challenging the infinite, Abélard flung the "broken arch" of his ambitious, restless thought. The reason why he could not help failing only appears when he is examined on another level. "With infinite regret," Adams asserts, "Héloïse must be left out of the story." Without her, nevertheless, the story as it is told to us would lose all its meaning. Not a "philosopher, she philosophized only for the sake of Abélard while Abélard taught philosophy to her not so much because he believed in philosophy or in her as because he believed in himself."[63] In the last words of this sentence we find a key not only to this particular "story," but to all of *Mont-Saint-Michel and Chartres.* Abélard's tragedy has its source, not in his mutilation but in his self-consciousness. With reason, as long as it remains a simple energetic instinct, there is nothing wrong. It is when Man becomes self-conscious that reason deteriorates into logic. Then Man is lost; self-centered, he is no longer able to lose himself in a bigger energy. Logic, according to Adams, is not only a degradation of instinct but the death of it: such is the moral toward which his psychological allegory tends.

Yet, as far as Abélard is concerned, his case remains amenable to the twelfth century which was "a childlike time"; he himself was

"childlike" in his use of theology, and if, against his better understanding, he questioned the divinity of the Mother, with what
youthful fervor he worshipped the Father, the Son, and the Holy
Ghost in his little oratory of reeds and thatch at the Paraclete, not
unlike the bower Nicolette builds for herself in the *Chantefable!*
Héloïse became "prioress of the Oratory of the Holy Trinity," still
—we must understand—ensuring a woman's presence in the
Trinity. What Adams implies is that, owing to the sheer force of
Héloïse's personality (she was "a French woman to the last milli-
metre of her shadow") Abélard could still yield, even in spite of
himself, to the emotional unity of his age. Thus, if, on a rational
level, Abélard's story appears to be that of a failure, because his
"logic" already contained all the seeds of modern multiplicity, on
an emotional (or medieval) level, it could still be the tale of a
victory. It is a paradox (but a revealing one) that here are the
only "lovers" of whom it is said in *Mont-Saint-Michel and Chartres*
that they will remain forever united by the grace of God. The
promise is in a letter ringing "with absolute passion," which Peter
the Venerable sent to Héloïse after Abélard's death and which
serves as a fitting conclusion to this particular chapter. One must
see it all as a myth. Confused, contradictory, human (indeed
"perplexing" as well as "fascinating") Abélard's mythic figure then
truly appears to be the best fulcrum on which Adams could rest
his diffuse meaning.[64]

In the following chapter, Adams shows how, during the golden
age of the Gothic, "the Mystics" reacted against the tendency to
abstraction, repressing it by the compelling force of their personality. These men did not need the "ignorance" of reason to
reach God; for them "the only way to reach God was to deny the
value of reason and to deny reason was scepticism." As Adams also
remarks in the same chapter: "Religious minds prefer scepticism.
The true saint is a profound sceptic; a total disbeliever in human
reason, who has more than once joined hands on this ground with
some who were at best sinners. Bernard was a total disbeliever in
scholasticism." True to the faith of his time Saint Bernard nonetheless chanted with all his heart the glory of the Virgin. And
even though Adam of Saint-Victor sang the theology of the Holy
Ghost in his verse, still, "the Holy Ghost, as usual, profited by it

much less than the Virgin." Indeed, the mystics of the school of Saint-Victor all knew that "in essence, religion was love; in no case it was logic." God could be known only "directly; by emotion." And this was even truer of Saint Francis, "the ideal mystic saint of Western Europe," for whom "Satan was logic." Saint Francis, Adams notes, "was elementary nature itself . . . he was Greek in his joy of life." Nearly verbatim the same words are applied to Clarence King in *The Education;* even more than King, and to the same degree as Mary of Chartres, the saint appears to be the very incarnation of "feminine" intuition: "Both" [Mary and Saint Francis] "were illogical and heretical by essence"; both were loved for their very heresies. The true psychological importance of Saint Francis, at this point of Adams' story, is that he represents the "ultimate expression" of instinct: "He carried to its last point the mystical union with God and its necessary consequence of contempt and hatred for human intellectual processes."[65] Yet Saint Francis' solution was too extreme, or to use Adams' own term, too "extravagant"; it could not prevail in a world where logic now made deep inroads. As Adams also notes, "long before St. Francis' death, in 1226, the French mystics had exhausted their energies and the siècle had taken new heart." It was the time when Saint Thomas Aquinas entered the medieval stage.[66]

Entirely devoted to the "Angelic Doctor," the last chapter of *Mont-Saint-Michel and Chartres* has been characterized by Michael Colacurcio as "in many ways, the most important in the book." And indeed, to Henry Adams himself, this was "the only thing I ever wrote which I almost think good." "As personal to me," he commented to William James, the volume "is all in the last chapter."[67] It was understandably easier to identify oneself—at least openly, by way of an extended joke—with this scholarly "doctor," rather than with Abélard, or even Saint Francis. Besides, Henry Adams' interpretation of "Thomism" as a cathedral helped him to bring *Mont-Saint-Michel and Chartres* to a forceful close. Adams adduces the encyclical of Pope Leo XIII, the *Aeterni Patris* of 1879, to prove his thesis that "on the wings of St. Thomas' genius, human reason has reached the most sublime height it can probably attain." It was, however, but a desperate venture; the equilibrium of Saint Thomas' Intellectual Church appears all too precarious and its collapse inevitable, just as was the collapse of the Beauvais cathedral, foreshadowed at the end of *Mont-Saint-Michel and Chartres:* "The equilibrium is visibly delicate beyond the line of safety; danger lurks in every stone." It also turns out that the architectural analogy had a direct bearing on Adams' approach to the *Summa Theologiae:* "The foundation—the structure —the congregation—are enough for students of art; his ideas of law, ethics and politics; his vocabulary, his syllogisms, his arrangements are, like the drawings of Villard de Honnecourt's sketchbook, curious but not vital."[68] As a result, Adams concerns himself with less than one-fifth of the entire body of Thomistic philosophy; by failing to discuss Saint Thomas' theories of law, ethics and politics, he in fact neglects what to many modern analysts seems the most "vital" and relevant item of this philosophy: the theory of natural law. Indeed, taking interest only in metaphysics proper, he selects but one argument, out of Saint Thomas' five proofs of the existence of God: the argument from motion.

A guiding principle in this choice is Adams' conception of architecture as energy; for how can one explain "motion" if not in terms of "energy"? Thus the architectural parallel will run into the very heart of Adams' discussion of God; metaphysical speculation is deliberately placed upon a practical plane by the use of technical or "scientific" comparisons, terms, and ideas. This cannot be done without some distortions. Strikingly enough, one of the grossest is in Adams' very exposition of Saint Thomas' argument: "I see motion," said Thomas: "I infer a motor!" The Latin word used by Saint Thomas is *movens,* which theologians normally translate as *mover.* No doubt such a rendering sounds a little ludicrous to the modern ear, "as if God were some sort of Supreme Freight Agent." Michael Colacurcio explains why it alone is acceptable: "*Movens* is, in form, a verbal noun; as such it points first of all to activity: it describes a being as an agent rather than as a nature. Thus *mover,* in the accepted philosophical jargon, signifies any being which acts in any way whatever to produce motion (change) of any sort whatever. *Motor,* on the other hand, with its unmistakable materialist and mechanist suggestions, is clearly inappropriate to Thomas' notion of God as Pure Spiritual Act."[69] But it precisely was because of these "mechanist suggestions" that Adams preferred the term.

Confronting the metaphysician with an "average mechanic," he could thus oppose: "I see motion . . . I infer energy. I see motion everywhere; I infer energy everywhere," or, in other words, "an infinite series of motors." And if Saint Thomas insisted that he could only infer, "somewhere at the end of the series, an intelligent, fixed motor," the mechanic's pragmatic rejoinder was hard to "floor": "No doubt . . . we can conduct our works as well on that as on any other theory, or as we could on no theory at all; but if you offer it as a proof, we can only say that we have not yet reduced all motion to one source or all energies to one law, much less to one act of creation, although we have tried our best." The direction of Adams' thought is clear enough. He adumbrated one of the main themes of *The Education*, that if faith did constitute the principal unity in the Middle Ages, twentieth-century "unity" could only be apprehended in a purely mechanistic, that is, inhuman, order. Indeed, this is already the gist of his comments on Saint Thomas' reasoning: "The scheme seems to differ little, and unwillingly, from a system of dynamics as modern as the dynamo. Even in the prime motor, from the moment of action, freedom of will vanished."[70] "Will," that is, the energy of Mary, who alone, thanks to her feminine intuition, could embrace all contradictions and unify the world, disappears, killed by Saint Thomas' ruthless "logic." There is no Liberty, no Love, no Faith, only twentieth-century multiplicity, which, at the end of *Mont-Saint-Michel and Chartres*, the dynamo already begins to symbolize. "Chaos," nothing but "chaos," will finally prevail.

A "SENTIMENTAL NIHILISM"?

According to J. P. McIntyre, *Mont-Saint-Michel and Chartres* is to be understood as a "stepping down," which the opening and closing images of the book illustrate. In contrast with the proud beginning: "The Archangel loved *heights*," there comes at the end the failure of the Gothic: "The pathos of its self-distrust and anguish of doubt is *buried* in the *earth* as its last secret." In reality, the Palace of the Virgin of Chartres, flinging up "the delight of its aspirations . . . to the sky," rises much above the spire of Mont-Saint-Michel, destroying all possibility for a descensional continuum. Let us accordingly keep the metaphor of a diagram—that of a diagram whose descending line projects considerably further down *ad infinitum*. As Adams explained to Albert S. Cook, in August of 1910:

The *Chartres* volume . . . was intended to fix the starting point, since, I could not get enough material to illustrate primitive society, or the society of the seventh century B.C. as I would have liked. I wanted to show the intensity of the vital energy of a given time, and of course that intensity had to be started in its two highest terms—religion and art . . . My idea is that the world outside—the so-called modern world—can only pervert and degrade the conceptions of the primitive instinct of art and feeling, and that our only chance is to accept the limited number of survivors—the one-in-a-thousand of born artists and poets—and to intensify the energy of feeling within that radiant centre. In other words, I am a creature of our poor Calvinistic, St. Augustinian fathers, and am not afraid to carry out my logic to the rigorous end of regarding our present society, its ideals and purposes, as dregs and fragments of some primitive essential instinct now nearly lost. If you are curious to see the theory stated as official instruction, you have only to look over Bergson's *Evolution Créatrice* (pp. 288, 289). The tendencies of thought in Europe seems to me very strongly that way.

The best point of reference is of course provided by *The Education*. The two volumes really go together, as Adams himself asserts, toward the end of the latter:

Any schoolboy could see that man as a force must be measured by motion, from a fixed point. Psychology helped here by suggesting a unit—the point of history when man held the highest idea of himself as a unit in a unified universe. Eight or ten years of study had led Adams to think he might use the century 1150–1250, expressed in Amiens Cathedral and the Works of Thomas Aquinas, as the unit from which he might measure motion down to his own time, without assuming anything as true or untrue, except relation. The movement might be studied at once in philosophy and mechanics. Setting himself to the task, he began a volume which he mentally knew as "Mont-Saint-Michel and Chartres: A Study of Thirteenth-Century Unity." From that point he proposed to fix a position for himself, which he could label: "The Education of Henry Adams: A Study of Twentieth-Century Multiplicity." With the help of these two points in relation, he hoped to project his lines forward and backward indefinitely, subject to correction from any one who should know better.

Thus, as he also stated in 1910, *Mont-Saint-Michel and Chartres* "began the demonstration of the law" which *The Education* illustrates.[71]

Still in 1910, in "A Letter to American Teachers of History" he formulated that law conclusively enough to enable his students to comprehend "the series." Defining history as "the Science of Vital Energy in relation with Time," Adams posited that, since thought, "the substance of history," is a force, it must be measured by the laws which govern all force. There is no need to dwell on the particulars of these laws.[72] It has been conclusively demonstrated that when he tried, as a scientific historian, to reconstruct human activity according to the rules of physics, Adams was choosing a blind path. It is not merely the fact that his superficial knowledge of science invalidates his hypotheses, or the fact that he continually mistook metaphor for scientific proposition. Indeed, if it were granted that thought is an energy, it does not at all follow that thought is subject to the second law of thermodynamics or any other "scientific" law, because thought essentially transcends the limits of matter. The logical paradox which confronts Adams and his position as historian nullifies the study of history; as W. H. Jordy puts it: "Holding that science was the degradation of art, he still insisted on a science of history. Once achieved, such a science apparently proved that the proper teaching of history eliminated the subject taught." Even if Adams was aware of this basic contradiction, it could hardly embarrass him, since paradox was not only "his constant defence" but the essence of his thought.[73]

The real issue is not here. For, with special reference to *Mont-Saint-Michel and Chartres,* it fundamentally matters little that Adams' scientific theories were untenable—or even that his vision of the Middle Ages turns out to be vitiated throughout. Of course the so-called unity which he purported to find in these times did not then any more exist than in many other given periods. A good case can be made, as has been done by Yvor Winters, in direct rebuttal of Adams' assumptions. Thus Winters points to the chaotic character of the feudal system as well as the contrast between the culture of the ruling class and the very primitive form of the peasant civilization, which in fact, remained pagan. Even the unity of the medieval church was, insofar as it has been achieved, "due less to the spirit of the age than to the mind of Thomas Aquinas."[74] Indeed, this explains the importance Adams attached

to Saint Thomas; here was the one case in point directly supporting his thesis, and he also used it to destroy it. As he said of his
philosophy elsewhere: "Thought alone was Form. Mind and unity
flourished . . . together." With proper adjustment, this holds true of
Adams' demonstration from beginning to end; there too, Thought
and Form are basically one, and interest us as such. The allegory
carries in itself its validity, irrespective of what the premises were.

"Unity is vision," Adams remarks in *The Education;* it is the
unity perceived by the child ("the child will always see but one")
as well as by the artist, that fount of ever-youthful intuition, and
it is also the real unity of *Mont-Saint-Michel and Chartres.* R.
Spiller has rightly pointed out that "Henry Adams was at heart an
artist first, an historian second; only in the *aesthetic* expression
of his position did he reach any degree of finality . . ."[75] It is not
yet the time, at this point of our study, to show how Adams succeeded in informing *Mont-Saint-Michel and Chartres* with an
aesthetic unity; what interests us here is the special quality of
the historian's vision, insofar as it was determined by the artist.
It is clear that Adams' philosophy of history actually *hinged* on
his use of the two root metaphors. Still in R. Spiller's words: "As
the power of the Virgin is humanity on the level of divinity, so
that of the dynamo mechanism raised to the infinite. In the one
case, the power operated on an impassive and nonhuman object,
the Cathedral of Chartres, which in a sense becomes a subordi-
nate or reflective symbol; in the other, the object of the mechanistic force is human, is Henry Adams made impersonal and
passive."[76] If the Virgin represents that aspect of nature, as an
active and vital process, which Spinoza called *natura naturans*—
nature begetting, the *élan vital* and creative evolution of Bergson
mentioned by Adams in his letter to A. S. Cook—the dynamo
cannot certainly be identified with Spinoza's complementary aspect of nature, *natura naturata*, nature begotten, the material and
contents of nature, its myriad external forms. There is no possible
dichotomy in Adams' vision. His dynamo is just as active and
vital as the Virgin and has for him the same ontological significance as is proved by the "Prayer to the Virgin and the Dynamo."
Yet what do they have in common except what Adams calls in
his chapter on "The Dynamo and the Virgin," in *The Education,*

the "attraction on his mind"? Defining them as two kingdoms of
force, which "had nothing in common but attraction," Adams is
then purposedly ambiguous, since he leaves us the task of decid-
ing whether by *attraction* he means their magnetic power on
mankind as a whole or—more credibly—merely on Henry Adams
himself.[77]

Although the power of the dynamo is that of a physical measurable force which can be gauged in units of horsepower, it is
evident that its effect—or rather the effect of all that it symbolizes—counts only inasmuch as it is personally experienced by
Adams. In the same way, for all the practical evidence (the millions invested in such costly, such magnificent cathedrals)
brought up as a measure of Mary's attraction on her medieval
worshippers, the only real measure remains the personal reaction
of the individual Henry Adams, who, in *The Education,* tells how
he too "invested" in the Virgin by buying a Mercedes and went
the round of her sanctuaries, "wooing" her as "an adorable mistress." His mind, Mabel Hooper La Farge observes, "might be
exercising in dynamic theories and mounting on dizzy flights, but
his soul had found a refuge, in which he could stay forever."[78]
Not that we should believe what his niece (herself a convert)
here suggests, that he was leaning to the Catholic faith and even
in the secret of his heart became a convert. This view was not
shared by her own brother-in-law, John La Farge, S.J., who often
met Adams in his later years and testified that he could never
quite "free himself from his own introspection and inhibitions."
If it was possible for a man, afflicted, as he said, with acute "Bos-
tonitis," to lose his youthful prejudices (he had never heard "of
the Virgin except as idolatry"), how could he have lost the very
nature of his personality?[79]

We might here join the critics who have examined Adams in
relation to his New England background, and in particular Paul
Elmer More, who saw in him the archetype of the latter-day New
Englander, one who has lost the positive faith of his Puritan
forbears yet is unable to rest easy in negation. Adams' dilemma,
P. E. More explains, came from the inconsistency of a "conscience
that has outlived faith, and has not found philosophy." His only
resource, eventually, would be a sort of "sentimental nihilism, a

compensation, genuine if inadequate, for a lost religion." ("A modern nihilist," Yvor Winters has said of him, "and hence a hedonist or nothing.")[80] This seems unfair to the man who wrote *Mont-Saint-Michel and Chartres*, for what is the meaning of the psychological allegory we have been reading if not that faith alone (call it "instinct") saves? From beginning to end, the book professes faith in the efficacity of faith—faith blind, unreasoning, as when it wrought miracles in the service of the Virgin. To be sure the symbol of faith which Adams extols seems not only unorthodox, heretical, and irrational but, we do feel, at times, plainly incongruous, as is the dynamo-worship in *The Education.*

Rather than smiling, or being shocked, at Adams' very peculiar form of Mariolatry, informed with personal memories, and his fanciful reduction of the mystery of the Trinity to all-too-human terms, we must respect the deep impulse which was behind it all, and realize that Adams had, after his own fashion, really found a "refuge in which his soul could stay." For his conscience was not exactly, as P. E. More said, "moving, so to speak, *in vacuo*, like a dispossessed ghost seeking a substantial habitation"; he was not, to use T. S. Eliot's simile, "seeking for education with the wings of a beautiful but ineffectual conscience, beating noisily in a vacuum jar."[81] Colacurcio has convincingly placed him by the side of Jonathan Edwards, Emerson, Hawthorne, and William James in a large American tradition which is that of fideism; he too "urge[d] the transcendent value of the 'heart.'" Even so, it remains to be stressed that this tradition was much more literary than "philosophical." At bottom Adams could not be any more of a "believer," even diffusely, than he was a thinker. One of the most correct remarks ever made about him is by Herbert L. Creek: "the mind of Henry Adams played with ideas rather than absorbed them."[82] Similarly, it seems, his heart *played* with faith (or faiths); absorption was on an altogether different level, and it is that one level which finally counts. Imagination was Adams' real "refuge"; therein is to be found the "unity" of *Mont-Saint-Michel and Chartres* without which there would be no "meaning." Instead of a sentimental nihilism, what we shall see is the triumphant affirmation of Art.

8
The "Unity" of
Mont-Saint-Michel and Chartres

"A SORT OF RAGBAG OF EVERYTHING"?

From Papeete in May, 1891, Adams writes to Mrs. Cameron: "I have entangled two centuries of family history, and got it wound up nicely. I have rewritten two chapters, making a very learned disquisition on Tahitian genealogy, mixed up with legends and love-songs. The thing would be rather pretty if I only knew how to do it, or perhaps it might be better if I were writing it on my own account; but as it is for Marau in the first person, I have to leave out everything risky." This is the beginning of his "Travels/Tahiti" which, as we know, are clearly at the origin of his "Travels/France." For the time being, it is but a mere "moment of amusement" for the "passing traveller" that he is; and Adams does not feel altogether equal to the undertaking. As he also then tells Mrs. Cameron: "The legends and poetry of the island can be made interesting only by stringing them on a narrative and Stevenson could have done it better than any one else, for he has a slight hand, when he likes, and can write verse as well as prose. My hand is too heavy for such work, and here I am anyway only a passing traveller trying to find a moment of amusement to vary the wild monotony of island life." The seed of another and bigger work is here; it would have to be done by several hands. Adams suggests it to John Hay, in a letter from Paris on January 9, 1892: "I will come home, and immediately, if you will join me in writing under any assumed name or character you please, a volume or two of Travels which will permit me to express my opinion of life in general, and especially of the French, their literature and their art. I won't do it alone. Such a book, to be amusing, needs variety of treatment and experience." If King could be induced to join in the writing, "so much the better"; this is after all "only our old scheme," the enlargement of an idea they played with when the "Five of Hearts" were still five, before Marian's death. Adams elaborates his proposal: "My notion of Travels is a sort of ragbag of everything; scenery, psychology, history, literature, poetry, art; anything in short that is worth throwing in; and I want to grill a few literary and political gentlemen to serve with champagne."[1]

Neither Hay nor King can then respond to Adams' plea "to keep me going"; yet the notion of "Travels" will persist. The Norman tour of 1895 gives Adams his real subject; years of slow accretion eventuate in his decision to start on the work alone; and the result, after several more years of "life in the Gothic," is *Mont-Saint-Michel and Chartres,* which contains something of all the subjects listed in the letter to John Hay, though nothing is simply thrown in. The 1891 "ragbag," in J. C. Levenson's words, "proved to be a silk purse and the casual project turned into a labor of infinite patience."[2]

Such a long gestation, and then so much solitary labor, have marked the structure of the book, no doubt the most severely organized of all of Adams' works. It is composed like a triptych, with the first three chapters neatly balancing the last three.[3] Adams' vision of eleventh-century art and his interpretation of thirteenth-century scholastic philosophy flank with due Gothic proportions the twelfth-century shrine of the Virgin. In fact, three architectural structures: the Romanesque abbey at Mont-Saint-Michel, the Gothic cathedral at Chartres, and the *Summa Theologiae* of Saint Thomas Aquinas, representing the Church Intellectual, itself equated with Beauvais cathedral, all combine into one dominant symbol, the Cathedral, which gives *Mont-Saint-Michel and Chartres* its informing unity. There is here more than a matter of what J. C. Levenson calls "linguistic organization," even if architecture does provide a vocabulary of metaphors throughout the book. John P. McIntyre has rightly stressed "the monolithic quality of this basic image which enables Adams to convey his myth," as well as it reveals his affinity with the American literary tradition: "In its way, the cathedral replies to Melville's 'great white whale' and Twain's apotheosis of the Mississippi."[4] Between these authors and Adams, though, an essential difference is to be discerned. For whereas the chapters on cetology in *Moby Dick* do not fully coalesce into Melville's narrative and the lack of unity and coherence in *The Adventures of Huckleberry Finn* is only too apparent, Adams' disquisitions, whether they be on glass, literature, or scholastic philosophy, certainly fuse into a whole; they are integral parts of his expanding symbol.

By and large, Melville, Mark Twain, and Adams work on similar planes, each tells of a terrestrial journey with a spiritual destination; and each has chosen to contain his subject within the medium of the personal narrative. The obvious disparity between their books cannot be explained merely in terms of geographical setting or by the different scope and color of the adventures they recount; more fundamentally, it has to be traced to the position of the narrator within the personal narrative itself. For unlike Ishmael and Huck Finn, who are helplessly carried along in their own adventures, "the uncle" always remains master of his direction; far more than the other two characters, he can thus command the form of the book in a way consonant with Adams' notion of writing a story, as he told William James in February 1908, "with an end and object, not for the sake of the object, but for the form." Manner, not matter, is all-essential to Adams, as is made clear by his letter to Mrs. Eustis, also dated February 1908: "Between artists or people trying to be artists, the sole interest is that of the form. Whether one builds a house, or paints a picture, or tells a story, our point of vision regards only the form—not the matter. The two volumes have not been done in order to teach others, but to educate myself in the possibilities of literary form. The arrangement, the construction, the composition, the art of climax are our only serious study." The volume bracketed with *Mont-Saint-Michel and Chartres* is *The Education*, in which Adams recognizes that "the form fails"; such a failure, if we accept Adams' judgment as well as his own notion of how a story should be written, must be ascribed wholly to the position of the central character in the latter volume.[5]

Although he is not himself the narrator, the "manikin" in *The Education* resembles Ishmael or Huck Finn in that he follows the course of his story more than he leads it; indeed "things happen to him" in exactly the same way as they will, according to Wyndham Lewis' definition, to the Hemingway hero. Never by his own choosing, but because his life is "a succession of violent breaks and waves, with no base at all," he appears to be jolted from one situation to another, without ever being able to provide the tale with more than a focal or passive unity. On the contrary, setting his own pace as well as the itinerary, and ever keeping the thread of the narrative in hand, the "uncle" plays an active, highly unifying role; he is Mentor, in a modern and even more efficient ("practical") transposition, guiding female Telemachi on a conducted tour of French medieval art and seeing to it that his charges get full profit out of their field study. The "base" of the book is that of a lesson; to quote John P. McIntyre, "it is a literary exercise in the development of historical imagination,"—an "exercise," let us add, conceived with great pedagogical talent.[6]

There are, in *Mont-Saint-Michel and Chartres*, three patterns of coherence—spatial, temporal, logical—providing a causal nexus between all phases of the study. For in spite of the apparent wealth of learned allusions ranging far and wide in nearly all corners of civilisation, the object of the study remains circumscribed within clear limits. Beginning at Mont-Saint-Michel and moving across Normandy and Ile de France to Chartres, with an extension to Assisi, the tour imposes a spatial unity. Similarly, a broad chronological pattern embracing three centuries is observed. As one gradually advances in time and space along parallel lines, convenient signposts are provided in the form of announcements, rapprochements, or reminders, which knit together the main topics (but few in number, they are made to appear temptingly simple) of what we may call the syllabus. A good instance is the capsule at the end of chapter 1: "At Chartres we shall find Charlemagne and Roland dear to the Virgin, and at about the same time, as far away as at Assisi in the Perugian country, Saint Francis himself—the nearest approach the Western world ever made to an Oriental incarnation of the divine essence—loved the French *romans,* and typified himself in the 'Chanson de Roland.' With Mont-Saint-Michel, the 'Chanson de Roland' is almost one. The 'Chanson' is in poetry what the Mount is in architecture."[7] If repetition is at the heart of pedagogy, so is the adherence to a simple method. In each chapter, the uncle, alias Professor Adams, proceeds from artistic effects to their social causes: the abbey on Mont-Saint-Michel as well as the *Chanson de Roland,* for instance, both serve to reveal the military character proper to eleventh-century society. Exposition precedes deduction in a way which J. C. Levenson characterizes as the constant "pull from tourist geography" (be the "geography" a monument or a book) "to poetic history."[8] Indeed, the device is so regularly used that it comes close to appearing artificial. If it does not, it is because it falls within a larger scheme. Added to the structural and rhetorical unity of *Mont-Saint-Michel and Chartres,* an even more fundamental aesthetic unity must be discerned.

"Taking architecture" (and not only architecture, but art in general) "as an expression of energy," *Mont-Saint-Michel and Chartres* records the energy of medieval art and society. This is Adams' subject matter; for as he says, "yet half the interest of architecture consists in the sincerity of the society that builds."[9] The methods by which he sets about exploring his subject matter consists, as we know, in arranging a series of documents. Thus, in *Mont-Saint-Michel and Chartres,* the historian bows to scientific objectivity in exactly the same way as he does in his *History of the United States during the Administrations of Jefferson and Madison.* "He typified," says W. H. Jordy, "the scientific approach in his emphasis on the historian's function as . . . a transparent eyeball to the past."[10] What apparently escaped him—or, at least, did not enter his definition of the scientific historian—is that the selection and arrangement of pertinent documents implicitly involves an aesthetic. A rapprochement which Max Baym makes with Michelet helps us to understand Adams' real attitude toward his data:

Implicit in romanticism is the idea that the recollection of the past, in spite of its chronicle-aspects (presumably matters of fact), is essentially an aesthetic process. The historian *selects* the facts in reconstructing the past; *i.e.,* he arranges, he composes his materials. His arrangement, his composition, is conditioned by the quality of his imagination which, willy-nilly, infuses into the facts the image he has of that which he is reconstructing. That image then colors the facts and creates for us, who read history, the appeal to our own imagination. Through the enticements of the historian, we are led to contemplate the past aesthetically. It is this process which creates our fascination for *Mont-Saint-Michel and Chartres* and links Adams to Michelet, both having started with an appreciation for the exact manipulation of facts according to *la méthode venue d'Allemagne.*[11]

It does not, however, seem that Adams made great use of Michelet's *Histoire de France* (which he mentions but once) in the writing of *Mont-Saint-Michel and Chartres.* There are obvious similarities, such as their conception of woman as a central power in the organization of society; yet, even if both writers do lend the color and movement of fiction to the history they recreate, their recreations remain strikingly different at least in one major essential. Michelet's Middle Ages really throb with the life of millions of French peasant ancestors, whereas, by his own admission, Adams only concerns himself "with the artistic and social side of life." Since this social aspect more often than not merely coincides with the life of aristocratic circles, the air we breathe in *Mont-Saint-Michel and Chartres* is much more rarefied. But another more direct reason for Adams' greater "aestheticism" in his interpretation of the French Middle Ages is that the only documents he cared to deal with were works of art.

In "The Aesthete Henry Adams," Ernst Scheyer quotes Friedrich Kainz's definition: "The aesthete is committed to an experience of aesthetic values in situations where other kinds of experience alone are suitable." This definition fits Adams particularly well, since, instead of basing his study of energy on more or less measurable data, such as the growth of population or the development of economy, he refers to data which ought to—and in fact can only be—apprehended in a purely intuitive, non-measurable way. For he uses works of art not merely to illustrate the progress of civilization but as "aesthetic verifications" of his " 'dynamic' theory of the rise and fall of mankind in general." At the very outset of the journey, he thus has to impose on his reader an aesthetic approach to the subject matter: "Religious art is the measure of human depth and sincerity; any triviality, any weakness cries aloud." Deploring the fact that "we have lost many senses," particularly the power to see and feel, Adams deprecates those tourists who would substitute mere facts for feelings: "To overload the memory with dates is the vice of every schoolmaster and the passion of every second-rate scholar. Tourists want as few dates as possible; what they want is poetry."[12]

To counteract the jaded sensibilities of twentieth-century man, Adams insists that the "tourist" of *Mont-Saint-Michel and Chartres* feels the emotion contained in medieval works of art. The theme of lost emotion and the inability to recover it recur throughout the tour. After the analysis of the *Chanson de Roland*, we are told: "Our age has lost much of its ear for poetry, as it has its eye for colour and line, and its taste for war and worship, wine and women. Not one man in a hundred thousand could now feel what the eleventh century felt in these verses of the 'Chanson,' and there is no reason for trying to do so, but there is a certain use in trying for once to understand not so much the feeling as the meaning. The naivete of the poetry is that of the society." Later, speaking of the spiritual value implicit in the *grisaille* windows of Chartres, Adams observes: "Grisaille is a separate branch of colour-decoration which belongs to the whole system of lighting and fenêtrage, and will have to remain a closed book because the feeling and experience which explained it once are lost, and we cannot recover either. Such things must have been always felt rather than reasoned, like the irregularities in plan of the builders; the best work of the best times shows the same subtlety of sense as the dog shows in retrieving, or the bee in flying, but which tourists have lost." The best that can be expected from the modern tourist is an attempt "to feel what he can." This is why, in order to further his niece's (or reader's) "sentimental" education, Adams focuses not on the fact but on the feeling: "It is the stamp we want to distinguish in order to trace up our lines of artistic ancestry." Just as the societies which he is studying disdained historical accuracy, so he concentrates on the aesthetic and emotional qualities of his literary and architectural documents; constantly iterated and controlling Adams' insight into all phases of cultural history, this aesthetic preoccupation informs the book throughout, giving it its severest unity—as well as its major value.[13]

"AESTHETICISM AS A WAY OF LIFE"?[14]

Although *Mont-Saint-Michel and Chartres* obliquely purports to be scientific history, it is clear that it nevertheless intentionally defines an aesthetic sensibility. The arcana of science undoubtedly provided Adams with a background of imagery and theme, but as a literary man, he was free to manipulate his materials in conformity with an aesthetic credo. To quote W. H. Jordy: "Whether or not Adams correctly interpreted his scientific evidence is in itself unimportant, since on the score of exactitude the literary man has always enjoyed considerable leeway. But where scientific data comprise the stuff out of which the image appears, and without which no image would exist, it is certainly mandatory to examine the choices made, the basis of choice, and the effect of this choice on the intended imagery. In Adams' instance his pattern of selection has particular importance, for he sought a tension between the scientific fact, the emotional image, and a personal reference. So must his critic."[15] Adams' success as a man of letters therefore depends not on the scientific or historical accuracy of his work but on the literary effect of this tension, which we are now, thanks to his teaching, in a position to feel.

How easy it is then, in this new context, to perceive how Adams' scientific imagery, with its insistent reference to the notions of force, energy, and degradation, truly acquired, despite its facility and imprecision, emotional depth as well as thematic relevance! For the conflict which engages Adams on the literary level reveals itself to be not the degradation of instinct as opposed to reason but what Ludwig Lewisohn, in *Expression in America*, calls the problem "of creative expression in any and all of its forms having nothing left to express but the narrowly individual, unrooted in any collective faith, binding, form, culture."[16] Adams' juxtaposition of the Virgin and the Dynamo, already at the heart of *Mont-Saint-Michel and Chartres,* and which is going to receive full exemplification with the completion of the "series," finds its psychological validity in that it proves a warning against the increasing mechanization of society and the coeval depersonalization of man.[17]

Caught not only in the "America of the nineteenth century" but in the twentieth-century dilemma between scientific specialization and the fragmentation of man, Adams, even when he is treating of the Middle Ages, never in reality loses sight of the "new American," as he is going to describe him in *The Education:* "The new American showed his parentage proudly; he was the child of steam and the brother of the dynamo, and already, within less than thirty years, this mass of mixed humanities, brought together by steam, was squeezed and welded into approach to shape; a product of so much mechanical power, and bearing no distinctive marks but that of its pressure."[18] It is this lack of human personality and individuality, accomplished so swiftly, yet radically, which has startled Adams into his "dynamic theory of history," as well as setting him on the road to Chartres. From a society controlled by coal, electricity, and machinery, he could only recoil in stupefaction. Indeed, if as Samuels declares, "the real destination of his 'Travels' was of course his own age," the movement was back and forth, Adams being at the same time fascinated and repelled.[19]

As we know, Adams attributes to human reason and masculine logic this unleashing of new and uncontrollable energies which so thoroughly transforms our universe and drives it toward catastrophe. That logic cannot harness force constitutes its failure and its limitation. From this aspect, Adams' grudge against reason becomes intelligible, as does his linking, in a letter to Whitelaw Reid, the end of *Mont-Saint-Michel and Chartres* and that of *The Education:* "The volume on Chartres is involved in the same doubt, for both go together, the last three chapters of *The Education* being Q.E.D. of the last three chapters of *Chartres.*"[20] Thought, divorced from emotion and taste, results in a mathematical universe which renders art sterile and men impotent.

Indeed, the debaucheries of reason which robbed man of his personal grandeur and individual dignity, by substituting mechanical force for personal love, directly affected Art. If, in a physical sense, man can only accelerate his path to oblivion, this also, he felt, held true in a much larger sense; the mathematical universe, with its conventional abstractions and calculated symbolism, would eventually push thought "to the limits of its possibilities." In "The Rule of Phase applied to History," he called this phase of degradation the "ethereal" phase, succeeding the electrical phase: "Thought in terms of Ether means only Thought in terms of itself, or, in other words, pure Mathematics and Metaphysics."[21] That is to say that the nadir of human degradation occurs when man can no longer really communicate. As W. H. Jordy aptly condenses Adams' own reasoning: "To think was therefore eventually to lose touch with life, or with art, which Adams came to identify with life."[22] Hence the thematic use of the notion of life—good, true, *full* life, in opposition to science (or reason), which is not only "sarcastic," as Robert Frost will say, but devitalizing. And hence, also, the literal exactness of Adams' aim, repeatedly asserted, which is to find what the Middle Ages, or rather man when he was "rooted" in a collective faith and culture, "had to say." *Mont-Saint-Michel and Chartres* is first and foremost a study in artistic expression, expression, not for expression's or art's sake, but as a superior form of life.

The burden of Adams' contempt for logic, as witnessed in his treatment of the schoolmen and their preoccupation with universals, emphasizes the intrinsic failure of reason to grasp existential reality. Logic proves little but undoes much. Consequently Adams prefers images; he admits in *The Education:* "Images are not arguments, rarely even lead to proof, but the mind craves them, and of late more than ever, the keenest experimenters find twenty images better than one, especially if contradictory."[23] The synthetic imagination which unifies *Mont-Saint-Michel and Chartres* supports Adams' contention. For, to express what he himself has to say, the author resorts not only to the towering symbol of the Cathedral and the compelling image of the Virgin: first in order of entry as well as perhaps in psychological value, there is the "emotional image" *par excellence,* that of the child. "The man who wanders into the twelfth century is lost," we are admonished (page 2) "unless he can grow prematurely young. One can do it, as one can play with children." It suffices that one is willing to become Wordsworth's eternal child again:

What is curious to watch is the fanatical conviction of the Gothic enthusiast, to whom the twelfth century means exuberant youth, the eternal child of Wordsworth, over whom its immortality broods like the day; it is so simple, yet so complicated; it sees so much and so little; it loves so many toys and cares for so few necessities; its youth is so young, its age so old, and its youthful yearning for old thought is so disconcerting, like the mysterious senility of the baby that

> Deaf and silent, reads the eternal deep,
> Haunted forever by the eternal mind

One need not take it more seriously than one takes the baby itself.[24]

Childlikeness and feeling are corollaries, indeed truly synonymous in an existential sense, as when Adams says of Chartres ("a child's fancy; a toy-house to please the Queen of Heaven") that "any one can feel it who will only consent to feel like a child." Only the child can adequately respond to the superior "naivety" of the Middle Ages, whether it is to be found in the "childlike intensity" of Norman art, in the "laisses" of the *Chanson de Roland* or the "lyrics" of Adam de Saint-Victor, which read "much like a nursery rhyme," or even in Abelard's "childlike candour."[25]

In the image of the child, Adams has found the emotional reference which best enables him to disclose what he really pursues in this study of medieval unity. As he explains in "The Letter to American Teachers of History:" "Simplicity may not be evidence of truth, and unity is perhaps the most deceptive of all the innumerable illusions of mind; but both are primary instincts in man, and have an attraction on the mind akin to that of gravitation on matter. The idea of unity survives the idea of God or of the Universe; it is innate and intuitive."[26] Thus, if for a moment we lose sight of the schematic premises which give a rhetorical outline—but not more, indeed, than its outline—to the book, the theme of *Mont-Saint-Michel and Chartres* can be restated in Robert Spiller's phrasing: "The result has been served as a study of the medieval mind; it is only now coming to be recognized for its insight into the universal mind."[27] The children whom we see "sporting on the shore" of Wordsworth's "immortal sea" at the outset of our journey turn out to be that one child who is Father to the Man.

The literary value of *Mont-Saint-Michel and Chartres* precisely lies in this simplified allegory which brings out the unity, in fact, not of the world, but of the human person. Adams' quest for unity in thought as well as in action clearly presupposes an emotional and intellectual unity in the individual. And much of the book's relevance depends upon our apprehension of a central fact —that this individual is only by accident, and for the time of the "tale," the man of the Middle Ages. Essentially he is Everyman, and even more essentially he is Adams himself. Indeed, if *The Education* reveals, Paul Elmer More says, "the portrait of a naked mind caught by some art of spiritual photography," it is even clearer that *Mont-Saint-Michel and Chartres* "has made the whole mental and emotional life of the twelfth century a vehicle for the same insatiate personality."[28] It is Adams' personality, giving dimension and meaning to symbols which, within the framework of the "architectural" journey, all mirror and reflect but different aspects of the same self. Just as, by equating the old man that he is with the broken arch, the "uncle" builds himself into the cathedral, he clearly becomes the Wordsworthian child at the beginning of the book, when he declares: "Our sense is partially atrophied from disuse, but it is still alive, at least in old people, who alone, as a class, have the time to be young."[29]

His interest in medieval documents, he admits, "is a sign of a futile mind, no doubt," but there is no better way for Adams to follow the true bent of his personality. A metaphor he also uses in the first chapter is that of the *"pons seclorum, the bridge of ages, between us and our ancestors."* When this metaphor changes at last to *"Pons sanctorum*—over which only saints and children can pass,"* the formal achievement of *Mont-Saint-Michel and Chartres*, "completes its self-definition." And it is not only the definition of the journey which is completed, but that of the traveler himself; "children and saints," and also Adams, the man of paradox—"can believe two contrary things at the same time." Here is the true essence of the book, and the supreme reconciliation of the author with himself, in terms of art.[30]

It would be tempting to substitute for this metaphor of the bridge another; through his own "looking glass" (the binocle), Adams, in true Lewis Carroll fashion, gains access to a world of fantasy which meets the secret requirements of his personality. This is a world not of nonsense but of childish (or aesthetic) logic. Much more than Lewis Carroll's, it is a deeply personal world. Drawing a comparison between Adams' "Study in Thirteenth-century Unity" and his "Study in Twentieth-century Multiplicity," Michael Colacurcio has brought out an "interesting paradox": "The work which seems to be history turns out to be a good deal more personal than the one which seems to be autobiography." Although there is much self-revelation in *The Education*, it largely operates through nuance and implication. Adams reveals, not *himself*, "but always some particular version of himself, some dramatized construct or persona"; and he is not above taking with the true course of his life whatever liberties his theme and purpose require.[31] On the other hand, there is no distortion—conscious or unconscious—in his characterization of the "uncle." If liberties are taken in *Mont-Saint-Michel and Chartres*, it is with the medieval scene itself—the real "dramatized construct" here —and it is less a matter of willful inaccuracies than of arbitrary selection. Adams chose to see what suited his own "aristocratic terms," and these terms, as Ferner Nuhn remarks, "presupposed a privileged elite, an established social class, a political hereditary system, that simply did not exist in the United States."[32] The Middle Ages provided him with a congenial background, a sort of "land of heart's desire" where his feelings could freely expand. As a matter of fact, he could see his own family drama reenacted, the fall of the House of Mary corresponding to what was, for this fourth-generation Adams, the Fall of the House of Adams. Thus the autobiographical relevance heightens the psychological and emotional unity of *Mont-Saint-Michel and Chartres*.

ADAMS' "MUNDO"

"As I do not care to imitate Carlyle, and Ruskin and Emerson and all the rest of our protesting philosophers by trying to make a living by abusing the society of my time," Adams writes to Charles

Milnes Gaskell, on April 28, 1894, "nothing remains but to quit it, and seek another."[33] He is going to find this other society in the Middle Ages; what must be stressed here is that it is a private retreat; no other man of letters, no "protesting philosopher" accompanies him. Seen in a literary light, Adams' "pilgrimage" appears to have been a rather solitary journey.

We know that his movement could not parallel Ruskin's. It is not only that their temperaments diverged; they did not shrink from the same worlds. How could Adams have echoed Ruskin's protest against the sheer ugliness of the Victorian scene and the defilement of the English landscape? American nature, owing to the very dimensions of the United States, did not then seem to run the same danger of total defilement. And Adams, besides, did not feel concerned about the living and working conditions of what Jacob Riis then called "the other half." Unlike Ruskin he could not find in art, whether medieval or universal, a social panacea, because the word "social" did not have the same connotations for him. Of all the characters who flock into the pages of *The Education*, there is only one laborer, the gardener who, at his grandfather's house, tells young Henry that he'll be thinking he'll be President too; conversely, the exclusiveness of the society of *Mont-Saint-Michel and Chartres* is by now quite apparent. More than of Ruskin, then, Adams should make us think of the English *fin de siècle* aesthetes who simply turned their backs on their age and lived for art's sake. But here again the rapprochement comes to naught.

One of the most disappointing papers ever written on Adams is probably Ernst Scheyer's "The Aesthete Henry Adams"; this is due not to the author but to his very subject—in essence most elusive. For, although Adams' pursuit was primarily aesthetic, he himself never really posed as an aesthete, that is, to use the simplest dictionary definition, as "one professing devotion to the beautiful." One of the most surprising characteristics of *Mont-Saint-Michel and Chartres* (even more surprisingly, it has never been recognized), is the assiduousness with which Adams avoids passing aesthetic judgments of his own, as for instance on Chartres Cathedral: " 'Surely the most beautiful monument of this kind that we possess in France," *says Viollet-le-Duc*." Its stained glass windows are "the finest ever made," Viollet-le-Duc and Durand "are positive" about it. And this holds true for the Charlemagne window as well, whose "execution *is said* to be superb."[34] It seems as if Adams always prefers to rely on someone else's taste.

An explanation for this apparent diffidence can be provided by a comparison with Walter Pater. Although the "smile" of Chartres ("whatever Chartres may be now, when young it was a smile") inescapably calls to mind Mona Lisa's, no two smiles could be more different.[35] In the smile of Chartres there is nothing morbid, or even mysterious, if it is true, as Adams says at the beginning of "The Virgin of Chartres," that "when people talk of mystery, they commonly mean fear." To feel "the Majesty of Chartres," it suffices to be capable of feeling the *atmosphere* of a little poem like the "Tombeur de Notre-Dame," that is, its "colour and quality —the union of naiveté and art, the refinement, the infinite delicacy and tenderness."[36]

Indeed, the notion of *naiveté*, as indistinguishable from art, on which Adams dwells, is the real key to his aesthetic response to the Middle Ages. No doubt it may appear a little farfetched, or at least too studied, and at the same time, in a literal sense, curiously *naive*. Unlike Henry James, who could write to him, a few months before the outbreak of war in 1914: "You see I still, in presence of life (or what you deny to be such) have reactions—as many as possible . . . It's, I suppose, because I am that queer monster, the artist, an obstinate finality, an inexhaustible sensibility . . ."[37] Adams, Ferner Nuhn asserts, was *not* "that queer monster, the artist"; he never gave himself "absolutely" to Art.[38] Perhaps it was precisely because he feared that abandon; he did not want to give himself to Beauty, at least the form of Beauty which is incarnated by the Gioconda.[39] Such a disquieting element cannot be found in *Mont-Saint-Michel and Chartres*. Even if the book was conceived at the end of the century, it is far from being *fin de siècle;* it has the élan of early romanticism as well as a youthful purity.

Yet in his one aesthetic reaction (as opposed to Henry James' reactions), that of the Wordsworthian child who stands at the pure wellspring of things, Adams was himself also truly "the artist." He adhered to the lesson which he had finally and fully perceived in the South Seas when, among the primitives, he drank in the *fun* and *color* of life; indeed, the very first step in his education, as he was going to reminisce, had been "a lesson of color," at three years of age, when "he first found himself sitting on a yellow kitchen floor in strong sunlight." In the introduction to *The Renaissance,* there is a strikingly parallel notation in Walter Pater's assertion that: "in its primary aspect, a great picture has no more definite message for us than an accidental play of sunlight and a shadow for a few moments on the wall or the floor."[40] The world of Chartres first and foremost conveys a similar message. The artists of the windows never cared "whether a green camel or a pink lion looked like a dog or a donkey provided they got their harmony or value," such harmony or value, we may add, as only the child (or the man who can feel like a child) is in a position to appreciate.[41] It thus turns out that after all, in spite of their contrasting visions (their angles of sight were different), Pater and Adams did look at Art with the same eyes.

The unity of the Middle Ages which Adams struggles to recapture is a unity of perception; the ideal *pons sanctorum* over which saints and children pass is also that of the artist, fusing all contradictions or discordances into a perfect harmony because art—real art—transmutes all the material it touches into *form.* This is what Walter Pater clearly implies when, in *The Renaissance,* he notes that "all art constantly aspires toward the condition of music." Pater's discussion of the imagination in *Marius the Epicurean* makes this point even clearer; an impassioned contemplation as well as an intellectual discipline, productive of the most perfect forms of life, imagination can ascend to the level of a "blessedness" of vision—a vision which comes to be "like a well-executed piece of music."[42] Such is Adams' "vision" of Chartres, as he vibrates with the "music" of the cathedral:

Sitting here any Sunday afternoon, while the voices of the children of the maîtrise are chanting in the choir—your mind held in the grasp of the strong lines and shadows of the architecture; your eyes flooded with the autumn tones of the glass; your ears drowned with the purity of the voices; one sense reacting upon another until sensation reaches the limit of its range—you, or any other lost soul, could, if you cared to look and listen, feel a sense beyond the human ready to reveal a sense divine that would make that world once more intelligible, and would bring the Virgin to life again, in all the depths of feeling which

she shows here—in lines, vaults, chapels, colours, legends, chants—
more eloquent than the prayer-book, and more beautiful than the
autumn sunlight; and thought without end into the art he has studied
a hundred times; but what is still more convincing, he could, at will,
in an instant, shatter the whole art by calling into it a single motive
of his own.[43]

Superimposed on all the other structural elements of *Mont-Saint-
Michel and Chartres*, whether outer or inner, indeed, unifying all
these very elements into one musical motive, here is the final unity
of Adams' work. If the earliest lesson of his childhood had been
one in color, the second step in young Henry's artistic education
was the one he took in Berlin when "he was one day surprised to
notice that his mind followed the movement of a Sinfonie. He
could not have been more astonished had he suddenly read a new
language. Among the marvels of education, this was the most
marvellous. A prison-wall that barred his senses on one great side
of life, suddenly fell, of its own accord, without so much as his
knowing when it happened."[44] The movement of *Mont-Saint-
Michel and Chartres* resembles that of a symphony, with the "exposition" (the part on Mont-Saint-Michel) striking the dominant
melody of the Gothic as well as the modulating theme of medieval
literature. Then, after a broad and smooth transition in another
key ("Normandy and the Île de France"), comes the "development," regrouping the figures into new types of phrase, modulating freely; the courtois poetry or the love of Mary, like cadence-
phrases in various rhythms, all combine into one sequential
process leading through its wide range of keys to a "peroration" in
most magnificent Haydn or Beethoven style.

Thus, the endless repetitions in *Mont-Saint-Michel and Chartres*
do not merely bear the stamp of the seasoned pedagogue; they
reveal the musician, skillfully modulating his fundamental notes.
And not only musicians can play so, but poets. Yeats, Pound, Eliot,
have since Adams developed such a technique, allowing meaning
to arise out of juxtaposed statements. Yet, more than of these
poets, it is of Wallace Stevens that Adams will make us think,
Stevens who, in "Peter Quince at the Clavier," explains: "Music is
feeling, then, not sound." In "The Man with the Blue Guitar"
Stevens gives a definition which might serve as a motto to *Mont-
Saint-Michel and Chartres*:

> ... Poetry
> Exceeding music must take the place
> Of empty heaven and its hymns,
> Ourselves in poetry must take their place. . . .[45]

"Music," "feeling," "poetry" all melt into what Stevens called "the Supreme Fiction," this world created by the union of reality and the imagination: "It is the *mundo* of the imagination in which the imaginative man delights and not the gaunt world of reason. The pleasure is the pleasure of powers that create a truth that cannot be arrived at by the reason alone, a truth that the poet recognizes by sensation."[46] The elderly man who fancied himself as a twelfth-century monk in a nineteenth-century attic, "looking down upon all of Europe as a 'menagerie' making a queer struggle for reality,"[47] and wrote *Mont-Saint-Michel and Chartres,* delighted in the same world. He did not dream. He really was the poet. As Gaston Bachelard says, in *L'Air et les Songes:* "The dreamer lets himself be borne along. A true poet is not satisfied with such fanciful escapism; he wants imagination to be a journey. Every poet owes us an invitation to travel."[48] On such a journey we accordingly go from Mont-Saint-Michel to Chartres.

"If you do not know where Hilo is," Adams wrote to Mrs. Cameron, on September 18, 1890 (he was then setting on his South Sea journey); "don't look for it on the map. One's imagination is the best map for the traveller."[49] It is still the best map for the traveler in the Middle Ages. For if Adams, as a disillusioned historian, proposed to record the decline and fall of man, what he in reality does now, as a man of letters, is to exalt the imagination. This is the timeless theme—or in musical terms, the "topic"—of *Mont-Saint-Michel and Chartres.* If the Virgin and Saint Thomas, who represent two aspects of a unified sensibility—the balance between thought and action—symbolize the "meaning" of the book, there is only one hero; only the child exhibits such spontaneity, simplicity, integrity to represent the *full* life and become an emblem not only of order but even of salvation. In Adams' dialectical imagery, the child, who is Everyman as well as he is the imagination, stands in the shade of the broken arch and before the humming dynamo. *Mont-Saint-Michel and Chartres,* as a spiritual autobiography, records the adventure of a man who, in the evening of his life, truly recaptured the spirit of the child and in so doing became "that queer monster, the artist," at least to the same extent as John Ruskin, Walter Pater, or Henry James, if not in fact much more. For in truly paradoxical fashion, he succeeded in informing his "summer amusement" with the only real form of life that ever lasts. *Mont-Saint-Michel and Chartres*, remarks R. P. Blackmur in his "Parallel" between Henry and Brooks Adams, "has its value for us precisely because it is a work of divination dressed out or enacted in the mode of rational imagination. Brooks had imagination like Henry but he used it conceptually before he wrote; Henry put his imagination in his book; so that the book seems finally, as we think of it, to divine its own substance." Blackmur adds, "You use Brooks Adams, and you proceed. You use Henry and he participates in your sensibility for ever."[50] And so, to be sure, does his *mundo*, the Middle Ages.

Notes
Bibliography
Index

Notes

The following abbreviations are used in the notes:

Beringause   Arthur F. Beringause, *Brooks Adams, A Biography*, New York: Alfred Knopf, 1955.

Cater   *Henry Adams and his Friends*, Introduction by Harold D. Cater, ed. Boston: Houghton Mifflin, 1947.

Chartres   Henry Adams, *Mont-Saint-Michel and Chartres*, A Doubleday Anchor Book, Garden City, New York: Doubleday, 1933.

Education   Henry Adams, *The Education of Henry Adams*, The Modern Library, New York: Random House, 1931.

Ford, I   *Letters of Henry Adams, 1858–1891*, Worthington C. Ford, ed. Boston: Houghton Mifflin, 1930.

Ford, II   *Letters of Henry Adams, 1892–1918*, Worthington C. Ford, ed. Boston: Houghton Mifflin, 1938.

Samuels, I   *The Young Henry Adams*, Cambridge: Harvard University Press, 1948.

Samuels, II   *Henry Adams: The Middle Years*, Cambridge: Harvard University Press, 1958.

Samuels, III   *Henry Adams: The Major Phase*, Cambridge: Harvard University Press, 1964.

N.A.R.   *North American Review*.

Preface

1. *Virginia Quarterly Review*, 38 (Spring 1962), 196. Since Lewis Mumford drops the *s* of the possessive in his references to Adams, I conform to this practice, which is followed by a majority of critics.

2. *Samuels*, III, 519.

3. "*Le Mont-Saint-Michel et Chartres* demeure sans doute le chef d'oeuvre d'Adams, un chef d'oeuvre qui ne se rattache visiblement pas aux ouvrages qui l'ont précédé, un livre d'enthousiasme et de poésie couronnant une œuvre historique sévère et sombre." Maurice Le Breton, "Henry Adams et la France," *Harvard et la France* (Paris, 1936), p. 89 (my translation).

4. Oscar Cargill, "The Medievalism of Henry Adams," *Essays and Studies in Honor of Carleton Brown* (New York, 1940), pp. 327–328.

5. *Chartres*, p. 66.

1. The Makings of Ignorance

1. *Education*, pp. 3–6; Edwin M. Bacon, *Rambles around Old Boston* (Boston, 1921), pp. 140–141; Harold D. Eberlein, *The Architecture of Colonial America* (Boston, 1925), p. 100.

2. Carl Becker, *The Heavenly City of the Eighteenth-Century Philosophers* (New Haven, 1963), p. 31. Walt Whitman, "By Blue Ontario's Shore," par. 12, l. 11; "Song of the Broad-Axe," par. 7, l. 18; "Spain, 1873–4," l. 4.

3. Claude J. Bowers, *The Young Jefferson* (Boston, 1945), pp. 218, 222, 373.

4. R. W. Emerson, *The Complete Essays and Other Writings of Ralph Waldo Emerson* (New York, 1940), pp. 128–133, 637.

5. George Mead, *Movements of Thought in the Nineteenth Century*, (Chicago, 1936), pp. 64, 55.

6. Agnes Addison, *Romanticism and the Gothic Revival* (New York, 1938), p. 135.

7. J. G. Lockhart, *Memoirs of the Life of Sir Walter Scott* (Boston, 1901), IV, 163–164; James Hillhouse, *The Waverley Novels and their Critics* (Minneapolis, 1936), p. 242; *The Letters of R. W. Emerson*, ed. Ralph L. Rusk (New York, 1939), I, 156.

8. *Education*, p. 39.

9. G. M. Young, "Scott and History," *Transactions of the Royal Society of Literature of the United Kingdom* (London, 1950).

10. cf. Addison, *Romanticism and the Gothic Revival*, p. 54: "He popularized and made bearable the Middle Ages and so helped form a public which would accept the more archaeologically correct buildings of the nineteenth century. He swept away the disagreeable idea of the Middle Ages which the Gothic tales had made prevalent. He took the Middle Ages from the misty, murky and uncomfortable past and peopled them with honest human characters who seemed life-like and understandable." It is interesting to observe how this judgment on Scott applies not only to the America Henry Adams knew but to the very construction he was himself to raise.

11. See David Randall, "Waverley in America," *The Colophon New Series* (Summer 1935), I, 39–40.

12. *Ford*, I, 270; II, 615.

13. Thomas Carlyle, "Sir Walter Scott," *Essays*, vol. I, *Scottish and Other Miscellanies* (London, New York, 1950), p. 102.

14. *Samuels*, I, 3; James Westfall Thompson, *A History of Historical Writing* (New York, 1942), II, 280.

15. Samuel E. Morison, *Three Centuries of Harvard* (Cambridge, 1936), p. 264; *Harvard Bulletin* (1854).

16. *Harvard Bulletin* (1855 and 1858); *Samuels*, I, 28; Professor Samuels calls this textbook *History of the Origin of Representative Government in Europe*, by the name of an English edition into which the *Historie de la civilisation* had been incorporated. Though the title was given in English, the text to be read was in French. We know from the catalogue of Adams' library, reproduced by Max Baym in *Colophon* (Autumn 1938), pp. 483–489, that in 1858 he owned Guizot's *Historie de la civilisation* (6 vols.). Only the first part was in his syllabus; the rest of the work, which deals with the history of France, was not assigned.

17. William Robertson, *A History of the Reign of the Emperor Charles the Fifth*, with *An Account of the Emperor's Life after His Abdication* by William H. Prescott (Philadelphia, 1880), I, 25.

18. *Education*, pp. 55, 300; Samuel E. Morison, *Three Centuries*, p. 347; John Davis Long, "Reminiscences of Seventy Years' Education," *Proceed-*

ings of the Massachusetts Historical Society, 42 (June 1909), 352.

19. *Harvard Bulletin* (1858); Max Baym, *The French Education of Henry Adams* (New York, 1951) pp. 47–48.

20. Frederick Harrison, *John Ruskin* (English Men of Letters) (New York, 1902), p. 7; "Harvard College," *N.A.R.*, 114 (January 1872), 110. These opening lines were left out when the essay was reprinted in *Historical Essays* (New York, 1891); see also *N.A.R.*, 43 (October 1836), 369.

21. Morison, *Three Centuries*, p. 267.

22. *N.A.R.*, 43 (October 1836), 369; ibid., 43 (April 1844), 347.

23. *Education*, p. 64; Martha G. van Rensselaer, *Henry Hobson Richardson and his Works* (Boston, 1888), p. 4.

24. "Holden Chapel," *The Harvard Magazine*, I (May 1855), 210–215.

25. Mason Wade, ed., *The Journal of Francis Parkman*, (New York and London, 1947), I, 101–103, 180; on Rome, see Van Wyck Brooks, *The Dream of Arcadia* (New York, 1958), p. 85.

26. *Journals*, pp. 194–195; this experience was also recounted by Parkman in an article published anonymously, "A Convent at Rome," *Harper's Monthly*, 81 (August 1890), 448–454.

27. *Education*, pp. 61–62, 74.

28. Charles Sumner had spent the years 1839 and 1840 traveling in Italy, Germany, and England and had then become quite enthusiastic about cathedrals, particularly those of England. (See E. L. Pierce, *Memoirs and Letters of Charles Sumner* (Boston, 1877) I, 164, and II, 153.

29. Le Breton, "Adams et la France," in *Harvard et La France* (Paris, 1936); Addison, *Romanticism and the Gothic Revival*, p. 129.

30. Thompson, *History of Historical Writing* (New York, 1942), II, 150, 161–167; Ranke himself never spoke of "seminars" but of "exercises" (Ubungen).

31. *Ford*, I, 1–3.

32. Ibid., pp. 22, 42, 46, 50.

33. *Education*, pp. 89–92.

34. *Ford*, II, 566; Lloyd C. Griscom, *Diplomatically Speaking* (Boston, 1940), p. 38.

35. *Education*, pp. 114, 149, 201; *Ford*, I, 99 (July 3, 1863).

36. *Education*, pp. 141–42; for later comments, see *Ford*, I, 352 (June 10, 1883).

37. *Ford*, I, 113.

38. *Education*, pp. 200, 207.

39. L. C. Lloyd, *The Borough of Wenlock (Shropshire)* (Shrewsbury, 1955), pp. 39–40; See also Rose Graham, "The History of the Alien Priory of Wenlock," *Journal of the British Archaeological Association*, third series, IV (1939), 117–140. H. P. R. Finberg, in *The Early Charters of the West Midlands* (Leicester, 1861), p. 197, remarks that "there are good reasons for doubting the accuracy of the accepted history of Wenlock. A letter written by St Boniface describes a vision of the after-life seen by a monk of his acquaintance who had recently died and come to life again "in the convent of the Abbess Milburga." "This shows," says Finberg, "that Wenlock, like Whitby and its continental prototypes was not a nunnery but a monastery for both sexes, ruled by an Abbess."

40. *Education*, p. 228; "Wenlock Abbey" had been bought by the Gaskells

in 1857, but it was only in 1863 that the place was "put in order" (though not in 1864, as Adams has it in *The Education*, p. 207). The first entry in the guest book is dated November 1863. Adams, who came one year later was not, as he says, "one of [the] first guests." Henry James' visits were on July 14, 1877, and August 13, 1878.

41. *Ford*, II, 519.

42. Roger B. Stein, *John Ruskin and Aesthetic Thought in America, 1840–1900* (Cambridge, Mass., 1967), p. 209.

43. Quoted by E. T. Cook, *The Life of John Ruskin* (London, 1912), I, 305, 539.

44. J. W. Mackail, *The Life of William Morris* (I, 38), quoted by Cook, *Life of Ruskin*, p. 311.

45. *Samuels*, I, 209; *Ford*, I, 203; *Ford*, II, 4. For other entries on Ruskin, see ibid., pp. 3 (January 11, 1892) and 623–624 (March 31, 1914).

46. See Cook, *Life of Ruskin*, I, 306, 443–444; as for the Oxford Movement, Adams does not appear to have taken the least interest in it.

47. *Education*, pp. 213–214; Stein, *Ruskin and Aesthetic Thought*, p. 149.

48. Cook, *Life of Ruskin*, II, 48, 56; Stein, *Ruskin and Aesthetic Thought*, pp. 147–156. D. H. Dickason has also treated of "the Society for the Advancement of Truth in Art," in chapter vii of *The Daring Young Men* (Bloomington, Ind., 1953), pp. 71–82. But, as R. B. Stein points out, Dickason is confusing Ruskinism and Pre-Raphaelitism; though closely akin, these were not exactly one and the same movement.

49. *Clarence King Memoirs* (New York, 1904), pp. 190–192 and 129–130. See also Dickason, *Daring Young Men*, pp. 92–98.

50. Stein, *Ruskin and Aesthetic Thought*, p. 170; H. James, "Venice," *Century Magazine*, 24 (November 1882), 3; *Clarence King Memoirs*, p. 319.

51. Stein, *Ruskin and Aesthetic Thought*, pp. 151–152, 209.

52. *Education*, pp. 308–310; *Literary History of the United States*, rev. ed., ed. R. Spiller *et al.* (New York, 1955), p. 1094.

53. J. C. Levenson, *The Mind and Art of Henry Adams* (Boston, 1957), p. 235.

54. *Education*, p. 313.

55. Van Wyck Brooks, *New England: Indian Summer* (New York, London, 1950), p. 191; Thurman Wilkins, *Clarence King: A Biography* (New York, 1958), pp. 130, 174–175; Stein, *Ruskin and Aesthetic Thought*, pp. 172–175. As Stein also puts it, "King's geological training led him to anatomize nature topographically, but his impulses led him to describe not the facts of nature but their effect upon him as the observer, which was something quite different" (p. 175).

56. C. King, *Mountaineering in the Sierra Nevada* (Boston, 1872), p. 192. Dickason, *Daring Young Men*, pp. 96–98, where this passage of "Style and the Monument" is quoted. See also, by Dickason, "Clarence King— Scientist and Art Amateur," *Art in America*, 32 (January 1944), 41–51.

2. Doctor Barbaricus

1. *Education*, p. 291.

2. *Cater*, pp. 44–45; *Ford*, I, 194.

3. *Samuels*, I, 203–207; Cargill, "Medievalism of H. Adams," in *Essays*

and Studies in Honor of Carleton Brown (New York, 1940); Ward Thoron, ed., *Letters of Mrs. Henry Adams* (Boston, 1936), p. 14; Charles Francis Adams, Jr., *Charles Francis Adams* (Boston, 1900), p. 379.

4. *Education*, pp. 294, 299; Ford, I, 194–195, 197–198, 200, 203–204.

5. *Education*, p. 307.

6. J. L. Laughlin, "Some Recollections of Henry Adams," *Scribner's Magazine*, 69 (May 1921), 578–579.

7. *Education*, p. 307; Ferris Greenslet, *James Russell Lowell*, (Boston, 1905), p. 122; see also C. E. Eliot, "James R. Lowell as a Professor," *Harvard Graduates' Magazine*, 27 (June 1919), 493.

8. Charles E. Norton, ed., *Letters of J. R. Lowell*, (New York, 1894), I, 237; II, 38, 57, 65.

9. William W. Wilkinson, *A Free Lance in the Field of Life and Letters* (New York, 1874), p. 91.

10. *Samuels*, I, 209–210.

11. "The Study of Modern Languages," an address to the M. L. A. Convention in Cambridge in 1889, in *The Complete Writings of J. R. Lowell* (Boston, 1904), XI, 155, 156.

12. *Letters of J. R. Lowell*, II, 46, 52, 64. Samuel Longfellow, *The Life of H. W. Longfellow* (Boston, 1891), III, 158–168.

13. W. D. Howells, *Literary Friends and Acquaintance* (New York, 1900), p. 227; Greenslet, *J. R. Lowell*, p. 133.

14. *Letters*, II, 79.

15. ibid., II, 86–87, 217; Greenslet, *J. R. Lowell*, pp. 126, 129.

16. *Education*, p. 300; Ford, I, 194. Gurney's able but sole assistant since 1868, Torrey had become a full professor after Eliot's accession to the presidency. Gurney, himself promoted to faculty dean, had to be relieved of the greater part of his teaching.

17. Charles A. Wagner, *Harvard, Four Centuries and Freedoms* (New York, E. P. Dutton, 1950), p. 138; for a complete list of the courses taught by Adams at Harvard, see *Samuels*, I, 339–341.

18. See Michael Kraus, *A History of American History* (New York, 1937), p. 307. Neither C. K. Adams nor Herbert B. Adams (of Johns Hopkins) was related to Henry Adams.

19. Ford, I, 198; Cater, p. 48; "Harvard College," *N.A.R.*, 114 (January 1872), and *Historical Essays* (New York, 1891), pp. 80–81.

20. Lindsay Swift, "A Course in History at Harvard College in the Seventies," *Proceedings*, Massachusetts Historical Society 1918–1919, LII, 69–77.

21. *Education*, pp. 301–305.

22. Ford, I, 211, 256.

23. Ibid. pp. 253, 235; *Education*, p. 302; cf. also ibid. p. 304: "He imposed Germany with a heavy hand."

24. See Thompson, *A History of Historical Writing*, II, 267–272, and Paul Frederick, "The Study of History in Germany and France," *Johns Hopkins University Studies*, 8 (1890), 70–94.

25. Ford, I, 236.

26. Ford, I, 251, and *Letters of Mrs. Henry Adams*, p. 131.

27. Ford, I, 236 (to Henry Cabot Lodge, January 2, 1873).

28. *Cater*, pp. 63–64 (to Sir Henry Maine, February 22, 1875).

29. *Education*, pp. 303–304; cf. also *Cater*, pp. 80–81.

30. *Cater*, p. xxxix.

31. Laughlin, "Some Recollections of Henry Adams"; *Ford*, I, 292. Herbert B. Adams, "Seminary Libraries and University Extension," *Johns Hopkins University Studies* 5, (1887), 491; Kraus, *History of American History*, p. 303.

32. W. S. Holt, "Henry Adams and the Johns Hopkins University," *New England Quarterly*, 11 (1938), 637–638.

33. *Ford*, II, 119.

34. See W. S. Holt, "The Idea of Scientific History in America," *Journal of the History of Ideas*, I (June 1940), 356–357.

35. *Education*, p. 302; Laughlin, "Some Recollections of Henry Adams."

36. *Education*, p. 225.

37. Edward N. Saveth, *American Historians and European Immigrants* (New York, 1948), p. 15; Charles A. Beard, "Turner's *The Frontier in America*," in *Books That Changed Our Minds*, ed. M. Cowley and B. Smith (New York, 1940), p. 62.

38. Herbert B. Adams, "New Methods of Study of History," *Johns Hopkins University Studies*, 2 (1884), p. 111; Henry Adams had already made use of the principle in his Harvard seminars. As Laughlin could then perceive, "the primitive communal holdings of the early Teutons turned up, persisting even through the feudal system in our towns of Boston, Nantucket or Salem." ("Some Recollections of Henry Adams").

39. *Samuels*, I, 247 (but, Samuels goes on, "though he accepted the general theory of Teutonic origins, he relentlessly questioned the weaknesses of its supporting details"); *Education*, p. 412.

40. Oscar J. Falnes, "New England Interest in Scandinavian Culture and the Norsemen," *New England Quarterly*, 10 (June 1936), 211–242.

41. Ibid.

42. *N.A.R.*, 120 (January 1875), 195.

43. Falnes, "New England Interest," pp. 233–241; *N.A.R.*, 54 (April 1844), 480–508.

44. *Chartres*, p. 3; Falnes, "New England Interest," pp. 233–241.

45. *Edinburgh Review*, 109 (1859), 501.

46. See *Cambridge History of English Literature*, 14, part III, pp. 56 ff.; Thompson, *History of Historical Writing*, pp. 290–292; H. Adams, "Freeman's Historical Essays," *N.A.R.*, 114 (January 1872), 193–196.

47. Cargill, "Medievalism of H. Adams," p. 318; *Ford*, I, 203. In this letter to Gaskell, dated March 27, 1871, Adams only refers to books dealing with architecture.

48. In the third volume of his own *History* (p. 425), however, Freeman harshly remarked on Frank Palgrave's "injudicious" editing of his father's works. The Palgraves may have taken exception at this criticism.

49. W. A. Dunning, *Truth in History and Other Essays* (New York, 1937), p. 157.

50. *N.A.R.*, 217 (October 1867), 641.

51. Freeman, *History of the Norman Conquest of England, Its Causes and Its Consequences* (Oxford, 1867–1869), IV, 60.

52. Freeman, *Some Impressions of the United States* (New York, 1883), pp. 15–16.

53. *The Letters of Mrs. Henry Adams*, p. 331.

54. Cargill, "Medievalism of H. Adams"; Herbert B. Adams, "Edward Freeman," *American Historical Review*, I (1895), 149–153; Samuels, I, 226–227.

55. "Freeman's Historical Essays," *N.A.R.*, 114 (January 1872), 193–196; "Freeman's History of the Norman Conquest," *N.A.R.* 118 (January 1874), 176–181.

56. "Maine's Village Communities," *N.A.R.*, 114 (January 1872), 196–199; "Stubbs' Constitutional History of England," *N.A.R.* 119 (July 1874), 233–244.

57. *Samuels*, I, 247–258.

58. *Essays in Anglo-Saxon Law*, ed. H. Adams (Boston, 1876), pp. 20, 36–37, 52.

59. *Essays in Anglo-Saxon Law*, p. 54.

60. *Ford*, I, 288; *Education*, p. 412; *Samuels*, I, 252.

61. *Education*, p. 368 (Here Lies/The Manikin Writer/ Barbaric Doctor/Henry Adams/ Son of Adam and Eve/Who First Explained/Socnam).

3. The Best Traveling Companions

1. *Education*, p. 316; *Letters to a Niece*, pp. 10–11.

2. *Education*, p. 369.

3. *Cater*, pp. lxii–lxiii.

4. Van Rensselaer, *H. H. Richardson*, p. 20.

5. Lewis Mumford, *The South in Architecture* (New York, 1941), p. 81; *Ford*, I, 361 (October 26, 1884, to John Hay).

6. Quoted by Royal Cortissoz in *John La Farge, a Memoir and a Study* (Boston, 1911), pp. 153–154.

7. Van Rensselaer, *H. H. Richardson*, p. 22; Mumford, *South in Architecture*, p. 86.

8. Van Rensselaer, *H. H. Richardson*, p. 28; *Samuels*, II, 242–243; *Democracy and Esther (Two Novels by Henry Adams*, Anchor edition, Garden City, N. Y., 1961), p. 262.

9. *Samuels*, II, 242, 298; *Ford*, II, 240.

10. *Cater*, p. cxv, n. 138; Mumford, *South in Architecture*, p. 98; H. R. Hitchcock, *The Architecture of H. H. Richardson and his Times* (New York, 1936), p. 272.

11. *Samuels*, II, 261–262.

12. *Cater*, p. lx.

13. *Samuels*, II, 292; *Cater*, pp. 165, 167.

14. *Samuels*, II, 302–304; *Ford*, I, 368.

15. *An Artist's Letters from Japan* (New York, 1897), p. 25.

16. *Ford*, I, 382.

17. *Notes of a Son and Brother* (New York, 1914), p. 88.

18. Cortissoz, *John La Farge*, p. 262.

19. *Democracy and Esther*, pp. 220–221.

20. *Education*, p. 369; on La Farge see also Dickason, *Daring Young Men*, pp. 144–153, and Ira N. Hayward, "From Tahiti to Chartres: The Henry Adams-John La Farge Friendship," *The Huntington Library Quarterly*, 21 (September 1958), 345–348.

21. Cortissoz, *John La Farge*, p. 67: "At Columbia University where his father sent him, still hoping that he would embark upon a liberal career, his professor of English happened to be an Oxford man and a former member of the 'Oxford Movement'; under his direction La Farge read widely 'anything that would bring up the beauty of the medieval ideal.' Before leaving College in 1835, he felt that he had been indoctrinated with 'the belief that eighteenth-century art and, in fact, everything that did not agree with the medieval was wrong.' "

22. Ibid. p. 85; Cecelia Waern, *John La Farge, Artist and Writer* (London, 1896), pp. 18–19.

23. Sadakichi Hartmann, *A History of American Art* (Boston, 1902), p. 183; see also Focillon, "John La Farge," *Art in America*, 29 (1936), 311–319.

24. Cortissoz, *John La Farge*, p. 185.

25. *Ford*, II, 139 (December 31, 1897); *Ford*, I, 418 (October 9, 1890); both to Mrs. Cameron.

26. *Cater*, pp. 195–196; *Ford*, I, 414 and 477 (both to Mrs. Cameron).

27. James Schevill, *Sherwood Anderson, His Life and Work* (Denver, 1951), p. 140.

28. *Education*, p. 289.

29. Waern, *John La Farge*, p. 84; *Samuels*, III, 11.

30. *Cater*, pp. 197–198, 217 (October 16 and November 16, 1890; both to John Hay); "The Frenchman," Adams adds, "would be given some middle-aged woman, more or less repulsive in person, and the mother of several illegitimate children, who would have to be his only consolation for losing the object of his desire."

31. Adams papers, Massachusetts Historical Society (Samoa, November 21, 1890).

32. *The Life of John Hay*, ed. W. R. Thayer (Boston, 1915), II, 86.

33. *Samuels*, III, 101.

34. *Ford*, II, 35.

35. Ibid., 329.

36. *Samuels*, III, 65–70; in "Henry Adams and the Gossip Mills," *Essays in American Literature and English Literature Presented to Bruce McElderry Jr.*, ed. Max F. Schulz *et al.* (Athens, Ohio, 1967), pp. 59–75, Ernest Samuels very convincingly disposes of the rumor that Martha Cameron was, in fact, Adams' daughter. On Adams' feelings for Martha, see Charles Vandersee, "Henry Adams' Education of Martha Cameron: Letters, 1888–1916," *Texas Studies in Literature and Language*, 10 (Summer 1968), 233–293.

37. *Samuels*, III, 71.

38. *Ford*, I, 9–10.

39. *Beringause*, pp. 44–45, undated but probably sent in April 1868.

40. "The Heritage of Henry Adams," in *The Degradation of the Democratic Dogma* (New York, 1958), p. 88.

41. *Beringause*, p. 94.

42. "The Heritage of Henry Adams," p. 94.

43. See *Beringause*, pp. 101–102; *Education*, p. 243.

44. *Samuels*, III, 118–119.

45. "The Heritage of Henry Adams," p. 91; cf. also *Samuels*, III, 127:

"Its effect upon Henry was electric, bringing to an end the period of intellectual torpor and irresolution, and it helped launch him upon the greatest effort of his thought. It brought his anarchic disgusts into focus, gave him a scapegoat, identified the enemy and supplied him with a scientific rationale for rejecting contemporary civilization."

46. *Beringause*, p. 182; *Ford*, II, 81 (June 5, 1895).

47. *Beringause*, p. 110.

48. *Education*, p. 339; see also Robert A. Hume, *Runaway Star* (Ithaca, N. Y., 1951), pp. 179–180.

49. *Education*, p. 339.

50. "The Gold Standard," reprinted from *Fortnightly Review* (August 1, 1894), 62, p. 242; see *Samuels*, III, 128–129.

51. *Beringause*, pp. 123 and 130.

4. Ignorance Triumphant

1. *Ford*, II, 71; see same page, note 2, for letter to Sir Robert Cunliffe (June 6, 1895); ibid., pp. 72–73 (July 11, July 25; both to Mrs. Cameron).

2. *Letters to a Niece*, pp. 79–80.

3. *Cater*, pp. 346–347.

4. *Ford*, II, 77 (August 29, 1895; to Mrs. Cameron); *Letters to a Niece*, p. 80 (September 1, 1895).

5. *Ford*, II, 77; ibid; pp. 84–85 (September 18, 1895; also to Mrs. Cameron).

6. *Education*, p. 354; *Letters to a Niece*, pp. 78–79; *Cater*, p. 347.

7. See *Cater*, p. 346 and *Ford*, II, 79 (September 1, 1895; to Gaskell).

8. See *Ford*, II, 79, on "cattle on two legs" ("I did penance for being one but what penance atones for such mortal sin"). Cf. also ibid., p. 87 (September 25, 1895; to Mrs. Cameron).

9. Ibid., p. 80 (September 8, 1895; to Brooks Adams).

10. *Education*, p. 238; on Tati Salmon, see *Samuels*, III, 41–42.

11. *Ford*, II, 35, 72; H. A. to Phillips, July 26, 1896, quoted in *Samuels*, III, 168; see also ibid., p. 358.

12. *Samuels*, III, 208.

13. *Ford*, II, 72, 74, 76 (July 11, July 25, August 13; all to Mrs. Cameron).

14. Ibid., p. 74 and *Samuels*, III, 208.

15. *Ford*, II, 77 (August 29, 1895).

16. *Education*, p. 420; *Samuels*, III, 357.

17. *Education*, p. 128.

18. *Education*, p. 354.

19. *The Restriction of Immigration*, Speech of Hon. Henry Cabot Lodge of Massachusetts in the United States Senate, March 6, 1896 (Washington, 1896), p. 8.

20. *Ford*, II, 79.

21. *Cater*, p. 349; *Ford*, II, 116 (August 24, 1896).

22. *Beringause*, p. 316, n. 2; *Ford*, II, 79.

23. See *Beringause*, p. 138.

24. Ibid., pp. 135–136; Beringause only quotes parts of these letters

which are in the Brooks Adams Collection, Houghton Library, Harvard University.

25. Ibid., pp. 135 and 136–137.

26. *Cater*, p. 349.

27. B. A. Collection; the passage concerning La Farge is quoted in *Beringause*, p. 138.

28. *Beringause*, pp. 162–163; all the other quotations are from unpublished letters, B. A. Collection.

29. B. A. Collection.

30. *Ford*, II, 170 (April 23, 1898; to Gaskell); *Education*, p. 389.

31. *Ford*, II, 81, 108 (this letter dated July 15, 1896).

32. *Samuels*, III, 135–136.

33. *The Law of Civilization and Decay* (New York, 1951), p. 349.

34. *Cater*, p. 388 (October 6, 1896; to John Hay); *Ford*, II, 112, 117 (August 3 and October 9, 1896; both to Mrs. Cameron).

35. *Letters to a Niece*, p. 89; *Ford, II*, 120 (January 4, 1897).

36. *Cater*, p. 372 (July 5, 1896; to Mabel Hooper La Farge); ibid., p. 376 (July 23; to Mrs. Rae).

37. *Cater*, pp. 411–412 (June 3, 1897; to Mrs. Lodge); 417–418 (July 29, 1897; to B. A.); 418–419 (August 8, 1897; to Mrs. Rae); 420 (August 26, 1897; to B. A.)

38. Ibid., p. 412 (June 3, 1897; to Mrs. Lodge); *Ford*, II, 135 (October 25, 1897; to Gaskell; also October 31, 1897; to John Hay); *Cater*, p. 424. In "Propos inédits sur la France dans les lettres de Henry Adams," *Revue de littérature comparée*, 41 (1967), 267, André Monchoux clearly sets the limits of Adams' interest in French cultural life: "Henry Adams a certainement négligé les meilleurs moyens d'entrer dans le vif de la vie intellectuelle française, littéraire ou politique. Il reste du moins sa lecture considérable, sa fréquentation des théâtres. Mais on retrouve ici l'amateur, qui dédaignerait un intérêt de critique professionnel; et qui, pour rester gentleman, évite d'aller beaucoup au delà de l'impression première. L'information de H. Adams ne répond donc pas aux possibilités qui lui furent offertes." (Henry Adams certainly neglected the best means for getting to the heart of French intellectual life, whether literary or political. Still, on the positive side, there is his wide reading and theater-going to be taken into account; but here again we find the amateur who would disdain stooping to the interest of the professional critic; and who, to retain his status of gentleman, avoids going much deeper than first impressions. The body of facts on which Adams relies thus falls far short of what could be expected from the resources at his disposal.) No doubt this was due in part to a certain lack of self-confidence betrayed by his jokes about the poorness of his French. Adams wrote to Martha Cameron on November 3, 1899: "Your small boy needs attention. He does not work near enough, and his French is getting worse and worse" (Vandersee, "Henry Adams' Education of Martha Cameron," *Texas Studies in Literature and Language*, 2 (Summer 1963), 262). But it is also consonant with Adams' attitude of mind, even when he was in his own country. Cf. Brooks, *New England: Indian Summer*, pp. 498–499: "Save for his little circle of friends, Adams had missed in his age the finest writers and artists that America produced. Had he heard of Emily Dickinson or Stephen Crane, Winslow Homer or

Ryder? He never referred to them in his books or his letters. Had he bothered to read even James or Howells, except for a novel or two? He mentioned them only once or twice. Convinced that he 'knew everybody,' that he was 'wiser than anyone else,' however ironically he said it, he shrank from meeting even the lights of the Sorbonne, the great authorities on the Middle Ages, whose conversation might have unsettled his mind. *Omne ignorantum pro magnifico*, and he was without a rival companioned by nieces, by ladies with whom he went shopping and adoring young men."

39. *Samuels*, III, 180; *Cater*, p. 424; *Ford*, II, 143.

40. *Samuels*, III, 183.

41. *Ford*, II, 163.

42. *Cater*, p. 461; the subtitle above is from a letter of Adams to May, Nov. 7, 1900, in *Ford*, II, 299.

43. Ibid., p. 463.

44. *Ford*, II, 227 (April 23, 1899; to Mrs. Cameron); *Cater*, p. 475 (September 5, 1899; to Mabel Hooper La Farge).

45. *Cater*, p. 465 (June 12, 1899; to B. A.); *Ford*, II, 243 (October 9, 1899; to Gaskell).

46. *Ford*, II, 240 (September 18, 1899; to Mrs. Cameron; *Cater*, pp. 468, 475–476. On Adams' relative solitude, see *Ford*, II, 239 (September 12, 1899; to Mrs. Cameron): "I had all sorts of invitations for Sunday; indeed a man of the world is going about Paris just now; it is I."

47. *Ford*, pp. 245 (October 23, 1899; to Mrs. Cameron) and 260 (February 1, 1900; to Cecil Spring-Rice).

48. *Samuels*, III, 217 (H. A. to Mrs. Cameron); *Ford*, II, 237, 240, 245.

49. *Samuels*, III, 217, 218 (H. A. to Mrs. Cameron) *Ford*, II, 249; to Gaskell.

50. "The Heritage of Henry Adams," in *The Degradation of the Democratic Dogma* by Henry Adams, with an introduction by Brooks Adams (New York, 1958, Capricorn Books), pp. 100–102.

51. *Cater*, p. 460; translated by Auguste Dietrich, Brooks' book was published by Atlan, Paris, 1899.

52. B. A. Collection.

53. *Ford*, II, 295; *Samuels*, III, 220.

54. *Samuels*, III, 122–123.

55. See *Cater*, p. 538, n. 2.

56. Ibid., p. 529 (August 10, 1902).

57. *Ford*, II, 269 (February 26, 1900), 301 (November 7, 1900).

58. Ibid., p. 317; for an analysis of the "Prayer," see *Samuels*, III, 228–236.

59. *Ford*, II, 317, 327 (February 25 and April 22, 1901; both to Mrs. Cameron); *Samuels*, III, 253–254 (January 10 and April 27, 1902; also to Mrs. Cameron).

60. *Samuels*, III, 255.

61. *Ford*, II, 392, 396, 403, 422 (December 3, 1902; February 8, March 13, January 31, 1903; all to Mrs. Cameron).

62. Ibid., pp. 423, 426, 432 (February 7 and 24, March 27, 1904; all to Mrs. Cameron).

63. B. A. Collection.

64. *Ford,* II, 453.

65. Moreene Crumley, "The Reputation of Henry Adams," unpub. diss., University of Chicago, 1954.

66. *Cater,* pp. 550–551 (June 5, 1904; to Mrs. Lodge); Ford, II, 440–441: "Since June I've been victim to a Mercedes, and life has been labor. Every day I've had to find some new place to visit, and have acquired chronic dyspepsia by living at provincial inns. I've run madly through centuries and have hunted windows like hares." (August 29, 1904; to John Hay).

67. Ibid., p. 498 (June 2, 1908; to Mrs. Cameron).

68. Ibid.

69. Ibid., pp. 614 (July 1913; to Mrs. Cameron) and 617 (November 1, 1913; to Gaskell).

70. Ibid., pp. 482, 579, 597.

71. *Cater,* pp. xcviii–xcix; cvi.

72. *Ford,* II, 608 (December 17, 1912; to Mrs. Cameron).

73. *Samuels,* III, 539–541.

5. A World of Architecture

1. *Chartres,* p. xvi.

2. Levenson, *Mind and Art,* p. 239.

3. Made by E. Fremiet, "Membre de L'Institut," in gilded copper, some fifteen feet high and immovable, the present statue was set up in 1897 to replace another statue supposedly destroyed in the eighteenth century and which, as the story went, was the gift of a pope, gold-plated, and turning with the wind. In fact, nothing of the kind ever existed, except in "l'imagination des voyageurs enthousiastes qui avaient beau mentir parce qu'ils venaient de loin." See Etienne Dupont, *Le Mont Saint-Michel inconnu d'après des documents inédits* (Paris, 1912), p. 84. There is a copy of this book in Adams' library, with the inscription: "To uncle Henry, from Edith W." (probably Edith Wharton).

4. *Cater,* p. 559.

5. *Education,* p. 74.

6. Henri Focillon, *Art d'Occident: le Moyen Age Roman et Gothique* (Paris, 1955), p. 170 (my translation).

7. Quoted by Yvan Christ in *Mont-Saint-Michel* (Paris, 1962) p. 1.

8. *Chartres,* p. xvi.

9. *Ford,* II, 245 (my italics).

10. Cook, *Life of Ruskin,* 1, 257.

11. There are eight entries, all in pencil, concerning Chartres; the first entry is typical:

Chartres—South Porch

Virgin enthroned and crowned seated over arch of center. Three
large figures on pier on other side seem
half male half female
One on each outside pier
All seem to wear crowns
Over side arches, each has a seated female figure, one holding
a book, the other a vase or bottle.

12. *Ford*, II, 498 (June 2, 1908; to Mrs. Cameron).

13. Ibid., 246 (October 23, 1899; to Mrs. Cameron); *Chartres*, p. 56.

14. *Chartres*, pp. 56, 2.

15. *Description de l'Abbaye du Mont-Saint-Michel*, p. 75; *Chartres*, p. 10.

16. *Chartres*, pp. 35–40.

17. Ibid., p. 11.

18. Buried beneath the nave, the primitive Carolingian (tenth-century) church, now known as Notre-Dame-sous-Terre, was discovered only in 1908, a few weeks after Adams' last visit, but on the same level, Saint-Martin's crypt and the Chapelle des Trente Cierges, both dating back to the eleventh century, were open to visitors, as well as Saint-Stephen's Chapel (eleventh–twelfth century).

19. *Chartres*, pp. 9, 34; when at Chartres, Adams makes another reference to the crypt, but it is merely to say that "if we went down into it, we should understand nothing"; so he will spare us the visit (p. 111). Rather inconsistently he will later comment, while telling of one of the Virgin's miracles: "We have seen at Chartres what a crypt may be and how easily one might hide in its shadows." (p. 283). Cf. also pp. 33, 35. About the Aquilon as a model for the scenery of Robert-le-Diable, see Paul Gout, *Histoire de l'architecture française au Mont Saint-Michel* (Paris, 1899), p. 161.

20. *Chartres*, p. 39.

21. Ibid., pp. 41, 42.

22. *Cater*, p. 559 (January 17, 1905; to Henry O. Taylor).

23. Brooks, *New England: Indian Summer*, p. 272; cf. also *Ford*, I, 113: "As for me, my old tendencies grow on me more and more. If we lived a thousand years ago instead of now, I should have become a monk and would have got hold as Abbot of one of those lovely little monasteries which I used to admire so much among the hills in Italy" (London, December 18, 1863; to Charles F. Adams, Jr.).

24. *Chartres*, p. 43.

25. Ibid., p. 7.

26. *Ford*, 11, 332 (May 4, 1901; to Henry O. Taylor).

27. Chauncey B. Tinker, "Arnold's Poetic Plans," *The Yale Review*, 22 (June 1935), 789; Cf. also Louis Bonnerot, *Matthew Arnold, poète* (Paris 1947), pp. 169–170.

28. *Chartres*, p. 37; for a description of an *abbaye*, see *Grand Larousse encyclopédique* (Paris, 1960), I, 10: "Les bâtiments des abbayes . . . sont toujours distribués suivant un plan type . . . Les bâtiments conventuels sont groupés autour d'un cloître-promenoir" (The abbey buildings are always arranged according to a standard plan . . . The conventual buildings are ordered around a cloister).

29. Christ, *Mont-Saint-Michel*, p. 58; *Chartres*, pp. 43–44, 9. Adams twice refers to the expensiveness of granite, though in fact a more luxurious material was employed by the builders. See Christ, p. 63: "In the 19th century, restorers working under Corroyer set about repairing the cloister with the stubborn determination characteristic of the disciples of Viollet-le-Duc, almost all the fine columns and their capitals were replaced in polished pink granite quite unlike the white calcareous stone quarried near Oxford in England from which the originals were made." Some of these early columns remain; Adams noticed none.

30. *Chartres*, p. 16.

31. Ibid., pp. 20, 22.

32. Ibid., pp. 29, 246–247.

33. *Samuels*, III, 217; cf. also *Chartres*, p. 117: "For us the world is not a schoolroom or a pulpit, but a stage."

34. Introduction to the Collier edition of *Mont-Saint-Michel and Chartres* (New York, 1963), pp. 9–10.

35. Cf. Louis Untermeyer, ed. *Modern American Poetry, Modern British Poetry* (New York, 1942), p. 207.

36. *Chartres*, pp. 8–9.

37. Ibid., pp. 6–7.

38. *The Darkening Glass: A Portrait of Ruskin's Genius* (New York, 1961), p. 67.

39. *Ford*, II, 468 (April 23, 1906; to Gaskell).

40. See "A School of Art," Chapter 3 of this book.

41. *Chartres*, p. 60.

42. Ibid., p. 120.

43. Ibid., p. 118.

44. The final statement in the volume suggests the theme of the whole: "Of the pure French Gothic of the twelfth century it is hardly too much to say that it is the most splendid architectural product that human genius and skill have thus far wrought in the world." (*Development and Character of Gothic Architecture*, New York, 1899, p. 428); on Moore, see Dickason, *Daring Young Men*, pp. 116–124.

45. Moore, *Development and Character of Gothic Architecture*, p. 8.

46. *Ford*, II, 80.

47. *Chartres*, p. 95, 38.

48. Ibid., pp. 8, 35, 115.

49. Ibid., p. 112.

50. Ibid., pp. 67, 74, 127, 53.

51. Ibid., pp. 54, 61, 70.

52. Ibid., pp. 73–74.

53. Ibid., pp. 74–75, 95.

54. *Letters of J. R. Lowell*, II, 57.

55. *Chartres*, pp. 82, 89.

56. "L'oeuvre de Huysmans rejoint les *Monuments du Midi et du Centre de la France*, de Prosper Mérimée. Le nouvelliste, devenu, sous le gouvernement de Guizot, inspecteur des Beaux Arts, s'associait volontiers au courant archéologique contemporain. Avec beaucoup de romantiques il est imbu d'un goût décidé de l'architecture, que d'ailleurs gardera sa postérité littéraire. Il le doit, comme Michelet et Victor Hugo, à la Fondation du Musée des Monuments français, créé au début du siècle par Alexandre Lenoir. Plus que les recherches bénédictines du XVIII siècle, autant que le *Génie du Christianisme*, le Musée des Monuments français a contribué à propager le goût du gothique dans le premier quart du siècle. Ces souvenirs agissent sur les intelligences de 1830: des comités se créent, des sociétés et des commissions s'élaborent. . . . Après Mérimée, après Cahier, c'est Martin, Viollet-le-Duc et Vitet, Daniel Ramée, Chapuy, Taylor et Guilhermy et tant d'autres. Huysmans est leur héritier direct. A son tour, il se fait archéologue." Helen Trudgian, *L'Evolution des idées esthétiques de J. K. Huysmans*

(Paris, 1934), pp. 278–279 (my translation).

57. *La Cathédrale* (Paris, 1898), pp. 189–192; *Chartres*, pp. 116, 81, 75, 141.

58. Adams could also use Abbé Clerval's *Guide Chartrain* (Chartres, undated) which he calls "a useful little guide-book" (*Chartres*, p. 196).

59. *Chartres*, pp. 82, 79; see Emile Mâle, *The Gothic Image* (*L'Art religieux au XIIIe siècle en France*, trans. Dora Nussey), (London, 1961), pp. 81, 89. First published in 1898, Mâle's work went through its second edition in 1902 and a third in 1910. It was, as will be seen later, only after this third publication that Adams heard of it, quite by accident.

60. "des chaumines et des chapelles, des manoirs et des ports. . . . une Sion pour bébés, une Jérusalem céleste naine." *La Cathédrale*, p. 197 (my translation).

61. *Chartres*, p. 121.

62. Ibid., p. 76.

63. Ibid., p. 78; Mâle, *Gothic Image*, p. 185.

64. *Chartres*, p. 92.

65. Etienne Houvet, *Chartres Cathedral* (Chartres, undated), p. 55.

66. *Chartres*, p. 85.

67. Mâle, *Gothic Image*, p. 343.

68. "I was aware that the portrait character of the sculptures on the Porche de France was disputed, and for my purpose, I am glad of it. The interest of the place depends much more on the popular version of it than on the facts. I wish that tradition had attributed some of the figures to Blanche herself. The Saint Anne would double in interest if the public had ever called it a portrait of the Queen." H. A. to A. S. Cook; "Six Letters of Henry Adams," *Yale Review*, 10 (October 1920), 139.

69. *Chartres*, pp. 86–87.

70. Friedrich Heer, *The Medieval World*, trans. Janet Sondheimer (New York, 1961), p. 400.

71. Otto von Simson, *The Gothic Cathedral: Origins of Gothic Architecture and the Medieval Concept of Order* (New York, 1964), p. 211; *Chartres*, p. 137.

72. "Il faut au contraire admirer l'adresse avec laquelle l'auteur de ce plan, dont les irrégularités ne sont sensibles que sur le papier, a surmonté les difficultés de sa tâche." *Chartres*, p. 132; Yves Delaporte, *Notre-Dame de Chartres* (Paris, 1957), p. 19 (my translation).

73. *Chartres*, pp. 139–140.

74. Walter Pater, *Gaston de Latour—An Unfinished Romance*, ed. Charles Shadwell (London, Macmillan: 1910), p. 28; *Chartres*, p. 162; for subtitle, see ibid., p. 156.

75. Ibid., p. 192.

76. Ibid., p. 141.

77. *La Cathédrale*, pp. 166, 315–320, 326.

78. *Ford*, I, 468.

79. It was among the chemicals used in her photographic darkroom that Marian Adams, herself a skillful amateur photographer, had found the means of her self-destruction (see *Samuels*, II, 276).

80. *Chartres*, pp. 141, 142, 146, 178.

81. *Education*, pp. 470–471.

82. *Chartres*, pp. 186 and 189.

83. Ibid., 146–147.

84. *Ford*, II, 332–333.

85. *Education*, pp. 371, 385; *Ford*, II, 235.

86. *Chartres*, pp. 147, 156, 172.

87. The "fragment of a great work" mentioned is Paul Durand, *Monographie de Notre-Dame de Chartres* (Paris, 1881). This text was intended to accompany the *Monographie de la cathédrale de Chartres*, published by the Ministère de l'Instruction Publique et des Beaux Arts (Paris, 1867), a collection of plates (incomplete). The other "authorities" are Ferdinand Lasteyrie, *Histoire de la peinture sur verre d'après ses monuments en France* (Paris, 1838–1857), Charles Cahier and Arthur Martin, *Vitraux peints de Saint-Etienne de Bourges* (Paris, 1841–1844), E. Viollet-le-Duc, *Dictionnaire raisonné de l'architecture française du XIe au XIVe siècle* (Paris, 1858–1868), IX, 373–462.

88. *Chartres*, p. 142. The new authorities mentioned are L. Ottin, *le Vitrail* (Paris, 1896), Nat H. J. Westlake, *A History of Design in Painted Glass* (London, 1881), Emile Mâle, *L'Art religieux du XIIIe siècle en France* (Paris, 1898).

89. A. S. Cook, ed. "Three Letters of Henry Adams," *Pacific Review*, 2 (September 1921), 274.

90. *Gothic Image*, pp. 348, 350; *Chartres*, pp. 184–185.

91. "Combat des Français et des Sarrasins. Il faut remarquer la forme un peu déprimée du casque des Français, leurs boucliers longs se terminant en pointe, à la partie inférieure et leurs cottes de maille, tandis que les infidèles ont un casque conique, un bouclier rond et des cottes formées par des lamelles. Le combat est terrible. Le roi franc, reconnaissable à la couronne qui accompagne son casque, tranche le tête du roi son adversaire, tandis qu'un Sarrasin va asséner un coup de hache d'armes sur Charlemagne que protègent ses compagnons. Le mouvement rapide des chevaux est bien exprimé; ils sont au grand galop." Durand, *Monographie de Notre-Dame de Chartres*, II, 162–165 (my translation).

92. *Chartres*, pp. 185–186, 188.

93. Ibid., pp. 170–171, 182–183, 197–198.

94. Ibid., pp. 151–152.

95. "Il existe sur les problèmes essentiels de la couleur dans le vitrail médiéval une admirable étude qui est aujourd'hui encore le fondement de toutes nos idées: c'est le célèbre article 'Vitrail' dans le *Dictionnaire Raisonné d'Architecture* de Viollet-le-Duc. Son étude est une explication, ou une interprétation rationelle et positiviste de l'art médiéval . . . Quelles que soient les réserves que l'on doive faire à la thèse générale de Viollet-le-Duc, on ne peut contester la remarquable pénétration de ses observations sur l'art du vitrail. Tous les auteurs précédents reprennent ses principales idées." Louis Grodecki, "La Couleur dans le vitrail du XIIe au XVIe siècles," *Problèmes de la couleur*, papers and discussions at the May 18–20, 1954, symposium, collected and edited by Ignace Meyerson (Paris, 1957) (my translation); Charles Connick, *Adventures in Light and Color* (New York; Random House, 1937).

96. *Chartres*, pp. 143–144.

97. Ibid., p. 145.

98. "Mediaeval Windows in Romantic Light," in *Essays and Studies in Honor of Carleton Brown* (New York, 1940), p. 38.
99. Ibid., pp. 39–40.
100. Ibid., p. 37.
101. *Chartres*, p. 174.

6. "La Cathédrale littéraire"

1. *Chartres*, p. 284; Baym, *The French Education of Henry Adams*, p. 284. The title of this chapter is taken from Gustave Cohen's introduction to Adam le Bossu, *Le Jeu de Robin et Marion* (Paris, 1935), p. 16: "J'ai toujours pensé que pour comprendre le grand XIIIe siècle, il fallait en faire ressortir du fond des temps, claires, lumineuses, blanches, irrisées, les trois cathédrales; l'architecturale, la littéraire, la musicale" (It has always been my belief that to understand the greatness of the 13th century one must call up from the depths of time, in all their proper clarity, radiance, whiteness, and irridescence, the three cathedrals: the cathedral of architecture, the cathedral of literature, and the cathedral of music).
2. F. B. Luquiens, "Seventeen Letters of Henry Adams," *Yale Review*, 10 (October 1920), III.
3. "L'étude scientifique des langues romanes est maintenant entrée dans le cercle des études universitaires aux Etats-Unis. Il y a un public assuré pour les leçons sérieuses sur les langues et les littératures romanes pendant la période du Moyen Age. Dans ces études les universités des Etats-Unis sont notablement plus avancées que leurs soeurs ainées d'Angleterre." *Romania*, 14 (1885), 312 (my translation).
4. "The Teaching of French in the United States," *The French Review*, 36 (October 1963), 86.
5. J. R. Lowell, "The Study of Modern Languages."
6. Watts, "Teaching of French in the U.S."
7. There has been so far only one book written by an American and wholly devoted to the subject: *History of Old French Literature from the Origins to 1300* (1937), by Professor Urban T. Holmes; as its author puts it, it is a manual "adapted to the needs of American students," that is, much more aimed at scholarly precision than at literary grace.
8. Baym, *French Education*, pp. 291–301.
9. Horace E. Scudder, *James Russell Lowell, A Biography* (London, 1901), II, 187.
10. *Chartres*, pp. 286, 253, 284.
11. Ibid., p. 272.
12. Luquiens, "Seventeen Letters," p. 111; Lowell, "The Study of Modern Languages."
13. *Cater*, p. 547.
14. Barrett Wendell, *Traditions of European Literature* (New York, 1920), p. 480.
15. *Chartres*, pp. 20–24; discredited by Bédier, who pronounced it a figment of the poet's imagination. *Légendes épiques* (Paris, 1926), II, 370, the episode of Taillefer singing at the head of the Norman troops is now held to have truly occurred by R. M. Pidal. *La Chanson de Roland et la tradition épique des Francs*, 2nd ed. (Paris, 1960, p. 271).

16. In what he picturesquely called a "Guide-Joanne du Roland," purporting merely to give the strictly indispensable data any traveler should be familiar with, J. Geddes listed 365 titles. *La Chanson de Roland* (New York, Macmillan, 1906), p. xci.

17. *Chartres*, pp. 25, 35; "Pour trouver un terme de comparaison à la *Chanson de Roland*, je ne penserais pas certes à l'art ogival, surtout en sa période fleurie ou flamboyante, à ses dentelles de pierre, à ses flèches vertigineuses, à ses murailles de pierre multicolore. Notre vieux poème évoque plutôt l'idée d'une église romane, solidement assise, peu ornée pure et sévère, dont la grandeur n'exclut pas une sombre élégance et qui touche fortement par sa simplicité même." Maurice Bouchor, *La Chanson de Roland traduite en vers* (Paris, 1899), p. 10 (my translation).

18. *Chartres*, pp. 27, 29; G. F. Jones, *The Ethos of the Song of Roland* (Baltimore, Johns Hopkins Press, 1963), pp. 41–42.

19. *French Studies*, 12 (1958), 362.

20. *Chartres*, pp. 35–36; E. Faral, *La Chanson de Roland* (Paris, 1934), p. 275.

21. G. Paris, *Extraits de la Chanson de Roland* (Paris, 1891), p. 105, n. 111; *Chartres*, p. 34.

22. Cf. G. Lanson, *Histoire de la littérature française* (Paris, 1952), p. 31: "Détachée à l'instant des mots qui nous les apportent, leur image réelle subsiste seule en nous: ils s'ordonnent d'eux-mêmes en une vision étrangement nette et subjective; on ne *lit* pas, on *voit*." (Their real forms instantaneously isolate themselves from the works and live alone in us; they order themselves into a vision that, strangely, is at once precise and subjective; we do not *read*, we *see*.) This is why William and his companions could "see the scene itself."

23. "Rien de plus monotone . . . rien de plus traînant comme ces couplets *assonancés,* comme ces *laisses* inégales où le rythme s'en va cahotant, où les consonnes se heurtent et s'entrechoquent avec un bruit de mauvais allemand, où le nombre même des vers ne semble avoir en vérité d'autre mesure que la longueur d'haleine du jongleur." F. Brunetière, *Etudes critiques sur l'histoire de la littérature française* (Paris, 1882, first series, pp. 17–18 (my translation); *Chartres*, pp. 29, 33–34.

24. Luquiens, "Seventeen Letters," p. 111; Luquiens' original "reconstruction of the Chanson de Roland" had appeared in the *Transactions of the Connecticut Academy*, 15 (1909).

25. "C'est nous qui devons aller vers cette époque, nous adapter au sentiment de cette forme d'art, sans prétendre que les hommes de ce temps éprouvaient anachroniquement à l'égard de la poésie des sentiments semblables aux nôtres." R. M. Pidal, *Chanson de Roland et tradition épique*, p. 501 (my translation).

26. *Chartres*, pp. 219–232.

27. "Sur les quatre ou cinq siècles que comprend le Moyen âge nous ne retiendrons que le plus grand de tous, le XIIe, et même la seconde moitié seulement de ce XIIe siècle, car elle représente pour nous l'apogée de la courtoisie. Avant 1150, en effet, le raffinement des moeurs, les bonnes manières ne sont pas encore à l'honneur. Au XIIIè siècle la *chevalerie d'amour,* comme la chevalerie tout court, va dégénérer et se ridiculiser avec cette forme de chevalerie errante dont la caricature se retrouvera dans *Don Quichotte.*

C'est donc à peu près au règne de Louis VII dit le jeune que nous limiterons cette étude. Et sans doute n'est-il pas inutile de rappeler ici que Louis VII avait épousé Aliénor ou Eléonore, fille unique du Duc d'Aquitaine, le plus grand seigneur du midi. . . . Aliénor apportait . . . son goût de la poésie développé dans le midi au contact des Troubadours. La reine Aliénor avait en outre deux filles dont l'une, Marie, épousera ensuite le puissant comte de Champagne. La reine de France, la comtesse de Champagne, voilà deux noms célèbres que nous retrouverons souvent." *Troubadours et cours d'amour* (Paris, 1950), pp. 9–10 (my translation).

28. *Chartres*, pp. 254, 267.

29. Ibid., pp. 215–231; Garreau, *Etat Social de la France au temps des croisades* (Paris, 1899), pp. 155–164.

30. "La prospérité matérielle, accompagnée d'une culture nouvelle, avait développé dans les cours dès la fin du XIe siècle une forme de vie sociale où le luxe, où les fêtes, où le jeu de l'esprit appelaient naturellement la participation des femmes. L'exemple vint, semble-t-il, du midi: il se propagea dans le nord à la faveur d'expéditions militaires entreprises en commun et à la faveur d'alliances matrimoniales. La femme prit alors dans la société une place de plus en plus relevée et de mieux en mieux défendue. L'homme s'avisa d'instinct que la femme ne pouvait plus se conquérir seulement par le droit de la force . . . Par une fiction qui allait devenir de mode pendant plus d'un siècle, il représenta la dame de son choix comme une suzeraine féodale dont il prétendait gagner les faveurs par sa soumission, par la fidélité et la ferveur de son service d'homme-lige. Voilà née la notion, voilà né le sentiment de ce qu'on appellera l'amour courtois . . . une mystique nouvelle, une exaltation de l'âme qui pour l'amour de la dame ne rêve que d'atteindre aux perfections de la vertu chevaleresque et de la pureté du coeur par lesquels l'amant méritera sa récompense. Et voilà du même coup la femme passée au rang de juge." E. Faral, in J. Bédier and Paul Hazard, *Histoire de la littérature française illustrée* (Paris, 1949), I (du Moyen Age au XVIIe sièle), pp. 27–28 (my translation); *Chartres*, p. 232.

31. Ibid., p. 233.

32. Ibid., p. 233.

33. Holmes, *History of Old French Literature*, p. 157; *Romance Philology*, II (1958), 221.

34. *Chartres*, pp. 234–238.

35. Ibid., pp. 241–243; Jean Frappier, *La Poésie lyrique en France du XIIe au XIIIe siècles*, Les Cours de la Sorbonne (Paris, undated), pp. 3–5 (my translation).

36. *Chartres*, pp. 243, 247.

37. J. Frappier, *Poésie Lyrique*, p. 173 (my translation); *Chartres*, p. 248.

38. A. Wallensköld, *Les Chansons de Thibaut de Champagne, Roi de Navarre*, critical edition (Paris, 1925), p. 44.

39. *Chartres*, p. 249.

40. Wallensköld, *Chansons de Thibaut*, p. 185; J. Frappier, *Poésie Lyrique*, p. 192.

41. *Chartres*, pp. 234, 247.

42. Wendell, *Traditions of European Literature*, p. 505; *Chartres*, p. 238.

43. Ibid., p. 224.

44. Paul Studer, ed., *Le Mystère d'Adam* (Manchester, 1918), p. xviii.

45. *Chartres*, p. 259.

46. Walter Pater, *The Renaissance*, in *Works of Walter Pater* (London, 1910), p. 17.

47. *Chartres*, pp. 254–267.

48. Pater, *The Renaissance*, p. 24; *Chartres*, p. 267.

49. Andrew Lang, *The Song-Story of Aucassin and Nicolette* (New Rochelle, N.Y., 1902), p. 4.

50. *Chartres*, p. 267.

51. Ibid., pp. 268–270.

52. Jessie Crosland, *Medieval French Literature* (Oxford, 1956), p. 242.

53. *Chartres*, p. 270; Crosland, *Medieval French Literature*, p. 242.

54. "Les jeunes filles y sont généralement présentées sans coeur et sans vergogne. Elles ont une pensée unique: conquérir un bel époux, et pour arriver à leurs fins tous les moyens sont bons. Pas un trait d'attachment filial, de dévouement, ne vient varier le tableau." Garreau, *L'état social de la France*, p. 156 (my translation).

"sont souvent de fameuses drôlesses: luxurieuses, effrontées, même brutales." I. Siciliano, *François Villon et les thèmes poétiques du Moyen Age* (Paris, 1934), p. 350 (my translation); (see all chapter 5, pp. 349–406). The same judgment applied to medieval *jeunes filles* is found in J. Bédier, *Les Fabliaux* (Paris, 1895), p. 322: "Les rares jeunes filles de nos poèmes sont des niaises ou des drôlesses . . . des drôlesses vicieuses" (The few young women in our poems are either ninnies or hussies . . . and vicious hussies at that).

55. *Chartres*, p. 256; as Blanche H. Dow remarks in *The Varying Attitude toward Women in French Literature of the Fifteenth Century: the Opening Years* (New York, 1936), p. 50, the Middle Ages ceaselessly "struggled in the clutch of two conflicting sentiments toward women which took opposing directions, the one to find expression in the violent diatribes against the sex of a Jean de Meun . . . , the other to seek its satisfaction in the romantic tale of courtly love."

56. Quoted by Dow, *Varying Attitude*, p. 49.

57. "On ne fut jamais doux avec la femme; au moment même où on conçut la création du monde, on le fit perdre par elle, par sa faute. L'antiquité . . . sut cependant garder le culte de sa beauté et lui conférer quelque grandeur tragique, mais le moyen âge fut sans pitié et sans justice. Il la traîna dans la boue, l'accabla d'insultes et de mépris, la couvrit de tous les crimes. La femme—plutôt que la Dame—fut vraiment sa créature et sa victime. . . . Les Pères de l'Eglise jetaient l'anathème sur la femme, le populaire s'en moquait bruyamment." Siciliano, *François Villon*, pp. 349-350 (my translation).

58. E. Mâle, *L'Art religieux au XIIe siècle* (Paris, 1922), pp. 374–376.

59. "Nos conteurs ont developpé a l'infini tout un vaste cycle de ruses féminines. C'est un véritable *strigveda* . . . Il ne s'agit plus de ce fond de rancune que l'homme a toujours contre la femme, mais d'un dogme bien défini, profondément enraciné que voici: les femmes son des êtres inférieurs et malfaisants." *Les Fabliaux*, pp. 319, 321 (my translation); *Chartres*, p. 217.

60. "Fossa novissima, vipera pessima, pulchra putrede, semita lubrica, res male publica, praedaque praede; horrida nectua, publica janua, dulce venenum, mil bene conscia, mobilis, impia, vas lue plenum; insociabile, dissociabile, litigiosum" (parody fragment of Bernardus Morlanensis, quoted by Dow, *Varying Attitude*, p. 60; my translation).

61. Dow, *Varying Attitude*, p. 52.

62. *Chartres*, pp. 272–274.

63. Le roman devait sans doute, dans la pensée de l'auteur, durer assez longtemps encore; Guillaume nous assure que la fin du songe "en était la plus belle partie." G. Paris, *La Littérature Française au Moyen Age* (*XIe–XIVe siècles*), Manual of Old French (Paris, 1888), p. 163. "Ecrite pour les cercles brillants et mondains du temps de la régence de Blanche de Castille, son oeuvre porte tout le temps le cachet du public auquel elle s'adresse: la morale en est assurément peu sévère." Ibid., p. 164.

64. Ibid., p. 166. Cf. also p. 172: "il clôt la littérature du moyen âge en y introduisant des éléments nouveaux dont quelques-uns, comme la connaissance de l'antiquité et la réflexion philosophique, feront partie intégrante de la littérature moderne" ("He brings medieval literature to a close by introducing new elements into it, and some of these, such as philosophic thought and knowledge of classical antiquity, are to be integral parts of modern literature)" (my translation). An interesting parallel is drawn by Henry O. Taylor, in *A Layman's View of History* (New York, 1935), pp. 65–66, between *The Education* and the *Roman de la Rose*: "the education which Henry Adams was to seek through experience of men and the reading of many books was meant, not only personal enlightment, but a rational explanation of the world. This becomes more evidently the theme of the latter half of the book, where nothing correspondingly concrete succeeds the exciting diplomatic narrative of a childhood. One may recall how the Voltairean wanderings of the second part of the *Roman de la Rose* follow the *precieux* but lovely idyll with which the poem opens." Needless to say, such a resemblance is just apparent; nothing could be more contradictory than the views held by the two authors concerning women.

65. E. Langlois, ed., *Le Roman de la Rose* (Paris, 1914–1924), III, l. 9155 *et seq.*

66. *Chartres*, pp. 274, 276.

67. Siciliano, *François Villon*, p. 362 (my translation).

68. *Chartres*, p. 16.

69. See *Samuels*, II, 44.

70. *Chartres*, p. 277.

71. Luquiens, "Seventeen Letters," pp. 123–124.

72. *Chartres*, pp. 16–18.

73. Ibid., p. 260; see also p. 27, 4th l. of quotation (*ermes*); p. 32, 3rd quotation, 10th l. (*se jut*); p. 223, last l.

74. Ibid., pp. 24, 254, 269.

75. Ibid., pp. 30 (last l. of quotation); 223 (5th l.); 224 (paraphrase of 2nd quotation); 250 (9th l.); 297 (2nd quotation, 5th l.); on p. 223, quotation, 1st l., *fols* is rendered by "rough," which is equally wrong. It may be noted that *rice* is elsewhere translated by "powerful" (p. 260) or "great" (p. 269), even though, in this case, it happens to mean "rich."

76. Cf. pp. 253, 241; as a matter of fact, Chrétien de Troyes' passage may

easily deceive an "outsider": ". . . . tant com une jame/Vaut de pailes et de sardines/Vaut la contesse de reines?" This passage is explained by W. Foerster in his edition of the *roman* (*Der Karrenritter*, Hale, 1899, p. 362): "Soviel Perlen und Sarden ein Edelstein wert ist, ebensoviel Königinnen ist meine Gräfin wert" (The value of my countess in queens is that of a gem in pearls and sards).

77. *Chartres*, pp. 30, 260, 262.

78. Cf. p. 240. Bartsch reads *Voesse*, whereas the accepted reading is now *voltice*.

79. Cf. F. W. Bourdillon, *Aucassin et Nicolette*, edited in Old French and also rendered in modern English (London 1887), p. 122; a footnote explains: "kermes-oak . . . *quercus coccifera*, the small shrub-like oak with prickly leaves, which abounds in Provence and along the shores of the Mediterranean. Its English name is derived from the kermès, the European cochineal insect, which is got from it."

80. William Morris, translator, *Old French Romances*, (New York, 1896), p. 88.

81. In a letter to John Neal (August 2, 1867); cf. Samuel Longfellow, *Life of H. W. Longfellow* (Boston, 1891), III, 94.

82. *Chartres*, p. 34.

83. Arthur S. Way, translator, *The Song of Roland* (Cambridge, England, 1913), p. 80; Leonard Bacon, *The Song of Roland* (New Haven, Conn., 1914), p. 84.

84. *Chartres*, p. 27; Way, *Song of Roland*, p. 79.

85. *Yale Review*, 10, p. 118.

86. *Chartres*, pp. 241–243.

87. George Moore, *Confessions of a Young Man* (London, 1940), p. 138.

88. *Chartres*, p. 66.

7. The Meaning of *Mont-Saint-Michel and Chartres*

1. *Ford*, II, 444; *Literary History of the United States*, p. 1080.

2. *The Catholic World*, 145 (April 1937), p. 46.

3. John P. McIntyre, "Henry Adams and the Unity of *Chartres*," *Twentieth Century Literature*, 7 (January 1962), p. 167, my italics.

4. *Education*, pp. 387, 451.

5. *Cater*, p. 544; see *Democracy and Esther*, p. 223.

6. *Ford*, II, pp. 542, 546.

7. R. Spiller, Introduction to *Esther* (New York, 1938), pp. v, xix (my italics); E. Samuels, "Henry Adams' 20th Century Virgin," *The Christian Century* (October 5, 1960), p. 1143.

8. *Education*, pp. 85, 87.

9. *Ford*, I, p. 354; *Samuels*, II, p. 160.

10. *Chartres*, p. 108; *Ford*, I, p. 223.

11. *Samuels*, II, pp. 25–26.

12. *Chartres*, pp. 106–107, 140.

13. Cortissoz, *John La Farge*, p. 244.

14. *Chartres*, p. 162.

15. *Ford*, II, p. 542; Robert F. Sayre, *The Examined Self* (Princeton, N.J. Princeton University Press, 1964), pp. 62–63.

16. *Samuels*, III, p. 640.
17. Ibid., p. 278; *Chartres*, p. 108.
18. Ibid., p. 308.
19. "Henry Adams' 20th Century Virgin," p. 1143; *Education*, p. 384.
20. Ibid., pp. 447, 441.
21. Ibid., p. 446.
22. *Ford*, II, p. 457 (August 11, 1905; to Mrs. Chanler).
23. "Henry Adams' 20th Century Virgin," p. 1144.
24. "The Heroines of Henry Adams," *American Quarterly*, 8 (Fall 1956), p. 239.
25. *Education*, p. 40.
26. "Why We Have No Great Novelists," *Forum*, 2 (February 1895), p. 619.
27. "The Novels of Henry Adams," *Sewanee Review*, 51 (1943), p. 297.
28. *Cater*, p. 544; *Education*, p. 370.
29. Cargill, "Medievalism of Henry Adams," pp. 326–327.
30. "The Expense of Greatness," in *The Lion and the Honeycomb* (New York, 1955), p. 90.
31. Spiller, *Literary History of the U.S.*, p. 1101.
32. On Adams' reading of William James, see Baym, "William James and Henry Adams," *New England Quarterly*, 10 (1937), 712–742.
33. *Chartres*, p. 8.
34. Ibid., pp. 1, 8.
35. *The Degradation of the Democratic Dogma*, p. 189.
36. *Chartres*, pp. 138, 187.
37. Ibid., pp. 288, 287, 290, 361.
38. Ibid., pp. 100, 105, 281.
39. Ibid., p. 307; *Literary History of the U.S.*, p. 1101.
40. "The Dynamo and the Angelic Doctor, the Bias of Henry Adams' Medievalism," *American Quarterly*, 17 (Winter 1965), 706–707.
41. *Chartres*, p. 276.
42. Levenson, *Mind and Art*, p. 278.
43. *Ford*, II, 485.
44. R. P. Blakmur, "The Harmony of True Liberalism, Henry Adams' Mont-Saint-Michel and Chartres, "*Sewanee Review,* 60 (Winter 1952), 1–27; John P. McIntyre, S.J., "*Mont-Saint-Michel and Chartres:* Structure and Meaning," M.A. thesis, University of Toronto, 1960; Michael Colacurcio, "The Dynamo and the Angelic Doctor: The Bias of Henry Adams' Medievalism," *American Quarterly*, 17 (Winter 1965), 696–712; see also Levenson, *Mind and Art*, pp. 278, and *Samuels*, III, 291–308.
45. J. P. McIntyre's article, "Henry Adams and the Unity of *Chartres*," in *Twentieth Century Literature* is a good digest of his M.A. thesis.
46. Colacurcio, "The Dynamo and the Angelic Doctor," p. 700.
47. Another book which he probably used, for his interpretation of Saint Francis, is Matthew Arnold's *Essays in Criticism, First Series* (London, 1883), "Pagan and Medieval Religious Sentiment," pp. 193–222; but he made no scorings or annotations on the copy, still in his library.
48. *Ford*, II, 562–563, 295.
49. "In his imaginative hypothesis Adams consistently misses or ignores basic Thomistic distinctions between essence and existence, matter and

form, act and potency, substance and accidents; and consequently his interpretation of Saint Thomas is not at all reliable. Above all, he does not grasp
the unifying principle of Thomism, the principle of *esse* or existence." (J.
P. McIntyre, M.A. thesis, p. 114); cf. also "Henry Adams and the Unity of
Chartres," p. 170.

50. E. Saveth, ed. *The Education of Henry Adams and Other Selected
Writings* (New York, Twayne Publishing Co., 1963), p. xxxiv.

51. J. P. McIntyre's M.A. thesis, p. 71.

52. *Chartres*, p. 321.

53. Ibid., p. 328.

54. Ibid., p. 329; as Max Baym remarks (*French Education*, pp. 184–185)
the knotty problem of Realism and Nominalism which comes up in all Cartesian discussions seems to have engaged Adams' attention as early as his
junior year at Harvard, when he read G. H. Lewes, *A Biographical History
of Philosophy* (London, 1852); on p. 61 of vol. 2, he underscored this passage: "We are here led to the origin of the world-famous dispute of Realism
and Nominalism . . . The Realists maintain that every General Term (or
abstract idea) such as Man, Virtue, etc. . , has a real and independent existence (apart from concrete instances). The Nominalists on the contrary,
maintain that all General Terms are but the creations of human ingenuity
. . . merely used as marks of aggregate conceptions . . . Plato was the first
Realist; M. Pierre Leroux is, we believe, the last."

55. *Chartres*, p. 358.

56. Cf. *Samuels*, I, 34.

57. "En regardant l'aveuglement et la misère de l'homme et ces con-
trariétés étonnantes qui se découvrent dans sa nature; et regardant tout
l'univers muet et l'homme sans lumière abandonné à lui-même et comme
égaré dans ce recoin de l'univers, sans savoir qui l'y a mis, ce qu'il y est
venu faire, ce qu'il deviendra en mourant; j'entre avec effroi comme un
homme qu'on aurait endormi dans une île déserte et effroyable, et qui
s'éveillerait sans connaître où il est et sans avoir aucun moyen d'en sortir."
Chartres, p. 359 (my translation).

58. Ibid., p. 326.

59. Ibid., p. 351.

60. "The Harmony of True Liberalism," p. 4.

61. Ibid., p. 6; *Chartres*, pp. 339–340.

62. See in this chapter: "A Psychological Allegory and Diagram" (quotation from William James' *Principles of Psychology*, II, 441).

63. *Chartres*, pp. 321, 335.

64. Ibid., pp. 321, 354.

65. Ibid., pp. 357, 361, 362, 378, 382.

66. Ibid., p. 384.

67. Colacurcio, "The Dynamo and the Angelic Doctor," p. 699; *Ford*, II,
485, 490 (December 9, 1907, and February 17, 1908; both to William
James).

68. *Chartres*, pp. 387, 389, 422.

69. Colacurcio, "The Dynamo and the Angelic Doctor," p. 701.

70. *Chartres*, pp. 390–391, 413.

71. *Ford*, II, 542, 546–547; *Education*, pp. 434–435; though Adams does
refer to the cathedrals of Amiens and Rheims in the last chapter of *Mont-*

Saint-Michel and Chartres (p. 388), it is with that of Beauvais that Adams' comparison really runs, because "the 'Summa Theologiae' is unfinished—like Beauvais cathedral." (p. 386).

72. See *The Degradation of the Democratic Dogma,* p. 150.

73. See Jordy, *Henry Adams, Scientific Historian* (New Haven, Conn., 1952), p. 158; *Samuels,* III, vii.

74. "Henry Adams or the Creation of Confusion," *The Anatomy of Nonsense* (Norfolk, Conn., 1943), p. 62.

75. *Education,* p. 429; R. Spiller, "Henry Adams, Man of Letters," *The Saturday Review of Literature* (February 22, 1947), quoted by Ernst Scheyer, "The Aesthete Henry Adams," *Criticism,* 4 (Fall 1953), 317.

76. *Literary History of the U.S.,* p. 1102.

77. *Education,* p. 383.

78. *Letters to a Niece,* p. 21.

79. Cf. Mrs. M. Whitcomb Hess, "The Atomic Age and Henry Adams," *Catholic World* (January 1951), p. 262; *Education,* p. 383.

80. P. E. More, *A New England Group and Others* (New York, 1921), pp. 139–140; Y. Winters, *Anatomy of Nonsense,* p. 57.

81. P. E. More, *New England Group,* p. 262; T. S. Eliot, "A Skeptical Patrician," *Athenaeum,* I (May 23, 1919), 361–362.

82. Colacurcio, 'The Dynamo and the Angelic Doctor," pp. 709–712; H. L. Creek, "The Medievalism of Henry Adams," *South Atlantic Quarterly,* 24 (1925), 88.

8. The "Unity" of *Mont-Saint-Michel and Chartres*

1. *Ford,* I, 487–488; *Cater,* pp. 263–264.

2. Levenson, *Mind and Art,* pp. 234–235.

3. Cf. *Samuels,* III, 291: "In external structure the scheme of the book suggests an almost Pythagorean use of the number three, dictated by the central mystery of the Trinity and symbolized by the 'mystic triangle.' The basic theological movement of the two centuries is exemplified in the fortunes of the persons of the Trinity, in the ascendancy of now one and now another of the aspects of the Three in One."

4. McIntyre, "Henry Adams and the Unity of Chartres," p. 171; in *Ishmael, A Study of the Symbolic Mode in Primitivism* (New York, 1960), p. 146, James Baird similarly comments: "The Cathedral of Chartres interpreted by Adams as itself a symbol of meaning, invested with the unifying mastery of meaning over disparate meanings, is to the art historian what the multiplex symbols of Moby-Dick are to Melville."

5. *Ford,* II, 490; *Cater,* p. 614.

6. *Education,* p. 312; McIntyre, "Henry Adams and the Unity of Chartres," p. 162.

7. *Chartres,* p. 13.

8. Levenson, *Mind and Art,* p. 241.

9. *Chartres,* p. 9.

10. Jordy, *Scientific Historian,* p. 13.

11. Baym, *French Education,* pp. 60–61.

12. Scheyer, "The Aesthete Henry Adams," p. 313; *Chartres,* pp. 4, 41.

13. *Chartres,* pp. 33–34, 174, 58.

14. "The humanistic message of myths acquires a special significance in our age in which the fragmentization and 'meaninglessness' of time and the self have caused . . . increasing concern and disturbance. According to this kind of humanism, whether ancient or new, the community of man would presumably not be defined only in terms of an immortal soul, a universal reason, or an ideal and idealized image of man. It would be composed of the common irrational, or non-rational aspects of human existence as well— the aesthetic images of which are reflected and 'celebrated,' as Thomas Mann would say, in the mythical tales and prototypes. *It would be an aesthetic humanism, a variety of aestheticism as a way of life*" (Hans Meyerhoff, *Time in Literature* (Berkeley, University of California Press, 1955, p. 84; my italics).

15. Jordy, *Scientific Historian*, p. 163.

16. Ludwig Lewisohn, *Expression in America* (New York, 1932), p. 344.

17. This, V. L. Parrington has admirably sensed: "Mont-Saint-Michel and Chartres is rich and tender and wise perhaps beyond anything else that his generation of Americans wrote, with a mellow scholarship that walks modestly because it has learned how little it knows. Yet in its very implication it is a sharp and searching criticism of Boston and America of the nineteenth century. It repudiates every ideal of a generation that had gambled away the savor of life—that does not comprehend 'and never shall' the greatness of that earlier time, 'the appetite' for living, the 'greed for novelty,' 'the fun of life.' " (*Main Currents in American Thought*, New York, 1930, III, 221.)

18. *Education*, p. 466.

19. *Samuels*, III, 290.

20. *Cater*, p. 623 (September 13, 1908).

21. "The Rule of Phase Applied to History," *The Degradation of the Democratic Dogma* (A Capricorn Book), p. 302.

22. Jordy, *Scientific Historian*, p. 250.

23. *Education*, p. 489.

24. *Chartres*, pp. 95–96.

25. Ibid., p. 349.

26. "A Letter to American Teachers of History," *The Degradation of the Democratic Dogma* (A Capricorn Book), pp. 237–238.

27. Spiller, *Literary History of the United States*, p. 1100.

28. P. E. More, *A Commemorative Tribute to Henry Adams* (New York, 1922), p. 4.

29. *Chartres*, p. 2.

30. *Chartres*, p. 5; Levenson, *Mind and Art*, p. 237.

31. Colacurcio, "The Dynamo and the Angelic Doctor," p. 697.

32. F. Nuhn, "Henry Adams and the Hand of the Fathers," *Literature in America*, ed. Philip Rahv (Cleveland, 1957), p. 248.

33. *Ford*, II, 46.

34. *Chartres*, p. 69.

35. Cf. Germain D'Hangest, *Walter Pater, L'Homme et l'Oeuvre* (Paris, 1961), I, 195; "Inversion romantique et macabre du thème de la reminiscence, la légende du vampire effleure le texte de Pater de son ombre sinistre, installant au sein même de la vie la hantise de la mort; et l'âme humaine, après avoir, de siècle en siècle, perdu sa fraîcheur, semble, lorsqu'elle s'in-

carne en Mona Lisa, n'avoir plus autre chose à lui léguer que ses maladies. . . La Joconde, on le voit, symbolise donc l'humanisme de Pater dans sa morbidité."
(The vampire myth—that romantic and macabre inversion of the idea of reminiscence—touches Pater's text with its sinister shadow and sets obsession with death on the very heart of life; all its freshness lost over the course of the centuries, when the soul of mankind comes to be embodied in the Mona Lisa it seems to have only its maladies left to bequeath to Pater . . . La Gioconda, it can be seen, thus symbolizes the morbid aspect of Pater's humanism.)

36. *Chartres*, p. 318.

37. Quoted by Ferner Nuhn, "Henry Adams and the Hand of the Fathers," p. 247.

38. Ibid., p. 248.

39. Cf. D'Hangest, *Walter Pater*, p. 196: "Sombre plante aux instables et multiples reflets, fleur du mal tardivement épanouie dans la demi-lumière d'une serre chaude, la beauté qui s'incarne dans cette figure ressemble à celle dont, quelques années plus tôt, l'image étrange et rare avait surgi dans les visions de Baudelaire; elle aussi appartient au monde fatigué du romantisme mourant et, comme l'autre, elle porte toutes les marques de la décadence qu'elle announce" (The beauty embodied in this face—a somber plant of manifold changing hues, a flower of evil that blossomed late in the dim light of the hothouse—resembles that beauty of which the strange and rare form had suddenly appeared in the visions of Baudelaire; it belongs to the weary world of expiring romanticism and, like the former, bears all the signs of decadence it heralds).

40. *Education*, p. 5; Walter Pater, Introduction to *The Renaissance*, quoted by Wendell V. Harris in "Pater as Prophet," *Criticism* (Fall, 1964), 358.

41. *Chartres*, p. 152.

42. Walter Pater, *The Renaissance*, p. 135; *Marius the Epicurean: His Sensations and Ideas*, pp. 110–111, in *The Works of Walter Pater* (London, 1910).

43. *Chartres*, p. 193.

44. *Education*, p. 80.

45. Wallace Stevens, *Collected Poems* (New York, 1954), pp. 89, 167.

46. Wallace Stevens, "The Figure of Youth as Virile Poet," *The Necessary Angel* (London, 1960), p. 58.

47. *Ford*, II, 299.

48. "Le rêveur s'en va à la dérive. Un vrai poète ne se satisfait pas de cette imagination évasive. Il veut que l'imagination soit un voyage. Chaque poète nous doit donc son invitation au voyage." Gaston Bachelard, *L'Air et les songes: Essai sur l'imagination du mouvement* (Paris, 1934), p. 11 (my translation).

49. *Ford*, I, 410.

50. R. P. Blackmur, "Henry and Brooks Adams: Parallels to Two Generations," *Southern Review*, 5 (Autumn 1939), 309.

Selected Bibliography

Writings of Henry Adams Cited in this Volume

Books, Articles, and Book Reviews

"The Anglo-Saxon Courts of Law," in *Essays in Anglo-Saxon Law*, pp. 1–54. Boston: Little, Brown, 1876.

The Degradation of the Democratic Dogma, with an introduction by Brooks Adams. (1st ed., New York: Macmillan, 1919); New York: Putnam Capricorn Books, 1958.

The Education of Henry Adams. (1st ed. privately printed, Washington, D.C., 1907; also published as *The Education of Henry Adams: An Autobiography*. Boston: Massachusetts Historical Society, 1918; Boston: Houghton Mifflin, 1918); New York: Random House, the Modern Library, 1931.

Esther: A Novel (1st ed. under the pseudonym of Frances Snow Compton, New York: Henry Holt, 1887); in *Democracy and Esther*, with an introduction by Ernest Samuels, Garden City, N.Y.: Doubleday Anchor Books, 1961.

"Freeman's Historical Essays," *N.A.R.*, 114 (January 1872), 193–196.

"Freeman's History of the Norman Conquest," *N.A.R.*, 118 (January 1874), 176–181.

"Harvard College," *N.A.R.*, 114 (January 1872), 110–147; reprinted in *Historical Essays*, pp. 80–121. New York: Charles Scribner's Sons, 1891.

History of the United States of America During the Administrations of Jefferson and Madison. 9 vols. New York: Charles Scribner's Sons, 1889–1891.

"Holden Chapel," *Harvard Magazine* (May 1855), 210–215.

"King," in *Clarence King Memoirs*, pp. 157–185. New York: G. P. Putnam's Sons, 1904.

A Letter to American Teachers of History. Baltimore: privately printed, J. H. Hurst & Co., 1910. Reprinted in *The Degradation of the Democratic Dogma*. New York: Putnam Capricorn Books, 1958, 133–259.

Mont-Saint-Michel and Chartres. (1st ed., Washington, D.C.: privately printed, 1904. Revised and republished, Washington, D.C.: privately printed, 1912. Also in an edition "by Authority of the American Institute of Architects," with an introduction by Ralph Adams Cram. Boston: Houghton Mifflin, 1913; Garden City, N.Y.: Doubleday Anchor Books, 1933.

"The New York Gold Conspiracy," *Westminster Review*, 38 (October 1870), 411–436; reprinted in *Historical Essays*, pp. 318–366. New York: Charles Scribner's Sons, 1891.

"The Rule of Phase Applied to History," in *The Degradation of the Democratic Dogma*, pp. 261–304. New York: Putnam Capricorn Books.

Tahiti, with an introduction by R. Spiller. New York: Scholars' Facsimiles and Reprints, 1947.

Selected Bibliography

Correspondence

"Henry Adams' Education of Martha Cameron: Letters, 1888–1916." Ed. Charles Vandersee, *Texas Studies in Literature and Language*, 2 (Summer 1968), 233–293.

Henry Adams and His Friends: A Collection of His Unpublished Letters. Ed. Harold D. Cater. Boston: Houghton Mifflin, 1947.

Letters of Henry Adams, 1858–1891. Ed. Worthington C. Ford. 2 vols. Boston: Houghton Mifflin, 1930–1938.

Letters to a Niece and Prayer to the Virgin of Chartres, with a Niece's Memories. Ed. Mabel La Farge. Boston: Houghton Mifflin, 1920.

"Seventeen Letters of Henry Adams," ed. Frederick B. Luquiens, *Yale Review*, 10 (October 1920), 111–140.

"Six Letters of Henry Adams," ed. Albert S. Cook, *Yale Review*, 10 (October 1920), 131–140.

"Three Letters of Henry Adams," ed. Albert S. Cook, *Pacific Review*, 2 (September 1921), 273–275.

Manuscript Material

Massachusetts Historical Society, Boston: Henry Adams to Mrs. Cameron, letters from the South Seas.

Writings about Henry Adams

Adams, Brooks. "The Heritage of Henry Adams," in *The Degradation of the Democratic Dogma*, pp. v–xiii, 1–122. New York: Putnam Capricorn Books, 1958.

Adams, James Truslow. *The Adams Family*. Boston: Little, Brown, 1930.

———— *Henry Adams*. New York: Boni, 1933.

Baym, Max I. *The French Education of Henry Adams*. New York: Columbia University Press, 1951.

———— "Henry Adams and the Critics," *The American Scholar*, 15 (Winter 1945), 79–89.

———— "The 1858 Catalogue of Henry Adams' Library," *Colophon*, 4 (Autumn 1938), 483–489.

———— "William James and Henry Adams," *New England Quarterly*, 10 (1937), 717–742.

Beard, Charles A. "Historians at Work: Brooks and Henry Adams," *Atlantic Monthly*, 171 (April 1943), 87–98.

Becker, Carl. "Henry Adams Once More," *Saturday Review of Literature*, 9 (April 1933), 162–168.

———— "The Education of Henry Adams," *American Historical Review*, 24 (April 1919), 422–434.

Blackmur, R. P. "Henry and Brooks Adams, Parallels to Two Generations," *Southern Review*, 5 (Autumn 1939), 308–334.

———— "Henry Adams: Three Late Moments," *Kenyon Review*, 2 (Winter 1940), 7–29.

————"The Harmony of True Liberalism, Henry Adams' Mont-Saint-Michel and Chartres," *Sewanee Review*, 60 (Winter 1952), 1–27.

———— *The Lion and the Honeycomb, Essays in Solicitude and Critique*, chap. vi: "The Expense of Greatness," pp. 79–97. New York: Harcourt, Brace, 1935.

———— "The Novels of Henry Adams," *Sewanee Review*, 51 (April 1943), 281–304.

———— "The Virgin and the Dynamo," *Magazine of Art*, 45 (April 1952), 147–153.

Blunt, H. F. "The Mal-Education of Henry Adams," *Catholic World*, 144 (April 1937), 46–52.

Bradford, Gamaliel. "Henry Adams," *Atlantic Monthly*, 125 (May 1920), 623–634.

Brooks, Van Wyck. *Sketches in Criticism*, "The Miseducation of Henry Adams," pp. 197–210. New York: Dutton Co., 1932.

———— *New England: Indian Summer*, chap. xii, pp. 256–283 and *passim*. New York: Dutton Co., 1940.

Cargill, Oscar. *Intellectual America*, pp. 551–569. New York: Macmillan, 1941.

———— "The Medievalism of Henry Adams," in *Essays and Studies in Honor of Carleton Brown*, pp. 296–329. New York: New York University Press, 1940.

Carpenter, Frederic L. "The Three Ages of Henry Adams," *College English* 15 (December 1953), 148–155.

Cater, Harold D. Biographical Introduction to *Henry Adams and His Friends*, pp. xc–cvii. Boston: Houghton Mifflin, 1947.

Colacurcio, Michael. "The Dynamo and the Angelic Doctor: The Bias of Henry Adams' Medievalism," *American Quarterly*, 17 (Winter 1965), 696–712.

Commager, Henry S. *The American Mind*, pp. 132–140. New Haven, Conn.: Yale University Press, 1950.

Conder, John. *A Formula of His Own*. Henry Adams's Literary Experiment. Chicago: University of Chicago Press, 1970.

Creek, Herbert L. "The Medievalism of Henry Adams," *South Atlantic Quarterly*, 24 (January 1925), 86–97.

Crumley, Moreene E. "The Reputation of Henry Adams," unpub. Ph. D. diss., University of Chicago, 1954.

Cunliffe, Marcus. "What Was the Matter with Henry Adams?" *Commentary*, 39 (1965), 61–71.

Dickason, David H. "Henry Adams and Clarence King: The Record of a Friendship," *New England Quarterly*, 17 (June 1944), 229–254.

Donovan, Timothy P. *Henry Adams and Brooks Adams*. Norman, Okla.: University of Oklahoma Press, 1961.

Eliot, T. S. "A Skeptical Patrician," *Athenaeum* (May 23, 1919), 361–362.

Glicksberg, Charles I. "Henry Adams and the Aesthetic Quest," *Prairie Schooner*, 25 (Fall 1951), 241–250.

———— "Henry Adams and the Modern Spirit," *Dalhousie Review*, 27 (October 1947), 299–309.

———— "Henry Adams and the Repudiation of Science," *Scientific Monthly*, 67 (January 1947), 63–71.

Hayward, Ira N. "From Tahiti to Chartres, the Henry Adams—John La Farge Friendship," *The Huntington Library Quarterly*, 21 (September 1958), 345–348.

———— "Henry Adams' Prose Style," *Utah Academy Proceedings*, 35. (1958), 25–38.

Hicks, Granville. *The Great Tradition*. New York: Macmillan, 1935.

Hochfield, George. *Henry Adams, an Introduction and Interpretation*. New York: Barnes and Noble, American Authors and Critics Series, 1962.

Homans, Abigail Adams. "My Uncles: Charles, Henry, Brooks Adams," *Yale Review*, 50 (1966), 321–346.

Hume, Robert A. *Runaway Star*. Ithaca, N.Y.: Cornell University Press. 1951.

———— "The Style and Literary Background of Henry Adams," *American Literature*, 16 (January 1945), 296–315.

Jordy, William H. *Henry Adams, Scientific Historian*. New Haven, Conn.: Yale University Press, 1952.

———— "Henry Adams and Walt Whitman," *South Atlantic Quarterly*, 40 (April 1941), 132–145.

La Farge, Mabel A. "A Niece's Memories," *Yale Review*, 9 (January 1920), 271–296; reprinted in *Letters to a Niece and Prayer to the Virgin of Chartres*. Ed. Mabel La Farge.

Laughlin, I. L. "Some Recollections of Henry Adams," *Scribner's Magazine*, 69 (May 1921), 576–585.

Le Breton, Maurice. "Henry Adams et la France," *Harvard et la France*. Ed. E. de Lévis Mirepoix and R. Doumic. Paris: *Revue d'Histoire Moderne* (1936), 74–96.

Levenson, J. C. *The Mind and Art of Henry Adams*. Boston: Houghton Mifflin, 1957.

Lewisohn, Ludwig. *Expression in America*, pp. 342–347. New York: Harper Bros., 1932.

McIntyre, John P., S.J. "Henry Adams and the Unity of Chartres," *Twentieth Century Literature*, 7 (January 1962), 159–171.

———— "Interpreting Henry Adams, An Answer to '20th Century Virgin'," *The Christian Century* (January 4, 1961), 18–19.

———— "*Mont-Saint-Michel and Chartres*: Structure and Meaning," unpub. M.A. thesis, University of Toronto, 1960.

MacLean, Kenneth. "Window and Cross in Henry Adams' Education," *University of Toronto Quarterly*, 28 (1958–1959), 332–334.

Mane, Robert. "Henry Adams," *Etudes anglaises*, 20 (1967), 29–37.

———— "Henry Adams et la science," *Etudes anglaises*, 16 (1963), 1–10.

Maud, Ralph. "Henry Adams: Irony and Impasse," *Essays in Criticism*, 8 (1958), 381–392.

Mitchell, Steward. "Henry Adams and Some of His Students," *Proceedings of the Massachusetts Historical Society*, 66 (1942), 294–312.

Monchoux, Henri. "Propos inédits sur la France dans les lettres de Henry Adams," *Revue de littérature comparée*, 41 (1967), 238–274.

More, Paul E. *A Commemorative Tribute to Henry Adams*, prepared for the American Academy of Arts and Letters (1920). New York: American Academy of Arts and Letters, 1922.

———— *A New England Group and Others*. Shelburne Essays, 11th series, pp. 115–140. Boston: Houghton Mifflin, 1921.

Mumford, Lewis. *The Golden Day, A Study in American Expression and Culture*, pp. 217–225. New York: Norton, 1933.

Selected Bibliography

Nuhn, Ferner. *The Wind Blew from the East*, pp. 164–194: "Henry Adams and the Hand of the Fathers." New York: Harper Bros., 1942. Also in *Literature in America*, pp. 247–267. Ed. Philip Rahv, Cleveland: World Publishing Company, 1957.

Parrington, V. L. *Main Currents in American Thought*, pp. 214–227. New York: Harcourt, Brace, 1930.

Quinlivan, Frances. "Irregularities of the Mental Mirror," *Catholic World*, 163 (April 1946), 58–65.

Rahv, Philip. *Discovery of Europe*, pp. 363–392. Garden City, N.Y.: Doubleday Anchor Books, 1960.

Samuels, Ernest. *The Young Henry Adams*. Cambridge, Mass.: Harvard University Press, 1948.

———— *Henry Adams, the Middle Years*. Cambridge, Mass.: Harvard University Press, 1958.

———— *Henry Adams, the Major Phase*. Cambridge, Mass.: Harvard University Press, 1964.

———— "Henry Adams and the Gossip Mills," in *Essays in American and English Literature Presented to Bruce Robert McElderry, Jr.*, pp. 59–75. Ed. Max F. Schulz *et al.* Athens, Ohio: University of Ohio Press, 1967.

———— "Henry Adams' 20th Century Virgin," *The Christian Century* (October 5, 1960), 1143–1160.

Saveth, Edward N. "Henry Adams' Norman Ancestors," *Contemporary Jewish Record*, 8 (June 1945), 250–261.

———— "The Heroines of Henry Adams," *American Quarterly*, 8 (Fall 1956), 231–242.

Sayre, Robert F., *The Examined Self*, pp. 44–327. Princeton, N.J.: Princeton University Press, 1964.

Scheyer, Ernst. "The Aesthete Henry Adams," *Criticism*, 4 (Fall 1962), 313–327.

———— "Henry Adams and Henry Hobson Richardson," *Journal of the Society of Architectural Historians*, 12 (March 1953), 7–12.

Shoemaker, Richard L. "The France of Henry Adams," *French Review*, 21 (February 1948), 292–299.

Simonds, Katherine. "The Tragedy of Mrs. Henry Adams," *New England Quarterly*, 9 (December 1936), 564–582.

Spiller, Robert E. "Henry Adams," in *Literary History of the United States*, pp. 1080–1103. Eds. Robert E. Spiller *et al.* New York: Macmillan, 1948.

———— Introduction to *Esther*, pp. iii-xxv. New York: Scholars' Facsimiles and Reprints, 1938.

———— Introduction to *Tahiti*, pp. iii-vii. New York: Scholars' Facsimiles and Reprints, 1947.

Stevenson, Elizabeth. *Henry Adams: A Biography*. New York: Macmillan, Collier Books, 1955.

Tanner, Tony. "The Lost America — The Despair of Henry Adams and Mark Twain," *Modern Age* (Summer 1961), 299–310. Reprinted in *Mark Twain, a Collection of Critical Essays*, pp. 159–174. Ed. Henry Nash Smith. Englewood Cliffs, N.J.: Prentice Hall, 1963.

Taylor, Henry O. "The Education of Henry Adams," *Atlantic Monthly*, 122 (October 1918), 484–491.

Selected Bibliography

Vandersee, Charles. "The Four Menageries of Henry Adams," *Arizona Quarterly*, 24 (Winter 1968), 293–308.

———— "Henry Adams (1838–1918)," *American Literary Realism*, 2 (Summer 1969), 89–119.

Wasser, Henry. *The Scientific Thought of Henry Adams*. Thessaloniki: University of Salonika Press, 1956.

Welland, D. S. R. "Henry Adams as Novelist," *Renaissance and Modern Studies*, 3 (1959), 25–50.

White, Lynn. "The Virgin and the Dynamo Reconsidered," *The American Scholar*, 27 (1957), 183–194.

Winters, Yvor. *The Anatomy of Nonsense*, pp. 23–87, "Henry Adams or the Creation of Confusion." Norfolk, Conn.: New Directions, 1943.

Miscellaneous

Adam le Bossu, dit de la Halle. *Le Jeu de Robin et de Marion* and *Jeu du pèlerin*. Ed. Gustave Cohen. Paris: Delagrave, 1935.

Adams, Brooks. *The Law of Civilization and Decay*. New York: A. Knopf, 1943.

———— "The Gold Standard, An Historical Study," *Fortnightly Review*, 62 (August 1894), 242–262.

Adams, Charles Francis, Jr. *Charles Francis Adams by His Son*. Boston: Houghton Mifflin, 1900.

Adams, Herbert. "Edward Freeman," *American Historical Review*, I (1895), 149–153.

Addison, Agnes. *Romanticism and the Gothic Revival*. New York: R. R. Smith, 1938.

Arnold, Matthew. *Essays in Criticism, First Series*, pp. 193–222, "Pagan and Medieval Religious Sentiment." London: Macmillan, 1883.

Bachelard, Gaston. *L'Air et les songes, essais sur l'imagination du mouvement*. Paris: J. Corti, 1943.

Bacon, Edward M. *Rambles around Old Boston*. Boston: Little, Brown, 1921.

Bacon, Leonard. *The Song of Roland*. New Haven, Conn.: Yale University Press, 1914.

Baird, James I. *A Study of the Symbolic Mode in Primitivism*. New York: Harper and Row Torchbooks, 1960.

Becker, Carl. *The Heavenly City of the Eighteenth-Century Philosophers*. New Haven, Conn.: Yale University Press, Yale Paperbound, 1963.

Bédier, Joseph. *Les Légendes épiques*. Paris: Champion, 1926.

———— *Les Fabliaux*. 2nd ed. Paris: E. Bouillon, 1895.

———— and Paul Hazard. *Histoire de la littérature française illustrée, du moyen âge au XVIIe siècle inclus*. Paris: Larousse, 1949.

Beringause, Arthur. *Brooks Adams, A Biography*. New York: A. Knopf, 1955.

Bonnerot, Louis. *Matthew Arnold poète*. Paris: Didier, 1947.

Bouchor, Maurice. *La Chanson de Roland traduite en vers*. Paris: Hachette, 1899.

Bourdillon, F. W. *Aucassin and Nicolette*. Edited in old French and rendered in modern English. London: Kegan Paul, 1887.

Selected Bibliography

Bowers, Claude, Jr. *The Young Jefferson, 1743–1789.* Boston: Houghton Mifflin, 1945.

Brooks, Van Wyck. *The Dream of Arcadia, American Writers and Artists in Italy, 1760–1915.* New York: Dutton, 1958.

Brunetière, Ferdinand. *Etudes critiques sur l'histoire de la littérature française.* Paris: Hachette, 1880.

Bulteau, Marcel (Abbé). *Description de la Cathédrale de Chartres.* Chartres: Garnier, 1850.

———— *Monographie de la Cathédrale de Chartres.* 2nd ed. revised and enlarged. Chartres: R. Selleret, 1887–1892.

Carlyle, Thomas. *Essays.* London: Dent, Everyman's Library, 1950.

Child, Ruth. *The Aesthetic of Walter Pater.* New York: Macmillan, 1940.

Christ, Yvan. *Mont-Saint-Michel.* Paris: Sun, Rainbow Collection, 1962.

Clerval, J. A. (Abbé). *Guide Chartrain.* Chartres: R. Selleret, 1896.

Commager, Henry Steele. *The American Mind.* New Haven: Yale University Press, Yale Paperbound, 1950.

Cook, E. T. *The Life of John Ruskin.* London: G. Allen, 1912.

Corroyer, Edouard. *Description de l'Abbaye du Mont-Saint-Michel et de ses abords.* Paris: Dumoulin, 1877.

Cortissoz, Royal. *John La Farge, A Memoir and a Study.* Boston: Houghton Mifflin, 1911.

Cowley, Malcolm, and Bernard Smith, ed. *Books That Changed Our Minds.* New York: Doubleday, Doran, 1940.

Crosland, Jessie. *Medieval French Literature.* Oxford: R. Blackwell, 1956.

Delaporte, Yves (Chanoine). *Notre-Dame de Chartres.* Paris: Hachette, 1957.

D'Hangest, Germain. *Walter Pater, l'homme et l'œuvre.* Paris: Didier, 1961.

De Rougemont, Denis. *L'Amour et l'occident.* Paris: Plon, 1939.

Dickason, David H. *The Daring Young Men.* Bloomington, Ind.: Indiana University Press, 1953.

———— "Clarence King — Scientist and Art Amateur." *Art in America,* 32 (January 1944), 41–51.

Dow, Blanche H. *The Varying Attitude toward Women in French Literature of the Fifteenth Century.* New York: Columbia University Publications of the Institute of French Studies, 1936.

Dunning, W. A. *Truth in History and Other Essays.* New York: Columbia University Press, 1937.

Dupont, Etienne. *Le Mont Saint-Michel inconnu d'après des documents inédits.* Paris: Perrin, 1912.

Eberlein, Harold D. *Architecture of Colonial America.* Boston: Little, Brown, 1925.

Emerson, R. W. *The Complete Essays and Other Writings of R. W. Emerson.* Ed. Brooks Atkinson. New York: Random House, the Modern Library College Edition, 1940.

———— *The Letters of R. W. Emerson,* ed. Ralph L. Rusk. New York: Columbia University Press, 1939.

Faral, Edmond. *La Chanson de Roland.* Paris: Mélottée, 1934.

Finberg, H. P. *The Early Charters of the West Midlands.* Leicester: Leicester University Press, 1861.

Focillon, Henri. *Art d'occident:* le Moyen Age Roman et Gothique. 3rd ed. Paris: Armand Colin, 1955.

————— "John La Farge," *Art in America,* 29 (1936), 311–319.

Frappier, Jean. *La Poésie lyrique en France du XIIè et XIIIè siècles.* Paris: Les Cours de la Sorbonne, undated.

Frederick, Paul. "The Study of History in Germany and France," *Johns Hopkins University Studies,* 8 (1890), 70–94.

Freeman, Edward Augustus. *The History of the Norman Conquest of England, Its Causes and Its Consequences.* Oxford: Clarendon Press, 1867–1879.

————— *Some Impressions of the United States.* New York: H. Holt, 1883.

Frye, Northrop. *Anatomy of Criticism.* Princeton, N.J.: Princeton University Press, 1957.

Garreau, Louis. *L'Etat social de la France au temps des croisades.* Paris: Plon, Nourrit, 1899.

Gilson, Etienne. *La Philosophie au moyen age.* 2d ed. revised and enlarged. Paris: Payot, 1952.

Graham, Rose. "The History of the Alien Priory of Wenlock," *Journal of the British Archeological Association,* 3rd series, 4 (1939), 117–140.

Greenslet, Ferris. *James Russell Lowell.* Boston: Houghton Mifflin, 1905.

Griscom, Lloyd C. *Diplomatically Speaking.* Boston: Little, Brown, 1940.

Grodecki, Louis. "La Couleur dans le vitrail du XIIè au XVè siècles," *Problèmes de la Couleur,* papers and discussions from symposium, May 18–20, 1954, edited by Ignace Meyerson. Paris: Publications de l'Education Nationale, 1957.

Harrison, Frederic. *John Ruskin.* New York: Macmillan, 1902.

Hartmann, Sadakichi. *A History of American Art.* Boston: L. C. Page, 1902.

Heer, Friedrich. *The Medieval World.* Trans. Janet Sondheimer. New York: A Mentor Book, 1961.

Hillhouse, James. *The Waverley Novels and Their Critics.* Minneapolis: University of Minnesota Press, 1936.

Hitchcock, H. R. *The Architecture of H. H. Richardson and His Times.* New York: Museum of Modern Art, 1936.

Holmes, Urban T. *A History of Old French Literature from the Origins to 1300.* Chapel Hill, N.C.: R. Linker, 1937.

Holt, W. S. "The Idea of Scientific History in America," *Journal of the History of Ideas,* 1 (June 1940), 356–357.

Hough, Graham. *The Last Romantics.* New York: Barnes and Noble, University Paperbacks, 1947.

Houvet, Etienne. *Chartres Cathedral.* Chartres: E. Houvet, undated.

Howells, William Dean. *Literary Friends and Acquaintance.* New York: Harper and Bros., 1900.

Huysmans, J. K. *La Cathédrale.* Paris: Plon Nourrit, 1908.

James, Henry. *Notes of a Son and Brother.* New York: Charles Scribner's Sons, 1914.

Jones, G. K. *The Ethos of the Song of Roland.* Baltimore: Johns Hopkins University Press, 1963.

King, Clarence. *Mountaineering in the Sierra Nevada.* Boston: J. R. Osgood, 1872.

Selected Bibliography

[King, Clarence.] "Style and the Monument," N.A.R., 141 (November 1885), 443–445.

Kraus, Michael. *A History of American History*. New York: Farrar and Rinehart, 1937.

La Farge, John. *An Artist's Letters from Japan*. New York: Century, 1897.

Lafitte-Houssat, J. *Troubadours et cours d'amour*. Paris: Presses Universitaires de France, "Que Sais-je?", 1950.

Lang, Andrew. *The Song-Story of Aucassin and Nicolette*, trans. from the ancient French. New Rochelle, N.Y.: The Eslton Press, 1902.

Langlois, Ernest. *Le Roman de la Rose*. Paris: Firmin-Didot, 1914–1924.

Lanson, Gustave. *Histoire de la littérature française*. Paris: Hachette, 1952.

Lewis, C. S. *The Allegory of Love: A Study in Medieval Tradition*. New York: Oxford University Press, 1958.

Lloyd, L. C. *The Borough of Wenlock (Shropshire) Official Guide*. Shrewsbury: Wilding and Sons, 1955.

Lockhart, J. G. *Memoirs of the Life of Sir Walter Scott*, Boston: Houghton Mifflin, 1901.

Lodge, H. C. *Life and Letters of George Cabot*. Boston: Little, Brown, 1877.

Longfellow, Samuel. *Life of H. W. Longfellow*. Boston: Houghton Mifflin, 1891.

Lowell, James Russell. *The Complete Writings of J. R. Lowell*. Boston: Houghton Mifflin, 1904.

—————— *Letters of James Russell Lowell*. Ed. Charles E. Norton. New York: Harper and Bros., 1894.

Mâle, Emile. *L'Art religieux au XIIè siècle*. Paris: A. Colin, 1922.

—————— *The Gothic Image*, trans. Dora Nussey. London: Collins, the Fontana Library, 1961.

Meyer, Andrew G. "Henry Adams Historian," unpub. Ph.D. diss., University of New York, 1948; chap. v., pp. 266–320, "The Illogical Virgin of Chartres," pp. 266–320.

Moore, Charles H. *Development and Character of Gothic Architecture*. 2nd ed. New York: Macmillan, 1899.

Moore, George. *Confessions of a Young Man*. London: Werver Laurie, 1940.

Mumford, Lewis. *The South in Architecture*. New York: Harcourt, Brace, 1941.

Paris, Gaston. *Extraits de la Chanson de Roland*. 6th ed. Paris: Hachette, n.d.

—————— *La Littérature française au moyen-âge (XIe-XIVe siècles)*, Paris: Hachette, 1888.

Pater, Walter. *Works*. 10 vols. London: Macmillan, New Library Edition, 1910.

Pidal, Ramón Menéndez. *La Chanson de Roland et la tradition épique des Francs*. 2nd ed. revised. Trans. from Spanish by I. M. Cluzel. Paris: A & J. Picard, 1960.

Poulet, Georges. *Studies in Human Times*, Trans. E. Coleman. Baltimore: Johns Hopkins Press, 1956.

Randall, David. "Waverley in America," *The Colophon*, new series, 1 (Summer 1935), 39–40.

Roques, Mario. *Aucassin et Nicolette*. Paris: H. Champion, 1962.

Rosenberg, John D. *The Darkening Glass, A Portrait of Ruskin's Genius.* New York: Columbia University Press, 1961.

Saveth, Edward. *American Historians and European Immigrants 1875–1925.* New York: Columbia University Press, 1948.

Schevill, James. *Sherwood Anderson, His Life and Work.* Denver: University of Denver Press, 1951.

Schorer, Mark, and Josephine Miles, eds. *Criticism: the Foundation of Modern Literary Judgment.* New York: Harcourt, Brace, 1948.

Scudder, Horace E. *James Russell Lowell, A Biography.* London: Macmillan, 1901.

Siciliano, Italo. *Francois Villon et les thèmes poétiques du moyen âge.* Paris: Armand Colin, 1934.

Spiller, Robert E. *The Cycle of American Literature: An Essay in Historical Criticism.* New York: New American Library Mentor Books, 1957.

———, ed. *Literary History of the United States.* New York: Macmillan, 1955.

Stein, Roger B. *John Ruskin and Aesthetic Thought in America 1840–1900.* Cambridge, Mass.: Harvard University Press, 1967.

Stevens, Wallace. *Collected Poems.* New York: A. Knopf, 1954.

——— *The Necessary Angel.* London: Faber, 1960.

Studer, Paul. *Le Mystère d'Adam, An Anglo-Norman Drama of the Twelfth Century.* Manchester: Manchester University Press, 1918.

Swift, Lindsay. "A Course in History at Harvard College in the Seventies," *Proceedings of the Massachusetts Historical Society,* 3 (1918), 69–77.

Taylor, Henry O. *A Layman's View of History.* New York: Macmillan, 1935.

Thayer, William R. *The Life of John Hay.* Boston: Houghton Mifflin, 1915.

Thompson, J. W. *A History of Historical Writing.* New York: Macmillan, 1942.

Thoron, Ward, ed. *The Letters of Mrs. Henry Adams, 1865–1883.* Boston: Little, Brown, 1936.

Tinker, Chauncey B. "Arnold's Poetic Plans," *The Yale Review* 22 (June 1935), 782–793.

Trudgian, Helen. *L'Evolution des idées esthétiques de J. K. Huysmans.* Paris: L. Conard, 1934.

Untermeyer, Louis. *Modern American Poetry, Modern British Poetry.* New York: Harcourt, Brace, 1942.

Van Rensselaer, Martha. *Henry Hobson Richardson and His Works.* Boston: Houghton Mifflin, 1888.

Von Erhardt-Siebold, Erika. "Medieval Windows in Romantic Light," *Essays and Studies in Honor of Carleton Brown.* New York: New York University Press, 1940.

Von Simson, Otto. *The Gothic Cathedral.* New York: Harper & Row Torch Books, 1964.

Wade, Mason, ed. *The Journals of Francis Parkman.* New York: Harper and Bros., 1947.

Waerm, Cecilia. *John La Farge, Artist and Writer.* New York: Macmillan, 1896.

Wallensköld, A. *Les Chansons de Thibaut de Champagne, roi de Navarre.* Paris: Champion, 1925.

Watts, George B. "The Teaching of French in the United States," *The French Review*, 37 (October 1963), part 2.

Way, Arthur. *The Song of Roland.* Trans. into English verse. Cambridge: Cambridge University Press, 1913.

Wendell, Barrett. *The Traditions of European Literature from Homer to Dante.* New York: Charles Scribner's Sons, 1921.

Wilkins, Thurman. *Clarence King: A Biography.* New York: Macmillan, 1958.

Wilkinson, William W. *A Free Lance in the Field of Life and Letters.* New York: A. Mason, 1874.

Winters, Yvor. *In Defence of Reason.* Denver: University of Denver Press, 1947.

Young, G. M. "Scott and History," *Transactions of the Royal Society of Literature of the United Kingdom*, pp. 74–81, London (1950).

Index

Index

141